See What the Lord Has Done

Elsie Popken

ISBN-13: 978-1-791734-21-3

"One generation shall praise Your works to another, and shall declare Your mighty acts. On the glorious splendor of Your majesty, and on Your wonderful works, I will meditate. Men shall speak of the power of Your awesome acts; and I will tell of Your greatness. They shall eagerly utter the memory of Your abundant goodness and shall shout joyfully of Your righteousness."

Psalm 145:4-7 NASB

God wants us to tell about His blessings and His love to generations following, to tell of His glorious kingdom and of His work in our lives so that all people will know about His mighty acts and glorious splendor. This is the reason for this book: to bring glory to our wonderful, awesome God.

Dedication

I wish to dedicate this book to my wonderful Lord and Savior, Jesus Christ. Without Him, these pages would be blank. There is no human way I can ever thank Him for all the wonderful, mighty ways in which He has blessed me, showing me His deep love. Many times, He has called me His "little one," and I still get choked up at His unbelievable love for me and my family. He wants you to know His deep love for you also, dear reader. May you come to the realization that what He has done for my family and me, He wants to do for you as well, over and abundantly.

CONTENTS

Acknowledgements

First, I would like to acknowledge my Lord and Savior, Jesus Christ, Who through His grace enabled me to write this book.

I want to thank my late beloved husband who supported me countless ways in my endeavors. He believed in me and my dream despite any setback I faced.

I wish to thank all five of my children who cheered me on, prayed for me, and supported me every step of the way. Your love means so much!

My two daughters, Kathy and Kristy, both spent numerous hours doing the busy legwork for this book from A-Z. From editing, research, giving advice, working with the editor, and more, all of your hard work helped me see my dream fulfilled. I deeply appreciate both of you! I'm also so thankful for Kathy's husband, Cliff, for providing much support with editing, formatting, and getting the book published.

Heartfelt thanks go to my editor, Mary Busha. Her many hours of work, patience, professionalism, and expertise helped greatly. She was an absolute joy to work with and is a shining example of Christ's light to my life.

Deep gratitude goes to my pastor and dear friend, Pastor Jackie Hartman. She has encouraged, prayed, discipled me, and laid her life down for me in countless ways. Only the Lord knows how my walk of faith has been strengthened through her love.

Finally, there are so many not mentioned here who have contributed to this book in selfless and unseen, yet pivotal ways. I cannot thank all of them the way they deserve, but I pray the Lord will bless them richly for their sacrifice.

JESUS IN MY HEART

"Jesus said to him, 'I am the way, and the truth, and the life; no one comes to the Father but through Me.'"

John 14:6 NASB

I couldn't stop weeping as I walked back to my place on the long, wooden pew in the quaint little Catholic church. Set among large evergreens on a hill, we could see the lush valley and river to the east. After having just received Holy Communion for the first time, all I could think of was, "I've got God in my heart; I've got God in my heart!" At age 9, I was so overwhelmed and so happy that the Creator of the whole universe would want to live in me, such a naughty, sad little girl, that tears of joy flowed. I was in 4th grade in the parish school of St. Anthony's Catholic Church, nestled in the country near West Point in northeast Nebraska.

My teacher, a small Franciscan nun named Sister Mercedes, prepared us for this wonderful privilege of receiving the Sacrament of Holy Communion. One of her statements that stood out was: "Do not be so happy because you get to wear a beautiful white dress, but that Jesus is coming into your heart." I took that seriously; however, I was still excited to be wearing the beautiful, white taffeta dress with shiny puffed sleeves, Peter Pan collar and 3-inch overlapping ruffles all the way down the skirt. A wide sash completed the special occasion dress. With it, I wore white shoes and long white stockings and a white dress-length veil. My older sister, Wilma, had worn it for her First Communion and I was happy it fit me for mine.

It was hard to focus on the fact that God was really coming to me. When I had gone to Confession for the first time in preparation for receiving First Communion, I was nervous because I was afraid I would forget to confess some of my many sins in my long life of 9 years. We had a kindly, older priest, Father Virgil, of whom I was rather afraid because he seemed so holy. He helped me remember and confess all of the bad things I had done, and I was much relieved to have that over and done with.

It rained cats and dogs the night before my big day, so I worried most of the night. "What if I don't get to church on time? What if we can't get there at all?" We usually could not drive up the long hill without our car getting stuck in the mud. I was relieved when my dad decided to carry me all the way up that muddy hill to meet our kind neighbors, the Kaups, who took me to church. It impressed me that my dad was so protective of me with my white clothes, and that the day was so important to him, that he would carry me at least a quarter of a mile.

When the great moment arrived on April 30, 1944, as I received the Communion Host Father Virgil placed on my tongue, I was in awe. I walked back to my place in the wooden pew, realizing something special had happened. From then on I wanted to be as good as I could be so that I could please this awesome God. I was afraid of Him, but also, I wanted to see Him someday in heaven. From the time I started school, I had a hunger for God, but I was frightened I wouldn't go to heaven. I became nervous and fearful about everything, it seemed, so I prayed almost continuously.

Despite my concerns, my heavenly Father already had plans for me that were beyond my wildest dreams and greatest fears. This is the story of my journey with Him. This is a story of His guiding hand.

CHAPTER 1

ANOTHER CHILD

"For You formed my inward parts; You wove me in my mother's womb. ... Your eyes have seen my unformed substance; And in Your book were all written the days that were ordained for me, when as yet there was not one of them."

Psalm 139:13, 16 NASB

I was born sometime after midnight on May 4, 1935 to John and Elizabeth (Betty) Hagedorn Luebbert in our tiny, 5-room farm house in the absence of our family doctor and my dad. My mother was blessed to have her spinster sister, Ann, at her side when I came into the world. There was no electricity, running water, or central heat, but the two brave souls did their best to bring about a safe delivery. Meanwhile, Dad drove the horse and buggy to retrieve the doctor since my parents did not have a telephone to make that important call.

I arrived quickly, right in the middle of the Great Depression. Mother told me one day, "I had to be really quiet so the kids upstairs wouldn't wake up." Years later, I wondered if my four brothers and my sister, Wilma, heard me crying downstairs.

My parents met at a barn dance near Mom's home outside West Point. My mom was living with her parents, sister and two brothers at that time. Her father had immigrated to the United States from Westphalen, Germany with his family and had homesteaded in St. Charles Township. His wife, Caroline, was of Czech descent, as her parents had come from Bohemia, and had also settled in St. Charles Township.

Together with two brothers and a sister, Dad had moved to Nebraska from his birthplace, Koeltztown, Missouri, in search of work. He was a hired hand at the time of their marriage, working for my brother's father-in-law. They wed on May 25, 1921, at St. Boniface Catholic Church in Monterey, Nebraska and began farming soon after, renting the land they worked, in St. Charles Township.

My oldest brother, Casper, was born in 1922, followed by the rest of my siblings: Leo, Irene, Fred, Bernard, and Wilma. In 1933, just two years before my birth, Irene died when she was not quite 7 years old. My parents and siblings were devastated because she had been such a dear little girl, drawn to the Lord at a very young age.

Because the doctor was not sure at the onset of Irene's condition what her serious illness was, he first diagnosed it as spinal meningitis, which required the family to be quarantined. Because of that, no one was allowed to attend the wake at our home to be with our grieving family, and the burial had to take place before the funeral services were held at the little country church. What a heartache that must have been!

A few weeks after Irene died, a new doctor arrived in town. After he conferred with the first doctor, he felt sure it was tuberculosis of her spine, a complication following the measles, which she had had only weeks before. Mom told my sister Wilma and me often, "Irene was so good. She was always trying to help me. She sat on a little stool and tried to peel potatoes when she was little, only around 5 years old, and she would always do other little jobs for me." Wilma and I always felt guilty because we weren't very helpful.

At her funeral, the priest related a beautiful story of Irene and her little friend Rita. During lunch hours, the priest observed the two going into the church nearby. Being curious about their activity in the church, he slipped in one day to check on them. The dear little girls were attempting to say the Rosary, a repetition of several Catholic prayers.

The priest also shared that Irene was so dear to the Lord that He chose to take her to heaven. He said, "She was a beautiful flower that the Lord wanted in His heavenly garden."

Though this story comforted my parents, my mother still grieved. As she neared the end of her life, she talked about how much she missed Irene.

CHAPTER 2

OUR HOME

Our home on the farm was a small 5-room, wood-frame house. Downstairs were two larger rooms with a tiny pantry and a washroom where we hung all our work clothes on nails pounded into painted boards. The washroom also had a wooden washstand, which held a 3-gallon bucket and dipper for cold drinks. The white enamel bucket with red trim and a matching drinking dipper sat next to a white enamel washbasin where we washed our hands and faces. When necessary, we took that same basin, set it on the floor and washed our feet. Then we'd use more water to rinse the basin out again for the next participant. With so many hands, faces, and feet being washed, the water didn't last long.

Always, there were Turkish towels (now known as terry towels) hanging on nails nearby. Some people had small pumps at the kitchen sink or in a room off to the side to fill buckets of water. Since we didn't have a pump or cold-water taps, Mom usually carried buckets of water in from the outdoor pump.

A galvanized steel washtub, placed discreetly behind the stove, was used for Saturday night baths prior to church the next day. A lot of water had to be heated on the cook stove. It took a long time to heat and a long time for everyone to get soaked clean. Mom supervised us smaller ones. She didn't want "potatoes growing in our ears," as the saying went, or bits of dirt left between our toes. Of course our hair had to be squeaky clean as well.

During the summer, we used a calf bucket with a hose attached to the bottom (where a nipple was attached for a calf to suck). We could stand in the tub near that bucket with a brush and take a makeshift shower, scrubbing off a week's worth of grime and sweat from work or play. The summer kitchen, which was separate from the house, was used for those baths. It also held drying sausages in the winter. Mom did the laundry in there too. Many other farm wives had an extra stove in their summer kitchen, a small wooden building built specially to cook daily meals. This kept the house cooler during hot summer days.

Mom was a wonderful cook. She prepared simple hearty meals during the hot summer months in the pantry on a small kerosene stove with two burners. Shelves built all across one wall from floor to ceiling in the pantry held most of our groceries, including rows of fruits and vegetables that mother painstakingly canned in glass jars. What jars the pantry shelves could not hold, Mom stored in the cellar, a cave dug underground, entered by wooden steps.

Our pantry always held a slop bucket where the used dish water went, as well as the contents of the wash basin when it needed rinsing or emptying. The bucket was carried outside for dumping during daytime, hopefully before it got too full and almost overflowed.

The cook stove had large, black stovepipes to vent the stove and four round holes with four lids to fit them. Each lid had a grooved hole in it for its iron handle. A shelf with another smaller door was under the lids with a pan for the dropping ashes, which of course needed to be carried out when full. Next to it, in front, was a long, low door with hinges to open the oven. There was also a warming oven (which was nice to keep leftovers) and a reservoir on the side, usually to hold extra water for washing dishes.

The warming oven was a good place for Mom to set the large, crockery bowl to raise her yeast bread dough. When the dough peeked over the edge of the bowl, she punched it down, deflating it with a "whoosh." Then she kneaded it for the second time and let it rise again. When the dough was ready, she shaped it into six loaves, resulting in delicious, crusty, golden bread for our hungry family.

Next to the stove stood a wood and corncob box that extended upward to hold a shelf for matches. It was necessary to use dried cobs as well as wood, so the box was usually kept well-stocked. Though a wood fire stayed hot longer, the cobs heated faster than the wood. This kept the stove hot for Mom to heat gallons of water to do the laundry, which she did by hand, using a scrub board. I sat near her and watched her wring out thick overalls by hand from the hot water, wondering how she could do that hard task.

Of course, Mom had many garments to iron and did it all with a sad iron, or flat iron. It had a clamp that released a handle she took off after heating the iron on the cook stove. A metal iron holder held the hot iron on the wooden ironing board while she readjusted the garment. At times, the iron sat waiting on the back of the stove for a last-minute job. Easy care polyester had not yet been created, so everything needed dampening and ironing.

I vividly remember Mom being so frustrated and discouraged from scorching the first garment because she didn't know just how hot that iron would be when she removed it from the stove. "Oh no, I scorched another one!" she lamented.

In that case, she would have to wash the clothes all over again and soak them in liquid starch. She dried the garments thoroughly, and then dampened them with a pop bottle filled with water. Once sprinkled, she rolled up each item so the moisture distributed evenly. Later, she ironed each one, leaving not a wrinkle.

Our large, sturdy wooden table, covered with colorful oilcloth, stood across from the stove. It held large meals to feed four hungry sons along with Dad and us two girls. The eight chairs fit around the table nicely but took up a lot of space in that kitchen.

The combination parlor-dining room was quite small. The old potbelly stove, our only other source of heat besides the kitchen stove, sat in the middle of that room. A lovely, round oak table stood in one corner and the matching china cabinet to display Mom's "good" dishes stood on the opposite wall with a leather couch against another wall. That room was also used to dry clothes when needed. I can still smell the wonderful scent of laundered clothes hanging on the temporary clothesline running from window to window across the room on cold winter days. This room was closed off unless we had company. Therefore, our makeshift laundry room was frigid cold in the winter. When Mom brought the clothes in out of the cold, they literally stood up straight from being freeze-dried!

Upstairs were three bedrooms: two tiny rooms, each holding a dresser and a double bed for the four boys to share, and one larger room with two double beds and a dresser. Wilma and I slept in one of the double beds and our parents slept in the other. We had two small closets for the three bedrooms. No hangers for our clothes were had in those days. There were nails on boards attached to the walls. Our garments, especially our woolens, always had obvious indentation marks either on the shoulders or necklines from the nails.

None of us had slippers, so during long winter nights before electricity, we dreaded going to bed in the unheated rooms upstairs. We sat in front of the open oven door of the wood burning stove, dozing off because we were so sleepy. Many times Dad scolded us. "You guys get to bed now. Quit sleeping by the stove." On bitterly cold nights, Mom heated up the sad irons on the stove, and then wrapped them in old towels to place in bed by our cold feet.

Being Catholic, each bedroom had special water in holy water fonts so we could bless ourselves as we got up or before we climbed into our beds. On Holy Saturday, the day before Easter, our priest prayed a blessing over fresh water. We were taught that if we made the sign of the cross (by touching our forehead, chest and both shoulders, forming a cross) as we dipped our fingertips into the blessed holy water, we would receive a blessing from the Lord. During the coldest months, the holy water turned to solid ice in those cups.

I remember being able to see our breath escaping in puffs in our dimly lit room. During those winter mornings, as we hit the icy floors with our bare feet, we grabbed our clothes and ran down the stairs as fast as we could to dress near the warm kitchen stove. In the early morning hours, Mom or Dad diligently built a fire long before we got up so the chill would be out of the kitchen. Sometimes, we almost burned our fannies from getting too close to the stove!

As we children grew older, my parents purchased a dark brown oil heater with glass panels gracing its front door. This replaced the old potbelly, which needed to be fed chunks of firewood almost continuously. Seeing the flames flickering through the door always gave me a comfortable feeling as the warmth radiated from it.

Eventually Mom and Dad bought a more modern black and white kitchen stove with a built-in reservoir to hold warm water. Mom also bought a new gas-operated iron, which proved to be rather dangerous. One time, my brother Leo wanted to help Mom by ironing his own dress shirt for a date with his future wife, Lorraine. Somehow, something went wrong. As he lit the iron with a match, it exploded with a loud bang and flames poured out of the side of the iron. His eyebrows got singed, but he was a good sport and laughed about it. Mom was just grateful that nothing worse happened. I was afraid of that thing from then on.

Mom soon graduated to a Maytag washing machine, a strong-smelling gasoline ringer type with a pedal starter. She had a hard time starting it, but that was certainly easier on her than scrubbing clothes by hand on a washboard!

To wash dishes, Mom poured hot water into a large enameled dishpan set on our large wooden table. "Girls, come and dry the dishes." She used a cake pan to set the dishes in for us girls to dry with her white towels. After the dishes were finished, the water was poured outdoors or into the slop bucket. Until regular dish washing detergent was available, Mom sliced homemade lye soap into the hot water.

Before we had electricity, our source of light in our kitchen and other rooms were dimly lit kerosene lamps. I was still quite young when a new gasoline lamp was brought home. The gasoline lamp, which operated on a combination of gas and air, held two fireproof mantels, little mesh, sock-like things Mom had to tie on with tiny drawstrings. These were situated on the pipes where the gas came out. The air was pumped into the tank that formed the base of the lamp. The light that emanated from the mantels was quite bright. If the light grew dim, Mom or Dad pumped more air into the tank and the light blazed bright again. The mantels gradually burned until dull ashes formed.

During warm, summer evenings, moths were attracted to the lights indoors. When a moth flew into the house, it immediately flew into one of the mantels, ruining it. The light went out and the moth met its fate. Mom would say, "Oh no, not again," and then she would stop whatever she was doing and replace the ruined mantel with a new one.

Outdoors, Dad used a portable lantern that burned kerosene which was absorbed into the wick from a small tank at the base. The lantern had a handle to hang it on nails in the barns. Even though the light was dim, it worked well enough while finishing chores like unharnessing the draft horses, or checking sows that were in labor, or milking the cows after dark.

Summer nights brought stifling heat into our upstairs bedrooms, so we slept on quilts placed on the kitchen floor in front of the screen doors. Mosquitoes serenaded us with their tunes before attacking, and many times we woke up with stiff, sore necks from sleeping in early morning drafts. Those mornings I just *knew* that I had polio, which was contagious and going around in those days before the vaccine became available.

When Mom's single uncle passed away in 1949, he willed his farm, the one we lived on, along with some cash to Mom and one of her brothers. Dad got a bank loan to buy the other half of the farm. Mom then hired a carpenter to build her longed-for built-in cabinets, which she painted ivory. She used light blue as an accent color and bought frilly, white curtains with light blue trim. I was 14 years old when our house was all wired for electricity. We were really living in luxury then and I often felt like dancing around the kitchen from sheer joy.

That is when Mom got a brand new General Electric range. She so appreciated her refrigerator, wringer-washer, iron, mixer and other wonderful electrical appliances. She was so excited, and we were all so happy for her.

Mom's work certainly was much easier after that. No longer did she have to carry in gallons of water. She had a double sink installed in her kitchen with a shower stall and an indoor toilet in the former washroom. How wonderful that we no longer had to run out to the dark, smelly outhouse with its inhabitants of spiders and flies. At long last, we actually had an indoor bathroom!

CHAPTER 3

FREE TIME

Evenings when supper dishes were finished, we'd gather around a battery-operated radio to listen to programs like "The Great Gildersleeve," "Fibber McGee and Molly," and "The Aldrich Family." More frightening programs were on Saturday evenings in the 1940's: "Gangbusters," "Dragnet," and the really scary one, "The Shadow Knows." One of my brothers always delighted in mimicking the Shadow, who laughed like a wicked fiend, or so I thought. After listening to that one, I was too terrified to even go into a dark room. Many times in the afternoons, we listened to soap operas like "Just Plain Bill" or "Portia Faces Life." During winter daylight hours, we spent a lot of time outdoors, making snowmen or sliding on the thick ice covering our large creek.

Our Catholic elementary school had a small library stocked with children's classics. That's when I became an avid reader. If I couldn't find new books, I read the old ones again. On cold, wintry Sunday afternoons, after the blessing of electricity came to the farm, we played board games like Uncle Wiggly, or Monopoly, or we'd play simple card games. Mom popped huge, enameled dishpans of popcorn from the home-grown popcorn in our fields.

Folks those days visited friends, neighbors, and relatives, who then in turn dropped by without an invitation just to socialize; most didn't have telephones to call ahead. Usually, a lunch of sandwiches, pickles, and coffee with cookies or cake was served. Sometimes, the hostess served a wonderful, full-course meal. We kids liked to go along or have company so we could play games with the other children.

Elementary school

I remember when I was five years old being so lonely that I begged my mom each day to let me go to school along with my siblings. My parents must have gotten tired of my complaining. After discussing it with other parents of the parish, who had children about my age, the day finally arrived when they allowed me to climb into our old car with my sister and brothers to start school.

Kindergarten had not yet been implemented in our area, so I began first grade with four boys and three girls: Bernard, Alfred, Leroy, Joe, Dorothy, another Dorothy and Virginia Grovijohn. I quickly became best friends with Virginia. I really liked school and loved to learn. We immediately started memorizing from the Catholic Catechism and we studied reading, arithmetic, grammar, spelling, and penmanship, along with music and art. Spelling, music, and art became my favorite subjects. With some effort, I made good grades in all of my subjects except for arithmetic.

Each week, our priest walked over from his home, built on the other side of the church, to teach us about God and the Catholic Church. I always wanted to be good so I could please him as well as Sister Mercedes, my teacher from first to fourth grade. I was in awe of the priest because we were taught by the sisters to have the utmost respect for him. When he entered the classroom or even walked over to us while we were on the playground, we stood in reverence and quickly said, "Good morning, Father," or "Good afternoon, Father" or whichever occasion deemed a respectful greeting.

By the time I began fifth grade, geography and history were added. I struggled many times to memorize answers for the various subjects, especially history. I couldn't seem to remember the important battles and dates. I was fearful of the nun because she seemed unkind and strict. She was especially impatient when I stumbled over history facts. Always I begged God to help me with my memorization.

Soon I became fearful of just about every challenge that came along. And when I became fearful, I felt sick to my stomach. Each morning I felt sick before school, so I missed many days. My parents even took me to a doctor, but of course he couldn't find anything wrong. At one point the nun threatened to hold me back a grade because I had missed about 12 days. I thought the only solution was to go to school feeling sick, so many mornings I wouldn't tell Mom how ill I really felt. I prayed hard for God to help me not throw up in school, since I went most mornings feeling nauseated. After history class I always felt better, however. And after fifth grade was completed, my stomach problems improved and I seemed better able to master my history.

I remember often being overwhelmed with fear, a pattern I would struggle with for many years. It seemed I was always nervous or afraid about something. Because of that I was not able to eat the nutritious food my dear mother sent with me each day to school. Invariably, I returned home with the black metal lunch bucket nearly full of cold, dried-up sandwiches. In those days, plastic bags were unheard of and waxed paper wasn't of very good quality. Mom was patient with me and so sweet, even though I know it must have concerned her that I only nibbled at those sandwiches of crusty, homemade, buttered bread with homemade dried sausage, or lunch meat, egg salad, or salmon salad. All she said was, "You didn't eat much today again."

Needless to say, I stayed scrawny during my entire youth.

Many years later, I learned that I actually had hypoglycemia or low blood sugar (the opposite of diabetes) all my life. Had it been diagnosed, Mom could have changed my diet and avoided a lot of sick days caused by nervousness and anxiety.

Most days, when we returned home from school, we were starving. Mom served us our favorite, warm slices of her freshly baked white bread. I remember vividly the fragrance of yeast and the crunching sound of the golden crust as she cut through slice after slice and slathered them with melted butter.

Winter fun

Some of the happiest memories of my grade school days are sledding on wintry days at lunch hour. In those days, we seemed to have a lot more snow. Most winters the snow drifts were as tall as our roof. The snow didn't melt all winter until the spring thaw sometime in March. The church, parish house, nuns' house, and elementary school were all built on top of the large hill overlooking the beautiful valley near the Elkhorn River, its banks bordered with many trees. Each day, the fathers struggled to drive up the steep parish hill with chains on their tires to drop off their school-aged children. The packed snow became slick as glass, making the hill perfect for sledding. All of us brought our wooden sleds to school and left them outside the building until the spring thaws came.

Whenever the lacy patterns of frost no longer adorned the window panes, we pressed our noses against the glass. Then we'd listen for the soft smashing and crackling sounds in the snow banks beneath, sure signs that spring was coming. Water dripped off the eaves of our house and the bare tree branches as the snow melted.

All winter and into March, we wore ugly long, cotton stockings held up with elastic garters. The long underwear we stuffed into those stockings left unsightly lumps on our legs. By March, we longed to wear anklets again. As soon as we were able to shed the long underwear, we also wanted to rid ourselves of those heavy cotton stockings. Sometimes, as soon as we got to school, we rolled those stockings, garters and all, down to our ankles and went around all day with that enormous doughnut resting right at the top of our shoes. Ah, we felt so much better, though we were probably a ridiculous sight. Before going home, of course, we pulled up those long stockings once again.

When we sledded, our toes and fingers went numb, and we girls could hardly waddle because of the long johns stuffed into those long stockings. Outdoors, our legs were covered with woolen snow pants over our stockings, usually lined with cotton flannel. We completed our fashion statement with colorful wool caps, mittens, and rubber overshoes.

We loved to whiz down that long hill at the speed of a bullet, not even minding that we needed to pull the sleds back to the top after each round. Though there were about 30 children in the entire school, we never ran over each other or had any accidents. The older children were careful around the smaller ones, and there always seemed to be plenty of room on that steep, wide, snow-packed hill.

Each time there was new fallen snow, we made footprints into large circles with paths across in a pie shape to play Fox and Goose. Or we would have snowball fights, making our mittens wet and soggy as we waited for the sledding hill to become slick as glass once again.

Father Virgil enjoyed children and photography, and probably had one of the first home movie cameras created. He enjoyed filling his reels with films of us gaily sliding down that hill. We were always delighted when he showed those movies at parish family nights, causing many childish giggles as he ran the film backwards for us to see ourselves speedily backing up the hill on those sleds to a sudden halt at the top.

During warm weather, the nuns organized a baseball team on the large grassy area next to the driveway. I was good at running, but terrible at swinging a bat, because there was no one at home to practice with me. None of the kids wanted to have Virginia or me on their team. Virginia wasn't much interested in baseball either, so a few times we sneaked off and sat in the two-holer outhouse, talking and giggling for most of our lunch hour.

Carefree spring days

It was always fun to be outdoors on spring mornings. Dew sparkled on the sprigs of grass and small weeds. Meadowlarks, wrens, robins, and sparrows sang, and mama rabbits stood up with paws dangling, long ears twitching and noses sniffing while their cute babies hopped about.

I always loved to watch little cheeping chicks hatch. They were adorable. Mom took them away from the clucking hens and raised them in a separate barn. Occasionally, some hatched out in a secret spot the mother hen had found to make her nest. She'd lead them proudly and call to them in her special "hen talk." She taught them to eat by pecking seeds or grain on the ground in front of her watchful eyes. Now, when I remember all of the chicks crowding under the mother hen's protective wings, I can visualize what Jesus describes in Luke 13:34 when He talks about protecting us like a mother hen protects her young. If we dared come near, she would jump up and come flying at us or at any predators such as dogs or cats, ready to peck any of us.

Springtime also brought lots of furry kittens of all colors, and I considered it important to tame each one. Of course, each had to have a name. I spent hours holding and petting them. Occasionally, we had a litter of darling, black and white, roly-poly, fluffy, yipping puppies. All of these small animals brought so much joy and laughter. I remember, though, weeping and questioning God when a sick or injured pet died. I had a private funeral service for each one. Usually, I buried them in a shallow grave unless rigor mortis had already set in. Then I just covered them with dirt.

Pet lambs were also a favorite, and I delighted in feeding the orphans with an empty catsup bottle with a large, rubber nipple pulled over the top. I loved watching their tails move up and down vigorously in contentment as they ate, almost like a pump handle. As they grew, my small hands could hardly hang onto the bottle. My arms ached as they hungrily slurped and jerked the bottle to drain every drop of milk, but I still loved that job.

Behind the large, red horse barn, the dirt was fine and smooth, which was perfect for making tiny dirt roads and cities. My brother Ben was so good at making those roads for his toy vehicles, sometimes finding the right shaped stick to resemble a car or truck. I really enjoyed that dirt. For hours, Wilma and I helped him make cities. He never seemed to mind our help and we were careful to follow his instructions to the letter, since he was the expert.

When Virginia came over, we'd build a playhouse behind the barn in our grove of trees with the canopy of leaves forming the roof. We used small, straight boards we "borrowed" from the corn crib to build a table. Together, we rolled tree stumps over to the location for chairs or stools. We strung baler twine between trees for room dividers and old fabric for unhemmed curtains strung between trees. Peach crates nailed to a tree for a cupboard were covered with old cloth curtains or rags. Of course, we always had our mud pies packed into Mason canning jar lids. We decorated each with locust tree leaves before letting them dry to release later into hard, flat dirt cakes or pies.

Many summer hours we took turns swinging under a tall tree. I loved standing and pumping on the notched board seat of the rope swing as I imagined being a trapeze artist. Swinging so high, it seemed I was flying almost horizontal as the wind whipped at my skirt.

Of course, I always had to have dollies to take care of and to mother. One was Judy and later, I received Shirley, named after my idol Shirley Temple. Though I really didn't know how to use my mother's old pedal sewing machine, I tried to make clothes for them by working that wheel by hand, one stitch at a time. Somehow, I got the seams put together, but the clothes never got facings, buttons, or trim. Safety pins made fine closures, I thought. I still have a peach-colored print doll robe, made on that old pedal sewing machine, from one of Mom's old bedspreads. It doesn't have buttons or facings, but my young granddaughter Grace thinks it's just lovely.

Many summer days, I hauled out all of my doll furniture to play house on the lawn. One day, a storm came up quickly and I didn't have time to get it all in. "Look what happened to Judy," I tearfully told Mom, showing her my rain-soaked dolly.

After Judy dried out, the skin on her face, which was made from sawdust and glue composition and painted by hand, cracked. I was heartbroken. I pretended then that she had a skin disease. I realized later in life that the Lord certainly had destined me to be a mother. Carefully I saved my toy doll furniture playing with all the pieces from Christmas to Christmas so that I would have all the necessary furniture to "mother" and care for my dollies.

When the summer days were unbearably hot, Wilma and I played in our large creek, shortening our skirts to keep them dry by stuffing them partly into our underwear. Sometimes Ben joined us. We could while away hours and hours in that creek, wading in the warm water or making small dams with the soft mud. In some places, willow trees hung low, shading the water. In other areas, the water spread out and ran wide and shallow, splashing over gravel. Sometimes if the creek water had formed into pools, we could see the minnows that occasionally nibbled at our toes.

When the creek was full of water, flowing high from heavy rains, we waited for the water to subside. Then we slid on the wet banks on our behinds, creating a mud slide. The soft dirt oozed between our toes. Almost daily many large turtles swam past. We poked them with sticks, getting them to snap. Occasionally various snakes floated by. I always ran away as fast as I could, praying they wouldn't suddenly come after me. With my vivid imagination, I worried they'd follow me up the dry creek bank!

Although strict, my dad had a kind heart. kindly driving me the two miles to Virginia's house for us to play. She and her family had a nicer home and a walk-in attic. That wonderful attic, which had two steps down from an upstairs bedroom, was my favorite room in her house. I was happy when she suggested, "Let's play in the attic," exploring it with me while I was there. It was never too dark, because they already had electricity, and the one small window gave us light as well. We were both fascinated with a trunk that held lovely old clothes and could not resist "dressing up," clunking around in high heels much too large for our feet.

I also delighted in playing with their doll buggy and Virginia's dolls. Her daddy was so kind to me. He smiled and chuckled at us a lot. Virginia's mother was a good cook, so I was always thrilled when I was invited to join the family for meals. They always made me feel welcome and loved. I especially loved to stay overnight and remember many times giggling in bed when we should have been fast asleep.

With money being scarce, we got few Christmas gifts in our family and never any birthday gifts. Still Mom and Dad saw to it that we always had wonderful Christmas celebrations. On Christmas Eve, while we were asleep, Mom decorated the small Christmas tree set up on the round table in a corner of the dining room. She always had a large supply of fruits and nuts, along with special baked goodies. And gifts adorned the table around the tree or sat on the floor nearby.

Because we never received more than two items, I was very careful with my doll furniture so I could add another item to my collection each Christmas. My brother Leo was a talented woodworker. One Christmas, a beautiful handmade toy table appeared as a surprise. My mother had him build a frame under two discarded china cabinet shelves butted together on the straight ends. She painted the table in ivory with red trim, and then applied some beautiful red rose decals on the curved corners for trim. How I loved that table!

When I was around 12, I asked for a small doll dresser from Santa. What a beautiful surprise I found on Christmas morning! Leo had diligently built one much larger than the tiny one I had spied in a store display. I was so overjoyed that I cried. In his hurry to finish it in his limited time after work, the paint was not quite dry. Though the whole family joked about that, eventually I caught on that he must have built it for me instead of Santa, so I no longer believed in Santa Claus. Years later, before Leo died, I was able to tell him how much that dresser meant to me and I thanked him for his loving work just for me.

Our birthdays were never really special. Everyone wished us a happy birthday and had to spank us. The custom came from saying that we would not grow properly the next year unless we had a spanking, so there would be one spank for each year and one to grow on. It was a real ordeal if all my brothers wanted to spank me. We did not receive any gifts, because Mom and Dad just could not afford it. And since Mom had not been raised having decorated cakes for birthdays, we never had birthday cakes either.

Since Virginia always got a special decorated cake, I longed to have one too, so I told my mom I wanted her to bake me a cake and decorate it for me. I will never forget how hard she tried. In spite of her always being so busy, for my eleventh birthday, she baked a sheet cake, and then frosted it with turquoise-colored frosting. I really did like it, but I was disappointed that it did not have frosting flowers, writing, or candles on it. I thought it sweet of her to sacrifice her time for me, but I never asked her again, because I didn't know how to explain what I wanted. Knowing Mom had taken her precious time meant a lot; I didn't want to burden her again. She was always kind and tenderhearted.

When I was small, my parents were recovering from the Great Depression and had their hands full feeding and clothing the six of us. We welcomed hand-me-downs, and Mom tried to sew for us girls when she had time. Any dresses she sewed were fashioned from flour sacks, which came in lovely, cotton prints. Because of her limited time, she'd buy us new dresses sometimes, though she always had to be practical. There was never money for frills or small luxuries; every dollar had to do the work of two.

When I was 10 years old, our parish church celebrated a 50th Jubilee of the years since the parish began. Though Mom did not enjoy sewing, she wanted us girls to have special dresses, and because she had received a larger egg check than normal, she bought some shiny, silky fabric in a medium blue print. I remember the bodice was made of matching blue lace that came to points attached to the print across my chest, which I thought made it look gorgeous. Since Mom was always extremely busy, I felt special because she had put so much work into that dress, one of my all-time favorites, and she did it just for me. I felt like a princess in my dress whenever I wore it.

I will always have fond memories of Mom's sacrifices for us kids. All the money for all of the groceries, clothes, shoes, and other necessities came from the 30-dozen eggs and some cream she sold each week at the produce store. Of course, in severe winters or hot summers, the hens did not lay many eggs, and her checks were quite lean. Most years, her egg money barely covered the many needs we children had, but somehow she "scrimped" so we could have new clothes if no hand-me-downs appeared from other families.

When I was about 12, I had grown out of my sister's hand-me-down coat. Mom had really hoped she could buy a new winter coat for herself, but spent the money on a much-needed one for me. One cold, snowy Sunday after church, I warmed myself near the oil heater from the chill of returning home in our old, cold car. The heat felt so good on my back, but alas, I smelled something funny. Lo and behold, I could see my coat smoking! I ripped it off as fast as I could. To my horror, I saw I had scorched my beautiful wine-colored, tweed coat, which now sported a huge, dark brown circle right in the middle of the back.

Mom was angry, of course, saying, "Why couldn't you be careful?" I cried about my carelessness, feeling terrible. I knew how she had sacrificed to get me that wonderful coat and now it was ruined. Fortunately, someone gave me a hand-me-down coat to finish out the winter. It didn't fit me very well, but I didn't complain. I certainly did not repeat the mistake of standing so close to that hot stove again.

Easter Sundays stand out in my memory as well. Mom boiled eggs and we colored them beautifully with boiling water, vinegar, and food dye. She also bought chocolate marshmallow eggs and the large sticky sweet, beautifully colored crème candy eggs, which she carefully placed in fresh straw hauled in from the barn in wooden fruit crates.

Each Easter season, she saved her egg money for weeks to buy us new spring outfits, usually ordered from mail order catalogs like Sears, Montgomery Wards, Aldens, or Spiegel. Our outfits consisted of a dress, coat, and a special coordinating hat, along with white anklets and new shoes. Many Easters, when the weather was cold, we wore coats over our lovely spring frocks. If we didn't have our warm coats on, we certainly hurried to the car to get out of the cold on those Easter Sundays.

We kids walked barefoot all summer because we only had two pairs of shoes, one pair for school and one for church. It was natural for us to stumble into thistles frequently in our bare feet. Those stickers could be painful, so almost daily we would have to sit and pick out dozens of them, one by one, before we could continue our adventures. My, how our feet hurt as we stuffed them into Sunday shoes each weekend after going barefoot all week.

We also spent hours in the large barn, which always held adventures, especially the hayloft. Hay was lifted into the haymow by a hayfork through the large door under the barn's peak. We would jump from a high place near the huge door onto the straw below, never being concerned that we might get hurt. We'd find kittens peeking out at us from their hiding places under the eaves, and sometimes a clucking mother hen with her fluffy yellow baby chicks scratched about the barn floor or under the horses' mangers.

On lazy summer days when hot air rose up in waves like heat from a stove, I enjoyed lying on my back in the shady yard. It was good to look up at the shapes of the clouds against a deep cornflower blue sky. The clouds were as white and fluffy as beaten egg whites on a meringue pie. Of course, I imagined all kinds of animal shapes as I watched the formations of those clouds. I'd think about God making all of His creation, realizing He was pretty awesome to do all that. Seeing the big and little dippers with the multitude of stars on warm, summer nights brought the same reaction.

While the guys were busy with field work, Wilma and I were assigned the job of bringing home the cows from the pasture for evening milking time. We were always careful to watch our step since we couldn't bear to step into a fresh cow pie, but you guessed it! "Oh, yuck!" We would hit one occasionally as we happened to look up from the well-worn path the cows had made during their daily trek for greener pasture grass. Then we'd have to wash our stinky, filthy feet in the horse tank which was stocked with goldfish that had outgrown the small fish bowl in our home. They were quite large, and their nibbles on our toes tickled as we washed.

During the school year, when we finished our homework or Mom didn't have chores for Wilma and me, I spent the time after school or Saturdays reading old classics from our school library or writing to my cousin Viola Boeckmann who lived in Missouri. Our paternal grandmother, Catherine Luebbert, convinced me to be pen pals with Vi. We remain good friends to this day, and still write or call one another by phone.

Singing was important to me from preschool days on. My mother loved to sing, and several of us inherited her gift. Her brothers were also quite musical and taught themselves to play mandolin and guitar. Everyone learned to play accordion as well. My brother Leo taught me a popular little song, "You Are My Sunshine," and one of my aunts (and my godmother), Clara Hagedorn, encouraged me to sing it to all of her relatives that visited when we were at their house. I was around 4 years old at the time. She'd say, "Elsie, why don't you sing for us? You can sing so good." Though honored, I was frightened and self-conscious.

Through the years, Mom, Wilma, and I sang and harmonized as we worked in the kitchen. One of us girls sat near the radio and copied the words of our favorite songs so we could join in singing. Years later, after my brothers Leo and Fred had taught themselves to play several instruments, they formed a small band with our uncles. They even rented a small dance hall for their polka dances. Sometimes I sang duets with my brother, Fred.

As a teen, I sang in our church choir with Wilma at my side. I never tired of attending choir practice, enjoying the many Latin hymns that accompanied our masses; I loved the beautiful English melodies as well. My favorite was "Holy God, We Praise Thy Name." Filled with joy, I felt so close to God as I belted out that song of adoration. Another we sang when we had evening devotions was a little melody, "Good-night, Sweet Jesus." I loved that one so much; I always got tears in my eyes when we sang it.

Another activity I enjoyed was art. I easily sketched pencil drawings from my coloring books. Since I had not traced them but did them freehand, my teacher honored me each summer by exhibiting my drawings and sketches on poster boards at our annual county fair. I was thrilled to receive blue-ribbon stickers for my efforts.

That annual county fair was the highlight of our youth. Always held the last week in August for five days, our family so enjoyed that event. It gave us a chance to see all the wondrous exhibits as well as the free nighttime shows, which featured a variety of family entertainment. These were held on a stage in front of a large grandstand with wooden bleachers. Following the acts were gorgeous, loud fireworks every night at 10 p.m. As a small girl, I always held my ears as tightly as I could because I was afraid of the loud booming noises. Mom and Dad kept a close eye on Wilma and me and warned us, "Don't hang around the carnival people. We can't trust them."

As Virginia and I grew older, Mom and Dad allowed me to meet her and hang out with her all day at the fair. Her relatives usually brought a picnic lunch with fried chicken and other delicious foods. We rode the carnival rides and, yes, we spent the little money we could beg off our mothers on the carnival games, wasting it for dinky little prizes.

Chapter 4

Chores

During late spring days, my mom put me in charge of watching and feeding little baby goslings. The goose eggs were collected and placed under hens to set on until the eggs hatched. Once the hens' hatching instinct kicked in, they were called clucks. Faithful to stay on the nests for several weeks, the hens left only briefly to eat or drink. When the goslings hatched, they were placed in a large cardboard box for the first few days to keep them from wandering off. I put in a shallow pan of water, teaching them to drink by dipping in their bills, and I gave them ground grain, called mash, to eat.

I'd lose all common sense and pet the fluffy, yellow darlings for hours, and sure enough they'd think I was their mother! Soon I grew tired of petting them, so when I'd sneak away for lunch or supper, they'd frantically peep most mournfully. I yelled at them, "Well, you dummies, I'm not your mother." Then when I couldn't stand it any longer and felt really guilty, I'd run back to comfort them until they nodded off to sleep. Each summer, I vowed not to let them get attached to me, but it happened every year. Finally, after several weeks, they'd busy themselves eating mash or catching insects and no longer needed me as their mommy.

The adult geese frightened me. They chased me when I least expected it. I was terrified of them because they snapped and pinched my legs with their large, strong bills, leaving black and blue marks. Their strong, flapping wings brought even larger bruises on the rest of me, causing me to scream and run to the house. I called on my mighty God, "God, get them away from me!" and I ran as fast as I could to get inside our fenced in yard.

One of my daily chores was filling the huge, wooden cob box. I would fill bushel baskets from the cob house to fill the cob box. If I wasn't careful, a mouse might accidentally get pulled in with those cobs, causing some squealing later as he tried to escape the cob box.

Mom needed a continuous fire for cooking and baking and heating water. In the harsh winter months, I brought in wood to fill the wood box. The box was built taller in the back, which was wise. Otherwise, I'm sure the cobs and wood would have spilled over on the back side as I carelessly emptied the bushel basket.

During summer months, when Mom was so busy canning hundreds of jars of vegetables and fruits, she'd have me gather eggs. Though I was uneasy about the hens pecking my hand as I reached under their fluffy feathers for their eggs, I was even more terrified of the large bull snakes lying in the nests, swallowing the eggs. Oh, how scared I was of those snakes! Then I prayed frantically, "Please, God; please, God." If I spied them slithering along the straw-covered floor on their way to the chicken nests (which were rows of handmade wooden boxes large enough for the hens to sit and turn around in comfortably), I'd tear outta there as fast as I could. I'd cry just enough so that Mom mercifully came out and helped me.

At times, the hens pecked my hands leaving red marks as they begrudgingly gave up their precious eggs. Those scary incidents did not relieve me of that frightening job, however.

As we grew older, Wilma and I got the job of washing the cream separator, which was standard equipment in most basements of farm families that maintained milk cows. The cream separators were powered by hand, with a lot of cranking involved to get the machine up to full speed and then still more cranking while the whole milk was poured into the large, stainless steel bowl that funneled the white stuff down into the whirling separator blades. It was our job to wash those blades once a day. We never failed to grumble and complain. Of course, if we had been smart, we would have washed the blades right after all the cream was separated, so the milk could have been easily rinsed off the blades. But invariably, we stalled until late afternoon the next day when all the milk was sour and curdled.

In the early '50s after our three older brothers had left home to get jobs as farmhands, Ben, Wilma, and I were assigned to milk the cows while our dad finished the field work until dark. The cows were quite tame and were anxious to be milked to relieve their aching flanks, so we parked them quite close together by nudging them until they moved into place. Then we began the rhythmic stroking of their teats as the milk plinked into the waiting pail. We sang songs and kept time with the beat of the music by the plinking of the milk in the pails. At that time, two of the latest hit songs played frequently on the radio were "On Top of Old Smoky" and "Goodnight, Irene."

We laughed as we harmonized those songs. "Irene, goodnight. Irene, goodnight. Goodnight, Irene. Goodnight, Irene. I'll see you in my dreams," plink, plink, plink of the milk. Or "On top of Old Smoky, all covered with snow," plink, plink, plink. The boring work of milking didn't seem nearly as bad if we passed the time by singing and keeping time with the plinking milk.

When the flies were particularly pesky, those cows swished their tails at our faces or demonstrated their discomfort with a stomp of their hooves, at times knocking over the bucket of foamy, white liquid or, worse yet, stepping into the bucket and wasting all of our efforts. The hungry cats always sauntered up close, hoping for a handout of fresh milk. We challenged each other to see if we could hit their mouths with a squirt of milk. Their tongues curled out to try and catch a mouthful of the warm milk, but many a time, the milk missed their mouths and hit their faces instead. That would bring about the frantic feline activity of licking themselves clean.

Planting and harvesting

Each spring, Dad plowed the fields, and then harrowed them to plant corn or sow oats. He used a two-bottom plow, called a sulky plow. Two wheels guided it through the field as he walked behind the plow, controlling the reins to the four draft horses by tying the four leather reins into a large knot. He'd then place the reins behind his head on his shoulders as he guided the horses down the field. He used a spiked-toothed harrow to break up the large furrows and flatten them for planting the corn. How exhausted he was when evening came from walking the fields all day long.

To plant the fields of corn, it was customary to use steel stakes (tapered rods with a catch about halfway up). The stakes were stuck into the ground as far as they would go, one on each end of the field. Attached to the stake was a long wire that stretched about a quarter of a mile with a woven knot or lug spaced every 40 inches. There was a mechanical trip on the planter, pulled by the horses. As the tightly drawn wire was fed through that trip on either side of the planter, it hit the lug and dropped a kernel of corn into the earth. Two rows of planter boxes held the seed corn, but one wire went through the trip to cause the corn seeds to drop from both sides. As he reached the end of the row and turned around with the horses, Dad got off the planter and moved the stake and wire in such a way that it switched from the right side to the left, or vice versa. Then he planted another two rows.

After the sprouted corn began to grow, there was a beautiful checkerboard pattern of green corn rows all across the fields. The horse-drawn cultivator had shovels to dig out weeds and was used when the corn was about 6 inches tall. The first time they went with the row. The next time they went across the row. Because the rows were all 40 inches apart, the horses could avoid stepping on the sprouted corn. With horses, only one row of corn could be cultivated, but when using a tractor Dad could cultivate two rows at a time.

To prepare the soil for the oats, he used a 10-foot disc with a seat on it that was pulled through the field with the horses to break up the cornstalks from the year before. He seeded the oats with an end-gate seeder placed in a wagon box. The oats in the wagon were shoveled into the seeder by my older brother as Dad pulled the wagon back and forth across the field. The oats provided nourishing food for our horses and cows after being separated by a threshing machine. Threshing also provided straw to keep all the animals warm in the cold winter months.

Before corn pickers were invented, when the corn was golden brown and the husks totally dried, it was picked in the fall by hand. Each man or woman strapped a leather device on their gloves that had a metal hook on the palm side, sometimes called a shucking peg. This hooked on the base of an ear of corn and pulled the husk off each ear. Then the ear was broken off the cornstalk with the right hand.

During my younger days, my dad had a team of horses pulling a small, 26-inch-wide box wagon with side boards, three feet higher on one side of the wagon. The horses were trained to pull the wagon through the rows of corn while my dad and his partner walked beside the wagon and picked all those ears by hand, heaving them into the wagon. About 125 bushels was the most they could pick during one day.

They then scooped all of the corn out of those wagons into a building with walls of widely spaced boards, called a corn crib. The spaces let the corn completely air dry. It took months into winter, sometimes 'til long after Christmas, to harvest the corn. The cold and snow caused much discomfort as the men struggled to finish the long harvest. I remember when I was older Mom going out to help pick, too. How hard that must have been for her to do that all day and still take care of the homemaking chores.

Before combines were invented, area farmers, including my dad, had "threshing bees" where several farmers met together and helped each other harvest their crops. In the hot summer months, when the silky, shimmering crop of bright green oats ripened to warm gold, it was time for threshing. A machine called a binder was used to tie the ripened oats into bundles that were pulled and then left on the field. Someone rode the back of the binder watching for the bundles. When six bundles were made, the helper pushed a pedal that dropped the tied bundles onto a pile. Then the bundles were shucked. Six of those bundles were set together in a pile resembling a teepee, with one on the top as the "roof."

The bundles were placed that way to dry thoroughly to prevent mold from forming. The farmers could only cut the amount of oats they could shuck before dark so that dew or rain would not ruin it. The shucks dried in three to four days; then a hay or bundle rack (a flat-bed type of wagon with lowered sides and high back and front) was used to haul them to another machine when it was time for the threshing.

The horses obediently walked slowly or stopped at the commands of the man throwing the bundles onto the wagon. When the wagon was full, the horses pulled up next to the threshing machine, and the men pitched the bundles onto the conveyer, which pulled them into the feed chute to separate the straw from the oats. The straw blew out of a 12-inch wide pipe to the back of the machine and the oats came out one side into the waiting wagon. It was a dirty, sweaty job for all.

If snakes hiding in the bundles, including deadly rattlers, didn't get a chance to nip at the men, they'd end up in the threshing machine. My husband, Marv, relates a time his grandfather was handling a bundle when a

4- to 5-foot bull snake crawled on the pitchfork handle and bit his grandpa right on his nose. He had the souvenir of two teeth marks at the end of his nose for a long time.

Most farmers did not have a threshing machine. They had to hire a neighbor to bring his threshing machine to do such a large job. At that time, the machine we used was owned and operated by one of my uncles, who lived in our neighborhood.

All the housewives prepared huge meals for at least 12 men while also providing rolls and dessert for their breaks in the mornings and again in the afternoons. Without an electric stove or refrigerator, it was a huge challenge for my mother to get bread, rolls, and pies made the same morning, and then put on a huge meal for all those hungry men. She used only a wood-burning cook stove.

Usually the threshing began after the dew dried on the shucks, about 10 or 11 in the morning, but a light rain could cause the oats to be tough, hampering the threshing machine from working properly. If that happened, the men postponed their work. That caused such stress for Mom because she never knew how to plan. Would all the men be coming or would they not? That was always the question.

Many times she'd be near tears, not wanting to have the food go to waste if the men didn't come, yet wanting to be ready for their huge appetites. Though we kids just loved all that wonderful fried chicken, mashed potatoes, gravy, corn, fresh beans, fresh bread, gelatin salads, wonderful fruit pies with delicious cakes, and other goodies, I always felt sorry for Mom and the other ladies for what they had to go through. I heard my mother exclaim many times, "Why can't the weather stay nice 'til we're done?" or "I wish I knew what I was supposed to fix."

My job was to run many errands to and from our cellar, a deep, earthen cave, which took the place of a refrigerator. I'd bring up jars of canned goods or fresh cream when Mom needed them. That could be quite scary because mice would take up residence wherever they could, and occasionally a snake slithered down the wooden steps to cool himself. Of course, in my case, snakes had the power to cause a screaming exit.

During the summer months, horses went to the pasture during the nights after they received long refreshing drinks from the horse tank and a supper of oats. Marvin told me of the time he held the leather strap while letting the horses drink from the large tank. This particular time, he propped up his foot on the tank with the strap wrapped around his leg. The horse, startled by a goldfish nibbling on his muzzle, reared back in fright, dumping Marv right into that tank!

Providing food

Each January brought butchering time when my father, older brothers, and sometimes a neighbor or an uncle worked together to kill several hogs. The large, iron cauldron outside had to be filled with water and heated to boiling by lighting a fire underneath the raised iron pot. The cauldron, which held huge quantities of meat, was called a feet cooker because they also used it to cook de-hooved, skinned, and cleaned pigs' feet. Yes, there was meat on pigs' ankles that needed to be used. Nothing was wasted in those days. Several men caught and killed the hogs, and then dipped them into the boiling water. The men then heaved the dead hogs out and placed them on boards to scrape all the hair off the hide before hanging them by their hind feet on a tree to cut them open and pull the insides out into a tub, which was later carried into the kitchen.

Mom endured cleaning the slimy, stinky intestines to make casings for all the sausages, dipping them up and down, rinsing them over and over in buckets of clean water. She then soaked them in salt water to get them clean and ivory white. Eventually she was able to buy the casings from the local meat market instead of doing all that unpleasant work. The casings came all shriveled up and stiff, but she soaked them in water for several hours to make them soft and stretchy.

Mom and Dad cut up the parts of those animals right on the kitchen table. Afterward, good ol' lye soap took care of that greasy, bloody table. (We had never heard of E. coli bacteria in those days.) The hearts, livers, and tongues were all soaked and the fat was trimmed off. The animals' bellies had lots of fat so they trimmed that off to make lard a few days later. They'd cut the fat into one-inch chunks and then boil the chunks in large kettles on the stove. This hot, melted lard was then strained through old white towels into large stone crocks or jars. The crumbling brown cracklings left in the cloths were thrown out.

It took days to cut up all of the meat by hand, using extremely sharp knives. Some was cut for roasts or chops. Spareribs were saved and cut smaller for serving with sauerkraut or seasoned catsup. The rest was ground to make homemade sausage. The head cheese was made by boiling the animals' heads until all the meat came off the bones. They then chopped it and seasoned it with spices, and added some of the broth back into it before pouring it into pans. After it was chilled, it became thick from the gelatin coming out of the bones. Mom had a wonderful recipe for homemade sausage – the finest I ever tasted.

The fun part for us kids was turning the crank of the cast iron sausage stuffer. The crank made the round press push down on the ground meat, causing it to come out of an aluminum pipe at the bottom. My mother slipped slimy, wet casings at the open end of a 4-inch by 2-inch diameter pipe attached at the bottom. As we turned the crank, the ground, seasoned meat filled the casing in long, fat, slick rolls. Dad tied them on each end, bringing them together in a semicircle and hanging them on poles. The wooden poles, the size of brooms, hung across wires strung from the ceiling in the summer kitchen turned smokehouse. After being smoked for several weeks, the sausages were wonderful to fry for supper, and later for sandwiches.

Mom was so patient with us kids because each time we helped, we couldn't resist turning the crank really fast a few times so that she couldn't control the flow into those casings. They burst every time. That particular sausage was fried for the next meal. She never scolded us. I like to think perhaps she liked to do that herself as a young 'un so she understood our antics. The homemade sausages were stored right in the lard in large crocks in our cellar until springtime. Even smoked hams were covered and wrapped, and then buried deep in oat bins in the granary to keep until spring.

In the summer, Mom heated the lard saved from winter butchering, stirring pure lye into it with a large spoon. The liquid foamed when the lye was added. As it cooled, it formed a soft cream-colored soap that eventually hardened. Mom then cut it into about 4-inch bars that she used to wash everything. To have it dissolve quickly, she cut it into thin slices with a sharp knife. We washed our hands with homemade soap, but not our faces. It was quite strong and harsh. It really worked well to cut grease and was good for laundry. Eventually, we were able to purchase Ivory or Lux soap, and later, Lifebuoy and Lava for our personal cleansing.

Preserving food

Canning time required our help in picking vegetables of all kinds from Mom's huge garden and hundreds of strawberries or other fruit along with the boring job of preparing them. We girls hated shelling peas, but then Mom got the idea to use the wringer washer to flatten out those pea pods after they had been scalded. That really worked well, though many peas went flying beyond her dishpan! Snipping ends off the mountains of green beans was even more boring, so we tried to lighten the load by singing or listening to radio programs.

Though our backs ached, each year we picked enough strawberries for 100-plus quarts of processed fruit along with apples or plums. I know that more went into our mouths than into the containers, but somehow Mom got enough to make lots of preserves. We never worried about cleanliness of the fruit in those days. We'd wipe the dust on the sides of our old dresses before popping it into our mouths. No worry about chemical sprays in those days – everything was "organic."

We raised over a hundred pounds of potatoes, which we kids planted and later picked up after our dad dug them up with the plow. He carried bushels of those potatoes into the cellar, and in the spring he carried many out again after they were sprouting. Mom cut up the sprouted potatoes in pieces, leaving two to three eyes on each piece to sprout during spring planting.

Mom lined the cellar shelves with hundreds of Mason jars filled with all kinds of canned vegetables she raised, plus peaches, pears, apples, apricots, plums, and strawberries. When chokecherries ripened, Wilma and I ate them all afternoon until our front teeth were stained totally brown. That was a telltale sign of what we had been up to every time. The jelly Mom made from those chokecherries was the best ever, especially on fresh, hot out-of-the-oven bread, sliced and slathered with melted butter. I'd love to have some right now. Along with canned meat from the butchering days of winter, we always had just enough food, even during the Great Depression.

CHAPTER 5

THE DUST BOWL AND GRASSHOPPERS

The summer before I was born, the temperature soared to 114 degrees. With no rain that summer our family endured another year of crop failure. The area fields had already gone several years without rain, which resulted in failing crops. My mother related that the dust from strong winds was so horrendous, they couldn't keep it out of their homes. Though they covered their windows and doors with sheets dipped in water or wet papers to keep the dust out, it would still sift through and eventually layers of fine dirt covered the floors and furniture. Poorly crafted windows had chinks and cracks letting the wind and dust in. It got into their food, too, giving it a gritty taste.

Sometimes the dust completely blocked out the sun and the men couldn't see their hands in front of their faces. They masked themselves with bandanas to protect their faces from the driving dirt and sand. Chickens went to sit on their roosts during the day because of the dark from the dust, and cattle gathered on the side of the buildings, trying to protect their eyes from the blowing dirt and sand. Dust began to pile up in drifts along barbed-wire fences, buildings, and anything in its path. Tumbleweeds were cut and stacked as food for the cows so they wouldn't starve.

Dad had a job for a few years building roads for the Work Progress Administration (WPA) set up by President Franklin D. Roosevelt. The job only paid a few dollars a week and there were no Social Security, pensions, or unemployment compensations to fall back on, but this job helped save our family and a lot of families from starving. Since our farm was leased from Mom's uncle, we didn't have a farm to lose as Marvin's father did. The price of corn dropped down to two cents a bushel, and Marvin's father's hogs all caught cholera and died. As a result, he couldn't pay the property taxes. The bank foreclosed and took the farm. This happened to many other farmers during that period. Many families left Nebraska and headed to California or other states in search of work. Somehow our family made it through those long years.

Besides the drought, there were unbelievable grasshopper hordes that took the crops of many farmers. They arrived in a huge cloud like nothing anyone had ever seen. The cloud looked like layers of snowflakes, but larger, thin, and glittery. It rose and fell and sent tiny sparks as it moved. It was not a storm but a mass of crackling, ugly grasshoppers that hit the ground like hail. Their long legs jumped with the noise of a hailstorm, covering the ground till there was not one bit of bare ground to step on.

They totally stripped the crops—the oats, the leaves, and tassels off the cornstalks, and they ate the garden plants, too. They chewed up everything in sight, including fence posts. The grasshoppers even made it difficult to milk the cows; when they hopped all over them, the cows became nervous and upset, and their milk would not flow down. These were unbelievably hard, depressing days, but our parents and community hung in there, optimistic and trusting God for better days to come.

World War II

My earliest recollection about the war was when I was 6 years old: the bombing of Pearl Harbor by the Japanese. My dad and mom were just horrified. We were all very much afraid because we didn't know when the Japanese would fly over and bomb here in the U.S. or if the Germans would attack. Apparently, German submarines were seen near the East Coast during that time period. I remember the terror we all felt.

Blackouts that restricted light were unsettling. Mom covered every window as tightly as she could with towels, and we used the dim lights of the oil lamps. I begged God for protection every night, while most of the evening Dad had the battery radio on trying to hear any news that he could. Dad had fought in the army for a year in France during World War I, so he could relate to the horror and possibility of America being bombed.

The rationing was hard on our parents as it was on every American. We couldn't get tires; the old ones were patched over. Rubber plantations in southeast Asia were seized by the Japanese, so tires and everything made with rubber was scarce. Gas, meat, coffee, sugar, white flour, and even shoes were rationed. Every family was issued ration book stamps according to how many were in our families. The stamps certainly were not plentiful. There would be long lines to wait in to get our rationed provisions, which could only be obtained with those special stamps.

The speed limit was set at 35 mph in order to save gasoline. Scrap drives were organized to collect unused scrap iron. The scrap would be dropped at a designated place in the city and sent to the factories where ships and planes were built for the war. We children even saved our small pieces of silver gum wrappers and turned them in at our school. We heard so much about the hardship our soldiers were going through in the war that we wanted to help in any way we could. The nuns at school must have been concerned as much as our parents were that Hitler would eventually come with his troops to invade our nation. I remember so well Sister Mercedes telling us, "Pray every day that you will be strong enough to die for your faith, if you're ever called to do so." That was always scary to me. I didn't think I had it in me to be a martyr.

I will never forget when we heard on our radio that President Roosevelt had died of a massive stroke on April 12, 1945. I was so frightened; it seemed like the end of the world. Soon we adjusted to having Harry S. Truman as our president. It was President Truman who ordered the atomic bombs to be dropped on Japan. I thought that must have been horrible suffering and I still think so. But it seems that the war would have lasted so many more years, and thousands more American and Allied troops would have been killed by the Japanese because they just would not quit fighting.

Finally, VE (Victory in Europe) Day arrived on May 8, 1945. The announcement came on the radio that the war in Europe was finally over. From our farm, we could hear church bells ringing for a long while. We were beside ourselves with joy and could hardly believe it. Then on August 15, that same year, the Japanese forces surrendered after the atomic bombs were dropped on two of their major cities. Finally, the soldiers could come home and begin a normal life, and so could we!

CHAPTER 6

LESSONS LEARNED

Many times, I walked barefoot on the 4-inch pipe that carried water from our windmill-driven pump to another tank in the hog yard. The hogs drank from the base of that tank with the cows drinking from it as well. I pretended I was in the circus, walking a tight rope. Dad repeatedly warned me, "You get off that pipe before you get hurt." I was so smug about my expertise that I disobeyed him often and walked on it anyway when he was out of sight in the field or in town.

One day, my disobedience caught up with me. As I did my act for my imaginary adoring audience, one foot slipped off and I came down hard on my crotch area. Talk about pain! I could not tell anyone or indulge in self-pity about my black and blue bottom, which actually bled. I knew I would get into big trouble for disobeying and, boy, was I scared! I quickly repented to God and prayed that I would heal. Eventually I did, and I never was interested in walking on that pipe again. I kept my secret well.

Then, one day when I was around 10, I hurt my neck when I foolishly decided to fly. I thought it would be fun to jump off the slanted roof of the chicken barn. Well, I fell wrong and hurt my neck. Again, I didn't have the courage to tell Mom or Dad because I was afraid of getting into trouble for being so foolish. Another time, I fell off our windmill from halfway up. By now I was terrified of heights and actually wasn't healed of that fear until I was an adult.

Another way I got into trouble was when I read library books. Dad wanted me to help my mother, so he scolded me when he saw me reading. Of course, I knew I needed to obey, so I asked Mom on many occasions if I could help her, and even wanted her to teach me how to cook. Her answer to my cooking request was always, "I don't have time now; some other time." She usually didn't have any ideas for us to help at those times either. When we saw Dad coming to the house, Wilma and I quickly scurried to pick up a broom and swish it furiously to make it look like we were helping. Sometimes I fumbled with something in the drawers to look like I was cleaning it, or I'd start setting the table ahead of time.

I knew better than to read in the summer time; however, I thought it would be alright if I read on school nights. Frequently, though, on those nights, while minding my own business, reading a good library book, one of my brothers would walk by and slug me on my shoulder really hard. In turn, I would exclaim rather loudly, "Ow!" and begin to cry. Dad would look up from his newspaper and say, "Oh, shut up, before I give you something to bawl about." This happened frequently, and Dad never corrected my brother even after I explained that he had hit me. Dad also told me frequently, when I couldn't seem to please him, "You're just worthless. If we tried to sell you, we wouldn't even get a penny for you." His words convinced me then that my dad did not love me.

Eventually, I believed that I really was worthless, and because of the unfairness of it all, I felt a lot of anger toward my dad. I had unforgiveness and deep resentment against both my brother and dad boiling up within me for years. This carried over into my teen and adult years, and would be a source of my emotional problems for years as depression took over.

Though my dad was strict, he didn't treat me that badly when I was younger, so I couldn't figure out why suddenly everything got worse in my relationship with him and my brother. Later, I came to realize it all started after I asked Jesus into my heart when I was nine. I've learned we all have a spiritual enemy, the devil, who comes only to kill, to steal and destroy (John 10:10). It must have been part of a demonic plan to destroy me. Apparently, the enemy was speaking thoughts against me in their minds. Dad, without realizing it, spoke those thoughts to me out loud. I have long ago forgiven them both. I know Dad didn't realize how much harm his words caused or he wouldn't have said them.

I was a nervous and sensitive child so I got my feelings hurt easily. I prayed almost continuously for God to help me feel better and to change the circumstances. I remember when Wilma was getting too old to play childish games with me, I would again feel lonely and sad. I would often walk back and forth in our grove of trees, weeping and crying out to God, "God, why can't someone love me?" I even remember wanting to die. I didn't realize at the time how much God Himself loved me or that those negative feelings came from Satan to harm me.

Prayer life and spiritual development

While Dad was strict and didn't seem very understanding, Mom was always kind and gentle. She was so overwhelmed with work, so she didn't have much time for us. But often I remember her praying while cooking or ironing. I remember her words so clearly. "Oh, Lord," and then quietly she stated her request to Him. Her prayers were more the begging kind but I also heard her talking to God as a friend. She prayed often during World War II that her four sons would not be drafted. My three older brothers did not pass their military physicals, so were spared. By the time Ben was old enough to be drafted into the army during the Korean War, I remember him telling my mother that it was important for him to serve his country.

The Catholic nuns were a great influence on our spiritual life, teaching us to pray at school. That, coupled with hearing my mother pray about her concerns, showed me how to go to our Father in heaven as well. During my elementary years, we went to church often, especially during Lent when we would attend four times a week.

On one weekend during Lent, a service was held named "40 Hours Devotion." We were usually assigned an hour of prayer to be spent in church before the Blessed Sacrament (Eucharist). Then each night, after supper, during the 40 days of Lent, our dad always made us all sit around the kitchen table and pray the Rosary. It would seem so long and boring. Somehow, almost every time, someone would make a funny expression or sound, and then someone would start giggling. Immediately, we kids all got the giggles, much to my dad's irritation.

During the school year, we kids attended daily Mass. By the time we were 10 years old, we were required to lead the Rosary in front of the whole school. I got so nervous because the nun expected us to get it right. I was always so glad that Virginia would choose to be my partner; I was more confident with her by my side.

The Rosary beads were used to count off three prayers – a short praise prayer of glory to the Father, the Lord's Prayer and the Hail Mary to the Blessed Virgin Mary. We were to meditate on various mysteries of the Lord's life on earth while reciting 10 of the Hail Mary prayers for the so-called five mysteries. Again, I was afraid of displeasing the nuns for any mistakes I made, and I would pray, asking God to help me. I believe He was faithful since I never did get into trouble.

I was so frightened and worried that I would go to hell because I wasn't good enough. I so wanted to know God better so I could please Him more. I felt I was not living up to His expectations. We were instructed that when we disobeyed or committed a small sin, it was called a venial sin. If we died while having unconfessed venial sin, we would not go to hell but would go to purgatory to suffer, in order to make up to God the punishment we deserved, and we would remain there until we were good enough to go to heaven.

I was always afraid I had committed a big sin, called a mortal sin, which I was taught would send me straight to hell if I died without confessing it to the priest. This meant we must be truly repentant for displeasing God rather than just being sorry for getting caught. I was constantly worried that I would go to hell, yet I was afraid to confess to the priest because I thought I should have been better, and the priest would think I was terrible.

I just did not feel good about praying to the Blessed Virgin Mary. I remember when I was about 10, Sister Mercedes had taught us that we should make an altar during the month of May to honor the Blessed Virgin Mary. I asked Mom for a small pedestal fern table where I placed a statue of Mary. We were also to pick flowers for a tiny bouquet to set before the statue. I picked some wild violets, blooming out on the lawn, and put them in a small tumbler of water.

As I was about to kneel down in front of the statue to pray as our nun had instructed, for some reason, I just couldn't seem to go through with it. I felt a little fearful but didn't know why. I never did kneel to pray before that statue or any other statue. Somehow, I remembered at one time reading in the Bible, Deuteronomy 4:16, "Beware lest you act corruptly by making a graven image for yourselves, in the form of any figure, the likeness of any male or female" (RSV), and Leviticus 26:1 that said we should not set up an image or bow down before a carved stone or image. I believed God wanted me to know that.

I really had a hard time with the custom of May Crowning as well. I felt nervous when I saw an older teen, who was chosen for the honor, place a crown on the statue of the Virgin Mary, and then kneel in front of the statue as a lovely hymn was sung, giving Mary our love. It really looked like she was worshipping the statue itself, which the statement in Deuteronomy 4 seemed to forbid. I never told a soul, though, because we were always taught that we are just honoring Mary as Jesus' mother. She certainly was a wonderful example of obedience and is to be admired and loved because of it. I greatly admired her but I felt then and still feel we need to be careful not to give her more importance than we do Jesus. He is the One who suffered so intensely and died on the cross to save us all from hell.

After training by the Catholic nuns, I learned good habits of praying. The entire four grades of children in our classroom stood up and said a prayer when we started our school day and again before we went out for recess, and then once more when we came back in for classes. Before and after our noon lunch, we said a prayer, and we prayed before and after the afternoon recess, and then again when we went home.

The habit of daily prayer taught me the importance of praying frequently. I came to truly value the sisters' discipline and good influence on me, and believe it has helped me obey God more easily over the years. Yet I was one of those little girls who begged God for this, and "Please, God! Please, God!" for that. There certainly wasn't much faith in my desperate little prayers.

Never, never gossip

When I was 7 years old, an incident happened that I have never forgotten and will not forget all the days of my life. Though it was a shameful, frightening lesson, it taught me to avoid gossip and to be extremely careful about keeping facts straight. One day, one of the 4th graders came to me as

I was packing my book bag for home, telling me that one of my classmates in the 3rd grade was lying.

I had overheard my mother saying that the mother of this 3rd grade classmate sometimes told lies. To comfort the 4th grader, I said, "Yeah, my mother says that her mother lies, so she lies, too." Then I left. Apparently the 4th grader wrote a note to this 3rd grader, telling her, "Dear _______. Elsie said your mother is bad and so are you." Unfortunately, she carelessly dropped it on the floor, or maybe she wanted it to be seen, because the nun picked it up and read it.

The next day, the nun had me get up in front of all four grades and stand before the offended party, my classmate, to tell her that I was sorry for saying she was bad. I still remember the shame and feeling of betrayal, because I had not actually said those words. My words had been twisted to be something worse. The hardest part was that this mother was extremely protective of her children and occasionally would come to scold the nuns if she disagreed with something they had done to or told her children. I was terrified she would tell my parents.

The next day, the girl came up to me. "My mother said she wants to see you after church on Sunday." Talk about fear! I was absolutely sick about it and dreaded to go to church that Sunday. I, of course, prayed my "Please, God; please, God" prayers all weekend so my parents wouldn't find out. Nothing ever did happen. The mother either forgot or just let it drop. To this day, I am careful to keep facts straight. I keep others' secrets when I'm told something in confidence. Throughout the years, I have heard scandalous things in confidence, but I have never repeated them to a soul, all because of that terrifying incident. Hard as it was, it was a valuable lesson for me.

Fervent prayer answered

When I was 13, I came to the conclusion that if I prayed to this big God long enough, and if I was a good enough little girl, and if it was His will, He would answer my requests. I didn't realize it then, but I see now that I actually did have some faith when I prayed. When I reached the 8th grade, my concern was to pass the 8th grade county exams given at our courthouse. It was a requirement everyone wanting to enter high school had to meet. Though our nun drilled us each day to prepare us for those dreaded exams, I was terrified I would not do well. I figured that if I prayed hard and long enough, maybe God in His mercy would help me pass.

When we had our 8th grade graduation ceremony at the country school before going to high school in a different parish, our priest proudly announced, "One of our students has received the second-highest test score in the entire county." When he spoke my name, I was so overwhelmed, I cried. I remember people staring at me, wondering why I was crying. God had certainly surprised this young farm girl. Though I was thrilled that He answered my heartfelt prayers, I didn't really feel I deserved the honor. That was when I started believing that maybe God did love me enough to do something so wonderful for me.

CHAPTER 7

HIGH SCHOOL

"In his heart a man plans his course, but the Lord determines his steps."

Proverbs 16:9 NIV

All summer long, after my 8th grade graduation in 1948, I thought about going on to high school. Virginia and the other girls were going, but I knew it was impossible unless God helped me get there. Dad was from the proverbial "old school" and believed that girls did not need further education. He believed girls should stay home and learn homemaking skills so they could become good homemakers and mothers.

Other than my nervous episodes, I really liked school, and even more than that, I loved learning new information about any subject. I also wanted to know more about homemaking and didn't think Mom would ever really have time to teach me her skills. Every time I asked her if she could show me how to cook, she always answered that she didn't have time right then. Because of my great desire to attend high school, I kept on praying that if it was God's will, I would somehow get to go.

It was the last weekend before Guardian Angels Catholic High School began classes when something unusual happened. My mother and I were waiting for Dad at our local grocery store where we shopped each Saturday night. It was nearing closing time when a long-time friend of Mom met us as we waited. She had been widowed at an early age many years ago. She asked if I was the youngest of the family. When Mom said yes, she asked my age. Mom answered that I was 13.

The lady's next question was whether I was going on to high school. My mom answered, "No, John won't let her go." The friend replied with a hint of indignation, "You need to let her go. I wish I could have gone when I was young. I wouldn't have gotten stuck with being a housekeeper for priests all these years. When my husband was killed, I couldn't do anything else to support myself because I didn't have a high school education. Don't you do that to her (meaning me)," she emphasized. "Let her go to high school to get more education."

I was shocked but amused, wondering what Mom would say and do about the suggestion. The next afternoon, I found out. Mom and Dad had a long discussion about my situation within my earshot. Mom was quite insistent and rather upset. They argued for a while, and then Dad finally walked upstairs to their bedroom to think about it. When he came down later, I heard him say, "We better call the nuns and see about boarding Elsie. I'm not going to drive her to West Point and back every day."

Inside my heart I said, "Hurray, You did it, God!" I felt like shouting and singing but I didn't know quite how to react, not wanting to irritate my dad more than he already was. I didn't want him to change his mind, so I stayed quiet. I did get concerned about what I could possibly wear. Here it was the day before school was starting and I didn't really have any suitable clothes.

That evening, my newly married brother Leo and his wife, Lorraine, dropped by. Mom and I both mentioned my dilemma, and Lorraine said she had some hand-me-downs that might fit. She graciously went back home to retrieve them, and I had my wardrobe. Though I was truly grateful, I was anxious as well. She was 10 years older than me, so, of course, her early 1940's clothes, though pretty, were totally outdated with their dropped waists that had once been stylish. I had no other choice but to start my new adventure at a boarding house and new school in 1948 with seriously outdated clothes.

Needless to say, to my utter shame, I got stares from the very girls I wanted most to impress. Not only did my outdated dresses hang on me like garments on wire coat hangers, but also my hair, which I rolled up on narrow aluminum curlers, became tight and unmanageable. It stuck way out from my head, looking wooly and dry, totally different from all the other girls' hairstyles. I had grown up using aluminum curlers, but my mother and I didn't realize that those were no longer used. Pin-curled hair was now the fashion. I noticed soon that even some of the guys gave me frowns. I definitely looked like the "drip," the uncomplimentary name the guys called me.

Boy, was I determined to learn how to do pin curls. I watched the other girls at the boarding house every night! I practiced twisting strands of my hair into curlicues and pinning them down with bobby pins, sometimes two, until I could do them all over my head (even in the back) without looking in the mirror. I got used to sleeping with those bobby pins stuck all over my head, all in the name of fitting in.

I liked most of my classes: Science and Biology, English, Social Studies and Typing and even Home Economics I. But I hated Algebra and Geometry, even though it was taught by my favorite teacher, Sister Frances, who had us dissecting frogs in Biology. She had a way of making every subject interesting, and she was so kind. I opted for both General Math and Geometry in my sophomore year because I could quit Geometry if I didn't like it, and quit it I did because I already had enough credits. The General Math was mostly review, so that was easy.

I was thrilled about learning to sew in Home Economics, which we took at the local public high school. I loved to sew and got an A, which I was really happy about. Mom was proud of me, too. I was excited about sewing things for myself, though I did blunder badly on my red corduroy vest, which was called a weskit in those days. I didn't know I had to lay all the pattern pieces on the fabric in one direction, so my finished garment was lighter in the back than the front. I had to rip it out, buy more fabric and cut a new piece to be placed in the back. Soon my efforts were quite presentable, even using Mom's old treadle sewing machine.

Boarders' house

My boarding experience where the teaching nuns lived started out well. Our food, which was served in the large dining hall, was agreeable with my palate; in fact, the food was quite good. The nun who did all the cooking was a good cook. After dinner, we used the long tables to do our homework from 7:30 to 8:30 p.m. An elderly nun, who was kind and sweet, watched over us to keep us out of mischief. She did a lot of crocheting each evening while keeping an eye on us students. I still have the little doily she helped me crochet.

Our dorm room with enormously high ceilings on the 3rd floor held six twin beds on each side of the room with its dark, oil-stained wooden floors, white painted, cracked walls, and several lavatories (sinks) and toilets. There were no closets. Makeshift racks made of pipes were provided to hang our coats and heavier clothes. Most of our worldly possessions were kept in our suitcase, which we daily slid under our beds.

Frequently after the lights were out, someone would start telling spooky stories while the trees blowing in the wind cast eerie shadows through the tall, oversized windows that were framed with thin curtains. The windows formed unusual shadow silhouettes on the walls around us. Our imaginations really got carried away. I actually felt fear sometimes as I remembered a sinister murderer in an old mystery movie, though I knew that no one could possibly reach us that far up. Someone invariably shrieked, followed by muffled laughter under the security of the bed covers.

Many times we got the giggles over some humorous anecdote. Of course, by then we'd hear a gentle rap on the steam pipes. The nuns tried to keep some "law and order," communicating to us by banging on the steam-heated pipes reaching clear up to our 3rd floor room. Woe to us if one of the nuns ever had to climb those three flights of stairs to discipline us, or so we thought. We'd listen for the squeaky steps which would surely tip us off that a nun decided to come upstairs.

When mornings arrived, our wakeup call was the sound of loud rapping on the pipes, which scared us out of our deep sleep. After breakfast, we all had clean-up jobs to do, which included dishes and sweeping the huge, wooden floor. As we worked together, the jobs were completed quickly. We also took turns cleaning the dorm room. The large clock in the church tower struck every hour and half hour so we had no excuses for ever being late for any meal, activity, Mass, or our classes.

After eight hours of school, we had our afternoon snacks of homemade cookies, and then we frequently walked downtown to window shop or around the scenic, wooded area nearby. At 5 o'clock, it was time to do homework at the senior assembly over at school. Supper was served at the boarders' house at 6 o'clock, after which we had KP (kitchen patrol) duty again before more homework was done on the long tables.

A large excavation in the woods nearby, called the Clay Pit, was where we frequently had wiener roasts, shuffling in the mounds of leaves in the cool, brisk autumn air. Parties or dances were held for us "inmates" several times during the school year across the alley at the high school, but at 7 o'clock each school night, one of the nuns would gather us together for fun at senior assembly again, which consisted of various activities like singing, dancing, basketball, kickball, playing games or even hand embroidering on special projects.

"O Lord, you have heard their insults, all their plots against me, what my enemies whisper and mutter against me all day long. Look at them! Sitting or standing, they mock me in their songs."

Lamentations 3:61-63 NIV

I did have some experiences at the boarders' house that deeply wounded my emotions. Also staying there throughout the school year was a classmate from another small town who had expensive clothes and lots of them. Her mother obviously spoiled her because we would hear her talking very disrespectfully to her mother when she came to take her home on weekends. This young teen was unkind and controlling. In our day, her type was called a "snot."

After she had been putting me down with her snide remarks and daily calling me "Feed Sacks," I was sick of her! One time, while singing one of our basketball cheerleading songs, she substituted the words, "G.A. will shine tonight, G.A. will shine," with "Feed Sacks will shine tonight!" I knew she was ridiculing my outdated clothes. The words felt like a knife in my heart and I felt so ashamed. Apparently, she felt superior when she could put someone else down.

None of the other girls ever stood up to her or came to my defense, so

I assumed they all felt the same way, and that crushed me. I felt inferior to everyone and I just couldn't be myself anymore. Most of the girls at the boarders' house tolerated me, but usually ignored me after school hours and/or during the activities. That rejection was tough to take; I longed to have Virginia there with me. I prayed a lot during those days just to get through. I never told Mom or Dad. I knew Dad would say, "Well then, quit."

One day after school, I went up to our dorm room to get something. As I opened the door, I saw that rude girl rummaging through my suitcase. I had just had it with her. I flew into a rage and screamed at her, wanting to know what she was doing. She answered in a sarcastic tone, "I was just looking for some bobby pins." I yelled at her to stay out of my stuff. I was hurt because again none of the other girls in the room defended me; they just stared at me. If it hadn't been for seeing Virginia during the day, I probably would have quit school. Eventually it got better when the rude girl quit high school the next year. I certainly was relieved that I didn't have to put up with her any longer.

Though school life became much easier with this intolerable girl gone, my pain was deep, and the inferiority I felt constantly was hard to overcome. At times, I still have problems with inferiority, though I am now in my 70's. I made a vow to myself way back then: "Someday, when I have my own money, nobody, but nobody is ever going to make fun of me again. I will have a lot of clothes so I can look coordinated and good all the time."

Now, more than 55 years later, I still shop and dress with great care. If my clothes, shoes and purse don't match perfectly or the colors are uncoordinated or don't fit me well, I feel compulsion to change several times until I feel like I look presentable. I still have fear that people, especially in my hometown, will gossip or ridicule me about my appearance. I hate it each time I go through that, but the compulsion is so strong, I know God has to change me.

My boarders' house experience came to an end at the beginning of my junior year when a neighbor boy, Hilbert Hunke, who lived about three miles beyond our farm, began his freshman year at Guardian Angels. His parents bought him an old car, and my dad paid him to stop at our driveway each day to pick me up. One of my classmates, Rose Ann (Rosie) Batenhorst Ortmeier, and her brother Kenny rode along as well. My high school life became much easier, and much more interesting and fun.

We would usually stop at the local drug store for ice cream bars or cones for an after-school snack. Rosie was kind to me, and many times she paid for my treat because Dad did not give me money. Rosie and I got along well, and I was most grateful to her.

As I rode to school each day, Virginia and I became more confident by comforting and strengthening each other. We developed good friendships with some of the other girls in our class and had more fun during our junior and senior years. Since I had learned to sew, I wheedled some money out of Mom (she was willing to dole out from her egg money for me to have some new things) for fabric and sewed some circle skirts. I found cute tops and sweaters in Montgomery Ward, Sears or Spiegel's mail order catalogs. I was able to dress more fashionably like the other girls, yet staying within Mom's budget. I even convinced Mom to buy me some new saddle shoes to go with my white bobby socks, which everyone wore those days.

For dress-up occasions, we wore silk or rayon stockings with dark seams running up the back. The stockings were held up with garter belts or even uncomfortable girdles. Always, we girls were checking our seams or asking each other if they were straight. Many times, horror of horrors, the hose would slither around until the right leg and left leg never matched, or even one or both seams would be crooked. Eventually, the lovely seamless nylons became available, long before panty hose were fashionable. Things were definitely looking up for me. I was able to dress more stylishly. Even a few of the guys started to flirt.

A boyfriend

It was during the summer before my junior year that a special guy came into my life. The grandson of one of the pioneer families who lived on a farm just two miles east of us, came to visit his grandmother and aunt and uncle for summer vacation. Bill became friends with my brother, which I really took advantage of! I flirted with him every chance I got. Soon, he wanted to take me out. I was only 15 and my parents had a rule: no dating until age 16. I had a serious crush on him so I coaxed my brother Ben to give me rides when he went out. He would drop me off wherever my new love interest happened to be.

By this time, Bill had decided to skip high school and live permanently at his grandmother's home rather than go back to his hometown. His uncle, who lived there with his grandmother and aunt, was not well and needed the young man's help with the farm work.

About that same time, when I turned 16, my brother Fred married his sweetheart, Marcella, on May 9, 1951. She asked me to be her maid of honor. It was a great honor, and I was thrilled to wear the pretty orchid bridesmaid dress with a matching picture hat. I loved dancing the night away at their wedding. Of course, I spent a lot of time with Bill. The very next month, my oldest brother, Casper, married his sweetheart, Theresa, on June 19. They had a lovely wedding in which my sister Wilma was a bridesmaid. Again, it was an exciting time, and I spent a lot of time that day with my guy.

Bill and I went together constantly after my 16th birthday, which really concerned my dad. Though he liked the young man, he was being protective of my morals, which I just didn't realize. It was then that Dad and I had so many fights. I thought he was too strict, so I manipulated him all I could. I also felt he was being unfair, so I became rebellious and disrespectful and didn't even try to please him anymore.

The situation was also hard on Virginia; I spent so much time with this young man that she felt left out. I had earned straight A's in high school until I started this relationship. After we started going out frequently, my grades slipped to B's. I was not doing my homework and was getting less sleep after staying out late at night. I have regretted letting my grades slip ever since.

Before graduation, in 1952, my brother Ben was drafted into the U.S. Army. He was eventually sent to Korea. His unit was with anti-aircraft, the unit in charge of protecting U.S. planes from enemy attacks by bringing down enemy aircraft. He and his fellow soldiers arrived in Korea in the middle of winter, so life was hard for him; however, the war soon ended and we were all relieved. I, for one, had missed him greatly. Because of our frequent double-dating with his future wife, Rita, Ben and I had grown close. We had so much fun together when I was a teen, even though he was five years older than I was.

CHAPTER 8

LEAVING HOME

Virginia and I turned 17 just before we graduated from high school. We were both ready for a new adventure by then. She soon joined her big sister and got a job in a large office at a meat packing plant, Geo. A. Hormel Co., in Fremont, Nebraska, sharing a room at a rooming house with her sister. We really missed each other. Virginia wanted me to move to Fremont as well, but, of course, my dad lost trust in me because of my disrespect and disagreements with him months before, so he wanted me to stay home where he could keep an eye on me.

The few secretarial jobs available in West Point were taken by my classmates who were better in shorthand than I was so I didn't feel there was much hope. After weeks of Mom trying to convince Dad that I needed to go to Fremont because there were more jobs available, he allowed me to go. I got a job at the Hormel office as well. I met a young woman, Laverne Semrad, renting a room at Mrs. Smith's Rooming House. She invited me to rent a room with her, which was a good arrangement and we became close friends.

Mrs. Smith, a widow, whose husband had died when her three children were small, was sweet and motherly and shared her wisdom with us. We could go to her with our problems, and she always gave good advice. We had kitchen privileges that allowed us to make our sack lunches for work each morning and to take turns cooking our suppers and eating together.

I learned so much from Mrs. Smith. She graciously tolerated our mistakes, even my stinky sauerkraut. After months of cooking the stuff, smelling up her whole house, she laughingly asked that I not cook that "smelly ol' stuff" any longer. I had not even realized that it was a problem for her; I was glad to stop. (That was her only complaint and she showed great patience, I thought.)

She was also unhappy that my work hours were so unusual. I worked from noon until 9 p.m. She was always concerned about me, a young single girl having to take a cab each night from the plant. All I did all day long was add up pages and pages of invoices with an adding machine called a comptometer.

Finally Mrs. Smith convinced me to quit. When I told my parents, they were really upset. I stopped at the Nebraska Unemployment Office in Fremont after quitting my job. The man in charge told me to practice up on my typing and then come back to see what jobs were available. As soon as the manager of the bookkeeping department at one of the banks told him they wanted to hire another bookkeeper, the man from the unemployment service contacted me. I was excited when he shared that this job didn't require any training and that the banker preferred to train me himself.

I began work there on December 1, 1952. I learned the work quickly, and really liked it. My boss was an easy-going guy who never scolded much. He even teased us girls a lot. Besides posting bank ledgers and statements (before the days of computers), there was a variety of other office work to do to maintain the customers' checking and savings accounts, so I never got bored. I liked most of the people I worked with, though a few gave me a hard time. I met many acquaintances and made many friends through that job of five years. All of the officers, tellers and secretaries were good to me.

It was at this time that I learned about budgeting. The hard way. My parents didn't realize that I needed some nice clothes to work at a bank, and I never mentioned it. I wore some of my old school clothes and some church clothes the first two weeks. I will never forget when I got my first paycheck. I promptly marched to a ladies' clothing store and spent nearly my entire paycheck. Oh, was that fun to have my own money to get whatever I liked!

A few days after my splurge, I realized that I did not have enough cash left to buy groceries, only enough for the bus trip home. That scared me, but fortunately my mother sent food from home to tide me over. I didn't dare tell my parents what I had done. I would have been in big trouble or at least been severely scolded for my foolishness. From then on, I certainly saved up more than enough for groceries before I shopped for more clothing. I actually began a savings account, which later helped me with wedding expenses and then travel expenses to join my husband in the military.

"For men are not cast off by the Lord forever. Though he brings grief, he will show compassion, so great is his unfailing love. For he does not willingly bring affliction or grief to the children of men."

Lamentations 3:31-33 NIV

A broken heart

I believe Mom's and Dad's prayers for me eventually won out because God broke up the relationship with Bill soon after I started working at the bank. The breakup in February before my 18th birthday certainly was not my choice. I was heartbroken because we had talked about marrying some day when we were older. I thought I truly loved him and felt he was "the one."

The emotional pain made me physically sick and I could barely function. I prayed diligently, begging God for my "steady" to come back to me, but this man was not in God's plan for my life.

One particular evening after work, I was really in the depths of despair. Laverne was out for the evening and so were the others. My thoughts of depression gave me a plan. I would buy a bottle of aspirin and take the whole bottle to kill myself. There was no way I could live any longer without this young man, I thought, and there was no chance of winning him back because he had fallen for my cousin (whom he eventually married).

As I was thinking about how to take my life, some other very strong thoughts, like a loud voice, interrupted my plans. "If you kill yourself, you will go straight to hell. This situation you are in seems like hell but it is only temporary. Hell is forever and ever. You will never, ever get out." I thought those words must be from God. I knew they didn't come from me.

I said to the voice, "But what should I do? I can't take this pain anymore." I then thought of St. Patrick's Catholic Church, which was located three blocks from the bank. I felt strongly that I needed to go there the next day after work to pray before walking home.

I was surprised when I got to the church to find about ten people quietly praying in various pews, and every one of those people got up at the same time and left quietly as I entered. I walked way to the front of the church to sit in the first pew to have more privacy, but no one else came in. As I told God how I felt, I sobbed from the heartache and pain.

Somehow after about 15 minutes, I felt strong enough to get through another evening. I got through the next day also after the same thing happened at the church. That scene took place every afternoon for several weeks. Each time, whether 2 or 15 people were in the church praying, they always finished their prayers and left when I came in. Since we never got off work from the bank at the same hour each day, the people must have been leaving at different times. I knew somehow this was God's way of helping me get through the pain as I cried out to Him. I believe He was graciously healing my emotional pain. I even kept my food down more often.

I also realized then how stupid the suicide plan had been. That experience actually helped me trust God more. I knew then He loved me and cared so much about how depressed and devastated I felt. In His great love for me, He wanted me to have the privacy of crying out to Him.

Years later, the Lord had me write to my former beau and his wife, a kind, loving letter, telling them how much better it was that they were married instead of him marrying me. Bill would not have been happy with me because of my emotional problems. I was able to tell them briefly how Marv and I had committed our lives to the Lord and how He had blessed us so much. Bill's wife thanked me, responding gratefully and kindly, and now we communicate comfortably whenever we see each other.

At the same time, my sister Wilma and her boyfriend, Paul Gentrup, got engaged. They enjoyed driving the 35-mile trip to Fremont to see me each week, which did wonders for me in my grief. They always invited Virginia along and sometimes they brought a friend of our family, a single older man who lived near my parents' farm. We had a lot of fun hanging out together; all that laughter did me a world of good. We usually saw movies or just drove around near Fremont or ate out together.

The dance halls

Soon my grief subsided and we started going back to our old hangouts, the large dance halls. I had learned to dance quickly and loved it. The music was beautiful, almost intoxicating. I liked nothing better than keeping time with the beat, many of which were the fast-paced polkas. In those days, if one did not have a boy ask her to dance, we girls danced together to "advertise" our dancing abilities. It was always a good way to practice our moves as well.

The guys standing around watched, whether we were pretty ladies or if we could dance well. Invariably, two of them would cut in. I never tired of dancing, so I never sat down to rest on benches set against the outer walls as many shy girls did. Dancing continued from 9 until 11:30 p.m., when there was a short intermission for the band to take a break. At this time, couples would go downtown to grab a hamburger and pop at a café. Many couples started their relationships during those intermissions. What could the guys lose by asking a girl to have refreshments together for that short period of time? They didn't have to spend much time with a boring intermission date. Dancing resumed at the hall again from midnight until 1 a.m.

Since I loved to dance, I had many guys asking me, and soon I was back in "circulation." My older brother, Fred, and his wife, Marcella, watched me when they attended the dances. Sometimes Fred told me later, "I saw you dancing with that one guy. Don't ever go out with him. He can't be trusted." I assured him that the fellow wasn't my type and I would be careful. I liked and appreciated advice from my big brother who cared about me and was so protective.

I learned later that two of the fellows had been waiting for me to break up with the "love of my life" so they could take me out. At the time, though, I had been badly hurt, so I determined I would not get serious with any guy for a long time. I was not interested in dating because I did not want to lead them on. I just wanted to dance with different guys and skip the dating.

Several kept asking so finally I went out with them. Later, I had to tell them that I could only be a friend, which hurt their feelings. In the meantime, gossips in my hometown asked my mother why I didn't date just one man. They had been insinuating that I must have loose morals. I explained to Mom that I didn't want to get serious with anyone, and then possibly get hurt again.

To get to those dances, Virginia and I would take the Greyhound bus home from Fremont to West Point, catch a ride with Paul and Wilma, Ben and Rita or someone else, and then get home between 1:30 and 2 a.m. Dad was kind enough to drive me or both of us to the train depot in West Point to catch the 4 a.m. train back to Fremont, so we didn't bother to go to bed. It was impossible to sleep on the noisy ride back on that rickety old train. The train engine made so much noise, as did the booming, jerking brakes as they screeched along, metal against metal, with the loud, shrill whistle as they stopped at the two little towns in between West Point and again at Fremont. They even whistled at every little road that intersected the railroad tracks to clear the track of cars or beasts.

That 35-mile trip by car took two hours by train, so we would arrive in Fremont at 6 a.m. and still have to walk with our bag or suitcase 10 blocks to our apartment. I had to be at work at 8:30, so all day my eyes felt like sand had been dumped into them. I joked that I could use a few toothpicks to keep my eyelids open. Somehow I always managed to get through the day. The fun we always had was worth the bumpy all-night train ride.

Chapter 9

Depression

"Even in laughter the heart may ache, and the end of joy may be grief."

Proverbs 14:13 ESV

During all that time of "playing the field," something began happening to me that I could not understand. At the dances or other occasions, whenever there were lots of young people around, I'd be filled with joy, loving the sound of the music and laughing with everyone at funny situations. As soon as I got home to my apartment, however, I fell into a depression, because, once again, the party was over. Hating to return to reality, I just never wanted the fun to end. It seemed I never felt satisfied.

Many nights, I cried myself to sleep. I knew this was not normal, but I didn't know what my problem was or what to do about it. I was laughing on the outside but crying on the inside. I never told anyone, not knowing how to even explain it. I was also very proud. I wanted everyone to like me, so I hid my feelings so no one would find out what I was really like and then reject me. Looking back, I believe it might have been connected to the perceived rejection and lack of attention from my father, since I seemed to thrive on the attention of all those guys at the dance halls.

Apartment dwellers

After Virginia's sister married my cousin in October of 1953, Virginia and I decided to rent a small efficiency apartment together. It had a tiny kitchen with built-in cupboards, a single wide sink, a small refrigerator and a small drop-leaf table. We had one small closet to cram our full-skirted dresses in, a full bath and a pull-out double bed. That bed didn't give us much room in our tiny living room, but it worked out well for us, and we got along great with our sweet, kind landlady and her husband.

Virginia and I started attending Saturday night dances at a hall in a small town near Fremont as well as the dances near our hometown. There we met a group of older, more mature fellows, well established in their work. They dressed really sharp and had nice cars. Best of all, they were superb dancers.

One of the fellows was especially kind and sweet to me; we had so much in common and liked each other from the start. We saw each other twice weekly that spring and summer. Virginia eventually married one of the fellows from that group of six.

Another wedding

In April of 1954, Ben arrived home safely from Korea – his military obligation completed. What a joyful time that was for Mom and Dad and for our entire family! He got home just in time be an attendant in the wedding of Paul and my dear sister, Wilma, on April 21. Again I was the maid of honor and I felt lovely in my beautiful blue bridesmaid dress. My new guy and all of his friends came to my sister's wedding dance. Virginia and I danced the night away, taking turns with all of them. My boyfriend didn't seem to mind when I danced with his friends, though I saved most dances for him. Boy, did some of the West Point girls ever stare at us, wondering about the handsome men we danced with! It sure did a lot for our egos as Virginia and I smirked at those who had put us down during days past, thinking, "Eat your hearts out, girls."

Another best friend

On May 2, right after Wilma and Paul's wedding, a friend and co-worker of Virginia's, Sharon Truelsen, came over to our apartment. She was all excited about her sister just having had a baby girl and wanted to tell Virginia all about it. Sharon and I clicked that first time Virginia introduced us, and we became the best of friends. Sharon has been faithful friend and a tremendous blessing in my life.

"Because of the Lord's great love we are not consumed, for his compassions never fail. They are new every morning; great is your faithfulness. I will say to myself, 'The Lord is my portion; therefore I will wait for him.'"

Lamentations 3:22-24 NIV

Another heartache

I continued to see my new beau all summer. When our relationship was getting serious, I started questioning him about his faith, knowing that my father would insist on me marrying a Catholic. My beau felt he could be just as good a person without attending church and told me about some hypocrites he knew who always attended their Catholic church on Sunday, yet lived like the devil all week. In a weak moment one night, he said, "Too bad you're Catholic. We could get married and raise a family. Now you'll have to go back to West Point and raise little West Pointers."

I knew then that while he may have loved me, he would not consider becoming a Catholic. I also sensed that drinking with the boys was important to him, which made me uneasy. He always said that he wouldn't take me out on Sundays, his evening to spend in the bar with the boys. I could just picture us years later, if we did marry. He'd be gone more and more while I stayed home on his farm alone with all of our future kids, doing all of the chores. I wanted someone who would attend Sunday Mass with me and our children, who would put me first rather than spend so much time with his friends. I decided then that I needed to break up with him right away. I told the Lord, "I need You to help me do this. I would like to be married someday, but I don't want to live like that." All I could figure was to just break it off fast and not give explanations.

When he called to see me again, I acted cold and refused to go out. Twice when he called, I refused, not giving any explanation, concerned that he would talk me out of my plan. Each time, after I hung up, I cried. It was hard, because I had fallen in love with him. Now, thinking back, I realize how I handled it was not fair to him. I should have told him the truth. I knew it would never work. I thought just making a clean cut would be better for both of us. I also realize that the Holy Spirit must have given me His wisdom when I knew how the marriage would have turned out; I learned many years later from this man's sister that I had been right.

I didn't stay lonely very long. Some of the girls at the bank arranged some blind dates for me, but nothing clicked. I met another nice, young farm boy from an area quite a distance away who started pursuing me. He was sweet, generous, kind, and handsome; however, no sparks flew. I didn't have the heart to refuse him, so we kept dating about once a week. I kept thinking that maybe I would fall for him, but he seemed more like a brother. My heart was still with the man I had just broken up with. Finally, one evening I realized I had to tell him that we were not meant for each other. I felt bad as he walked away, looking down, his shoulders sagging.

CHAPTER 10

MY ONE AND ONLY

"My beloved is all radiant and ruddy, distinguished among ten thousand."

Song of Solomon 5:10 RSV

It only took six more weeks for the Lord to bring me my future husband. Laverne, my former roommate, planned her wedding to Amiel Schmale for October 16, 1954. Our mutual friend, Sharon, convinced her father, a widower for many years, to drive us to the wedding dance. There, Sharon and I sat in a booth, chatting. Soon two young fellows asked us to dance. Marvin Popken asked Sharon, and I danced with his Army Reserve buddy Dennis Wachal. Marvin's friend was fun and a good dancer, yet, during the brief interlude before the next melody began, Sharon, a Lutheran, exclaimed to me, "The guy I danced with is Catholic. Why don't you dance with him and I dance with your guy?"

I thought, "How do you know they will ask us again?" Sure enough though, Marvin asked me to dance and his buddy asked Sharon. Though I thought Marvin was handsome and fun – he was in such a jovial mood – I mistook his enthusiasm with bragging and was turned off. He was telling me his dream. He said, "I intend to have $10,000 saved by the time I get married," and a few other boastful sentences. Judging his age to be in the early 20s, I almost scoffed, because in those days, $10,000 was quite a sum of money.

Sharon and I accepted the two guys' offer for refreshments at a downtown café during the intermission. It was fun joking with the three of them, but I decided to forget Marvin.

A few days later, he called me for a date. I refused, making up some lame excuse. He called the following week. I could see that this one wouldn't give up so easily so I decided, "Okay, I will go and get it over with. He'll be so bored, he won't ask me again, and then I will be rid of him."

Wow! To my utter surprise, the evening turned out wonderful. He was such a gentleman and so attentive. We had so much to talk about, and he was a lot of fun; we laughed all evening. He also scored favorably on one of my conditions: he didn't try to kiss me on the first date. If a guy was all over me, trying to kiss me on the first date, I marked him off as being only interested in my body, and I would never go out with him again.

On our second date, Marvin and I had another wonderful evening together, and this time he gave me two gentle goodnight kisses. Oooh la la, that got my attention! We continued our courtship from then on. I observed he had many of the qualities I wished for in a husband. For one thing, since I was old enough to think about marriage, I always wanted to marry a farmer because I liked the quiet and peace of farm life. Most of the farm boys seemed so humble and easy to talk with, which I liked. I wanted someone who would understand my sensitive emotions and be romantic and attentive. I wanted a hard-working man and a good provider. Best of all, Marvin was a Catholic man, a prerequisite for my dad and mom, and for me as well.

On Valentine's Day, he brought me a dozen gorgeous red roses. Impressed, I thought, "This man really knows how to treat a lady!" I noticed he always got so excited about little things he wanted to surprise me with that he could hardly keep a secret from me. That showed he had a caring, imaginative quality, which I liked. Things were definitely looking up. He even brought me to his farm home to meet his parents; I believed I made a good impression. I especially liked his dad, who was shy but warm as he asked all about my family. I was relieved they were farm people as well because we had quite a bit to talk about.

Sometime in late spring, Marv decided to test how I felt about him. One evening, while driving me to a dance, Marvin said, "You know, we have three Elsie's in our family already (referring to his three aunts), so one more wouldn't hurt, would it?"

I said, "Do you realize what you just said?"

He said, "Yes, I do."

I just said, "Oh, we'll see," trying to be coy, but I smiled delightedly back at him.

Engaged

Soon after, Marvin cooked up a secret plan with his married sister Betty and her husband, Richard Glodowski, to pop the question at their home near Fremont. It was May 3, 1955, the night before my 20th birthday, when Marvin suggested we stop by his sister's home. As we sat together on their sofa, he handed me my birthday gift. When I saw that the gift-wrapped box held a smaller, tiny box, I said, "Oh, my gosh!" Then I gasped when I saw the lovely diamond set in a heart design. He took my left hand, slipped the ring on my finger and said in a loving way, "Let's grow old together."

I said, "Okay, it's yes!" Then Richard snapped our picture.

How excited I was! By then, I really was head over heels in love with this man. I felt like my heart was singing as in the Scripture, Job 29:13, "And

I caused the widow's heart to sing for joy." (ESV). I told him right away we needed to wait a year to be married because my dad had always told all of us kids that he would not sign the marriage license for us; we all needed to be of age. I had also desired all my life to have a May wedding. Spring was my favorite time of year. Marvin was alright with that plan.

Not long after our engagement, we invited his parents to have dinner at my parents' home. The two couples hit it off beautifully. They all had a lot in common and chatted continuously, which made Marvin and me happy. It was fun to extend our courtship a year while I busied myself with our wedding plans and continued to work as a bookkeeper at the bank.

Virginia married her fiancé, Richard Wolfe, in September of 1955. Rather than live alone in the tiny apartment, I decided to move in with a former high school classmate, Bernice Gentrup. She had rented a second-floor room from a retired couple, not far from my apartment, after her roommate married. Bernice and I had kitchen privileges, which worked well for us. She met her future husband, Leonard Wadas, while I was living with her so we were not always at home the same evenings. We became quite close, and she, too, was always good to me. We had lots of fun together.

Since I was so thin, I knew I would have a problem finding a wedding gown that fit well without a lot of alterations. I decided to consult a seamstress who had sewn almost a hundred weddings through the years. I planned to have Virginia, Sharon and Bernice as attendants; however, it meant a lot to Marvin's only sister Betty to be in our wedding, so I skipped asking my friends and had Wilma and Betty as my attendants, along with my little niece, Marlene Luebbert, as my flower girl.

It was good that I had a seamstress, because Wilma found out she was expecting her second baby and needed a special gown, which my seamstress designed. We talked about having Richard as Marvin's best man, however, we thought the two couples would have more fun if the ladies could be escorted by their husbands. Mom and Dad offered to pay for all of the reception and dinner expenses, which was quite a blessing. I took care of the flowers, my wedding dress with the veil and all the rest of the smaller expenses.

This was such a wonderful time in our lives. Marv and I loved each other so much. The depression I had felt seemed to disappear because of Marv's strong love. Our time of engagement passed quickly with all of the busy activities getting ready for our big day.

CHAPTER 11

WEDDING BELLS

"He who finds a wife finds a good thing."

Proverbs 18:22 NASB

Finally, the big day arrived, our wedding day. I woke up too early at my parents' house and couldn't go back to sleep. I had been worried during the night, wondering if I had remembered everything, and thinking about all the decorations, arrangements and the supplies waiting in the City Auditorium at West Point, where the reception was to be held. I pictured every item I had packed into my faithful blue Samsonite suitcase for our honeymoon, knowing it was much too small but grateful that Marvin had a rod to hang over the back seat of his blue Ford to hold our extra clothes.

Because of all my concerns, I couldn't eat much the night before; I felt weak and shaky, and as usual, I felt big knots in my stomach. Soon, I smelled bacon frying down in the kitchen, which made me nauseous. I became fearful. "What if I'm too weak to walk down the aisle with Marvin?" "What if I faint?" "What if I throw up?" I started praying my "Please, God, please, God," prayers. Soon, who should come bounding upstairs but my beloved Marvin! Mom had told him to go upstairs to see me when she found out that I was feeling poorly. Marvin was all smiles and so excited. "This is our wedding day!" When he saw my sad face, he said, "What's the matter?"

I answered, "I feel sick. I don't know how I can walk down the aisle today." I started to cry.

He gave me a big hug and said, "Aw, don't worry, you'll be just fine."

I said, "You think so?"

He said, "I know you will. You have always made it other times. You can do it this time too."

Oh, did his confidence in me help! I started relaxing and felt better right away. He met me downstairs after I changed from pajamas to jeans and a shirt. I was even able to eat a little, and then get back upstairs to dress in my lovely gown that Mrs. Hendrickson had so painstakingly designed and sewn. My shoes and undergarments had been all set out the night before. I was thinking that the veil was still rather wrinkled, but later when Marvin's sister, Betty, offered to press it, I was too afraid that Mom's iron would scorch it, so I went to my own wedding in a wrinkled veil.

Fred and Marcella brought little Marlene, my flower girl (who was not yet 4), already in her long dress, to the farm to ride with us. Marcella helped her upstairs to wait where the rest of us added last minute touches to my attire. Paul, Wilma's husband, carried Marlene down the long stairs so she wouldn't trip. She looked like a beautiful little princess in her white polyester, dotted-Swiss dress designed to look similar to mine with her matching picture hat. When I saw Wilma and Betty in their gowns, I thought they looked like Southern belles with their large picture hats. I was pleased I had chosen the pretty shade of robin's egg blue for the dress fabric. Marvin and his attendants looked so handsome in their navy-blue suits. Even our ringbearer, Bruce Popken, Marvin's 5-year-old cousin, had his own navy-blue suit. He was such a handsome little boy.

I knew Marvin would see me in my wedding gown anyway, so we all rode to church in two cars. We were in Marvin's car, chauffeured by our best man, Paul, and my sister Wilma, our matron of honor. Following us were Richard and Betty, Marvin's sister, and our other attendants, who brought our flower girl, Marlene. As we drove to St. Anthony's Church, where I had been baptized and taken part in all of the important religious events of my life, I realized our day was absolutely gorgeous. Fluffy white clouds floated in a beautiful blue sky on this bright, 80-degree sunshiny day.

"God answered my prayers," I thought joyfully. When we arrived and the "Wedding March" began at 9 a.m., I felt such happiness and peace. I smiled so much, the priest, Father Virgil, actually whispered at one point, "You need to take this ceremony a little more seriously." Well, I knew one thing for sure, Marvin was "The One" for me and I was so happy.

The day went by quickly from then on. My mom served a light breakfast for us at our home, and after a lovely meal that noon at the West Point City Auditorium, we went to a photographer's studio to pose for pictures before the reception. I had also hired another photographer from Fremont to take candid shots all day. Aside from the wrinkled veil, everything went well.

The wedding dance was held in the same dance hall where Marvin and I had had so much fun dancing together. The hall held so many happy memories of our courtship. I never sat down that evening, having many long-time friends wanting to dance with the bride. And I was so very proud of my new husband.

"Therefore a man leaves his father and his mother and cleaves to his wife, and they become one flesh."

Genesis 2:24 RSV

Honeymoon

The next day, we started out on our honeymoon. Marv was so excited to take me to Colorado, and I was excited to see mountains. He enjoyed his Army Reserve Camp training held at Fort Carson in Colorado Springs three summers before and wanted to share it with me. I was delighted to see the Rocky Mountains. What a gorgeous state! I loved the scenery. We also drove through Wyoming on crushed rock rather than concrete and even on some cinder roads. We saw many lovely sights there as well as in South Dakota, including Mount Rushmore. The '54 Ford with its "overdrive" and 6 cylinders made it just fine throughout the trip. Soon our wonderful week was over. We arrived home to work and back to reality.

Marv had rented a little bungalow in Fremont that our landlady just happened to have recently built. I thought it so interesting that before we were married Marv told me several times that he wanted to give me a new home, so here we were, in a brand-new house. Who cared if it only had one bedroom and no basement for storage? He excitedly took me to a large furniture store at nearby Omaha and bought several rooms of furniture for the tiny house. I went back to my bookkeeping job at the bank and Marv started his new job with a plumbing company in Hooper, his hometown. Oh, we were gloriously happy in that tiny little house until…

CHAPTER 12

ARMY DAYS

A few weeks after we returned from our honeymoon, on July 19, we received some unwelcome news from the U. S. Selective Service of Dodge County, Nebraska. We were devastated to read the following:

> Dear Mr. Popken:
>
> We have received notice from the UAAR ADVISOR SUB-OFFICE, Fremont, Nebraska, that you have been ordered by them to report for a physical examination 31 July 1956 and that you will go on active duty on or about 6 September 1956.
>
> Very truly yours,
> Ada E. Sorensen, Clerk
> Dodge County Local Board no. 27

The date for induction to Fort Leonard Wood, Missouri, was changed to September 17. We thought our hearts would break when we had to say good-bye. Marv got through his eight weeks of basic training as well as he did because he had been used to hard physical work on his parents' farm. During those eight weeks, the loneliness and depression of missing him so much got to me. I couldn't eat because of depression and nerve problems. I kept getting nauseous when I tried to force down food. Soon I was actually throwing up each time I tried to eat. One of my brothers warned me that I needed to get a hold of myself or I would end up in an insane asylum. Oh, my! I believed him, and that made me even more afraid. To make matters worse, I didn't know what to do about myself. I didn't want to tell Marv or he would worry too much. I felt weak and was down to 92 pounds, skinny as a rail. I thought my brother had a point, but I still didn't know what to do.

One evening, I called my dear friend Sharon. She was preparing for her own wedding in a few weeks so she couldn't take the time to come over to the house, but she did call her family doctor, who was God's answer to my "Please, God; please, God" prayers. Her doctor actually made a house call the next evening. I told him my troubles, and just like a kindly daddy, he advised me that I shouldn't worry about not keeping down any food.

"When we have expectant ladies with morning sickness who can't keep anything down, we bring them to the hospital and feed them intravenously for a while until they are alright. We can always do that for you. Besides, even when you throw up, your stomach is never completely empty."

"I can give you sugar pills, and you can get better because you think they are helping, but you can also just do what I used to do. When I was a young intern, I had to make house calls. I would get so scared, I'd feel like throwing up. I didn't dare throw up in front of the patients, so I just had to swallow the hot stuff again. That's what you can do. Each time you start gagging, just keep swallowing until you can keep it down."

"Okay, I will try." I thanked him profusely and he left. I realized, years later, that he never even sent me a bill. I kept an orange down that day, and I have never again thrown up from nerves, thanks to that dear man's humility in telling me that he had the same problem. I never knew anyone who had the problem like I did, so it was wonderful to think that a well-known doctor, who became a heart specialist, experienced the same thing. What a blessing he was! I still can't eat when I'm nervous and I get a huge knot in my stomach, however, I am alright when I don't force down food. When I am relaxed again, I eat something soothing like soup or a banana, and then my stomach heals and I am back to normal. God is so good. He really did answer my prayers.

Once that problem was solved, I was blessed to drive to Missouri to visit Marv on Veterans Day weekend just before he graduated from basic training on November 26. My father and Uncle Gus accompanied me and visited their relatives near the Army Base during the time of my stay. Marv was then assigned to Germany. In the meantime, we enjoyed a whirlwind furlough from December 22 to January 4 of '57, after which he was flown from McGuire Air Force Base, New Jersey, to Rheine Main Air Force Base in Frankfurt, Germany.

He was assigned to the Second Armored Division at Mannheim to replace the supply clerk in that unit. It was a blessing for Marv to be able to work as a supply clerk while the other soldiers were out in the field on maneuvers. He issued supplies to the other soldiers and did not have to march or dig ditches as their unit continued training in the area around Heidelberg. He enjoyed sightseeing in the beautiful Black Forest and quaint villages while stationed with that unit.

Meanwhile, I moved from our little house to a small apartment and continued my job as a bookkeeper. I enjoyed my work at the bank, however the evenings were long and lonely. It helped to pour out my heart to Marv in the daily letters we sent to each other. On Friday nights, I would take the Greyhound bus home to West Point where my dad would pick me up at the bus station, and then I'd take the bus back again to Fremont on Sunday nights. I also spent a lot of time with another young married lady, Eleanor Wulf, who worked at our bank. She lived with her parents on a farm while her husband also served in the Army at Germany. Her parents were kind and I really enjoyed spending weekends at their farm. I also visited Marv's parents many weekends.

In August of 1957, a new unit, the 246th Transportation Army Aircraft Maintenance Co., was activated in Augsburg, 40 miles north of Munich. Marv was transferred to the unit as the new supply clerk and was promoted to Specialist 4th Class. There he met another young married man, Mervin Eastwold, of Ottawa, Illinois, who was assigned as the company clerk in the new Transportation Company. The two young men became fast friends. They worked their office jobs side-by-side with a kind father figure, Captain Roden Bentley.

Both men were raised on farms, both were the same age and both were married without children. They went everywhere together during their free times. Life was tolerable because their jobs were easy and enjoyable, and they had lots of fun together. As friends, they cheered each other up while missing us wives back home in the States. Mervin's wife, Phyllis, was busy working back in Illinois as I was in Nebraska.

Early in 1958, tragedy struck for Merv and Phyl. When Merv was drafted, Phyl moved from the lovely little trailer home they had bought as newlyweds to live with her parents. All of their furniture and wedding gifts were stored in that new trailer, waiting until his return from the military. One night the trailer burned along with all of its contents. No one knew what happened, though they thought there had been a problem with the wiring. Fortunately, they carried insurance on it all. Merv was so depressed; all he could think of was having his wife with him to start their lives over again. She didn't feel comfortable going to Germany unless I went too, so Marv called me at the bank one day in March of 1958, asking me to join him at Augsburg.

Adventures in Germany

I will never forget that day. Not having any modern satellites to relay the call, I could hardly hear Marv. When my fellow employees at the bank noticed, they all stopped the clatter of the bookkeeping machines and typewriters to stay quiet during our intercontinental conversation. They all cheered when I told them of Marv's exciting invitation. I quickly ran upstairs to talk to the vice-president and to some of my teller friends to get their advice. They all encouraged me to go. They explained that it was one thing to visit a foreign nation but quite another to live there; it would be a broadening experience I would never forget. I was also advised what to do and where to start, which was get to that important passport as well as necessary medical shots.

That evening I called Marv, which was, by then, the middle of the night in Germany. Again, it was hard to hear as the lull and a loud "wheesh" of the ocean waves could be heard against the transatlantic cables buried on the ocean floor. Though Marv and his friend were not the partying type, never drinking alcohol, I just couldn't believe he was serious in wanting me to spend all our savings and fly over there. I jokingly asked him if he'd been drinking.

Our mutual plan at the time of his induction was that I would save all of the money I could so he could buy farm machinery when he was discharged. He assured me that he was serious. We had missed each other so much. I prayed most of that night, deciding, like Gideon in the Bible, to put out a fleece before the Lord so I would know what He wanted me to do. I kept thinking of the banker's advice so I was really torn.

I told the Lord that I would know if I were to go if He had the passport come quickly. Then I would buy the airline ticket for the round trip, costing $725, which was quite a price in those days. My passport arrived in record time and I was glad to get the necessary shots. All of the bank ladies gave me a lovely shower/farewell dinner with many beautiful, personal gifts. I felt so loved and honored. Everyone was happy for me. I quit my job at the bank in March, a few days before I was to leave, and moved the contents of my apartment to Mom and Dad's place.

When Dad picked me up, he was angry that I was going. He had hoped that I would come to my senses and wait the last six months until Marv would be discharged. He yelled at me all the way home, telling me I was crazy for spending all of our savings. He also said other sharp words. "Why can't you wait until he comes home? He will be home in six months. You've waited this long; why can't you wait just a little longer?"

I cried and said, "I can't back out. It's too late now. Marv wants me to come." I told him that I didn't think it was right that he scolded me since it was our money I was spending, not his. He didn't talk to me the rest of my stay that weekend. That really wounded me. My oldest brother, Casper, and his family came on Sunday afternoon to say good-bye. That meant so much. My mother was also kind the whole time. She never objected and even offered to send blankets along or whatever I would need in Germany. When I left the next morning for Omaha, she was so happy that I could go, but Dad walked outdoors and wouldn't say good-bye to me. That was hard.

I thought, "I could get killed in a plane crash; doesn't he even care about that?" Months later, when I returned from Germany, Paul told me he thought my dad was just so afraid to let me go because of the possibility of a plane crash. He had even consulted Father Virgil, who had told him since we were married, it was only right that I be with Marv, my husband. Apparently, Dad did not agree with the priest. When I considered why he was so upset, I was able to forgive and forget. Fortunately, Marv's parents were happy about me joining their son in Germany.

On March 29, 1958, I took my very first plane flight, bound for Germany to be with my sweet husband. Though I was nervous about changing planes in Chicago, it all went well. Several ladies were on the flight with me who were joining their soldier husbands. I was glad to follow them at the airport since they seemed to know what they were doing.

While waiting at the Idlewild Airport (now John F. Kennedy Airport) in New York City, an announcement came over the intercom stating that the first jet passenger flight ever flown had just arrived from Brazil. That was an historic moment, and I wondered just how quickly it would happen again. When I boarded the Pan American DC-4, a prop plane, on the way to Frankfurt, I was impressed when we flew over the Statue of Liberty, thinking that I just may not come back, but I had a strange peace about it all. I felt close to God and was not afraid.

My feelings were different after the 18-hour flight and we landed at Frankfurt to change planes for the last leg to Munich. Oh my! I got so nervous, I felt like throwing up. I did lose a little in my paper bag just before landing. I had not seen my beloved for over 15 months, and it was almost overwhelming. Oh, the joy we both felt when my plane landed in Munich and I walked down the portable steps and onto the tarmac. There he was to hug and kiss me. He thought I looked great in my gray wool, Pendleton suit and perky little black hat with black pumps and matching purse. I had saved quite a while to buy the ensemble for this happy occasion. He showed up in his light blue suit he bought in Germany. He had gained weight, and I thought he was quite a hunk.

Before we wives arrived in Germany, the guys went in together and bought a used Mercedes that used to be a police car. It had the "Mox-Nix sticks," which were sticks used for turn signals that extended from posts behind the doors, and all kinds of fun gadgets still attached. That was a good little car and the guys never really had any trouble with it. When we went back to the States, Merv kept it and later sold it to another American couple right before he returned to the States.

I was delighted when Marv brought me to the apartment he and Merv had leased at 35 Leisenmahd Street in Haunstetten, a suburb of Augsburg. The two bedrooms, kitchen, and a tiny bathroom were on the third floor. I thought it was so cute because there was a tiny efficiency two-burner electric stove, a tiny apartment-sized refrigerator, a large, white oak buffet (like a dresser without the mirror) for our dishes, and a small, rectangular, white enameled table with two wooden chairs. In one corner sat a brown leather Davenport with a headrest on one end.

I learned quickly that the tiny oven only worked when I had the large burner off, so I had to start cooking early in the day to finish our meals on time. After the first time, I also learned the difference between Centigrade and Fahrenheit degrees. I overheated the stove so much, the knob got scorched. Oh, my!

Our bedrooms each had a small, pot-bellied, wood-burning stove. The solid wood single beds were covered with flannel sheets and a feather bed comforter on the mattresses. The first night, the comforter got tossed on the floor when we turned over in bed so we were left in the cold. To remedy that situation, Marv brought some twine home from work and tied the bottom two corners of the comforter to both bed posts at the foot of the bed. It was still quite cold out when I arrived, so Marv and I were happy to snuggle in one twin bed to stay warm.

No closets were built in. Instead, we had a large wardrobe with a full-length mirror on one of the doors. One side of the wardrobe held our clothes and the other side had narrow drawers. It was quite nice, really. There was also a wicker chair in one corner of our room, and the floor covering was a rug-sized, cheaper type of linoleum. Occasionally, we bumped our heads under the slanted ceilings.

At the end of a long hall was the bathroom. I got pretty frightened with my first experience of using the toilet. The reservoir was above the stool. A handle was fastened on a chain, which, when pulled, let the water drain down from the reservoir through a 1.5- inch pipe leading to the toilet to flush it. I gingerly pulled that chain because I couldn't find the handle to flush it. Eeek! The noise really scared me. It sounded like Niagara Falls above my head. The guys sure got a laugh out of that and so did I.

The bathtub, though new, was old-fashioned on claw legs. It had a hand-held hose with a nozzle for spraying (a makeshift shower), but it worked nicely, even for shampoos. The water heater was quite different as well. To have warm water, we built a small fire at the bottom, underneath the tank. The water took at least half an hour to heat to a comfortable temperature. We were always building fires, it seemed, because there was no running hot water.

We often left our shuttered windows open when the weather warmed up. We never had a problem with flies, but we'd have honey bees come in frequently. We realized why many farmers had their barns attached to their houses. They didn't have fly problems! It rained a gentle shower almost every afternoon, but soon the sun would come out and everything was pleasant again. Occasionally, it rained much of the day, but usually the weather was lovely.

Ten days after I arrived, Phyllis flew in. We were compatible right from the start. Phyl studied and soon received her Military Driver's License, which was great. We took turns cooking by the week and would plan our meals so that we could buy together at the Army commissary and split the cost. It worked well, except that I made large farmer meals, even at noon. The others felt those were rather fattening, so when Marv left for the States and I was left behind to fly back a week later, I noticed Merv and Phyl had more lunches than huge meals, which was much easier. I wondered, "Why didn't I do that?" Even I had gained 16 pounds during those five and a half months.

Each day, after we had our work finished, like the dishes, hand laundry, ironing, or picking up our rooms, Phyllis and I took off with Phyl manning the Mercedes to explore new areas of the city. We had great fun as we shopped or just drove around. The guys got used to us dropping them off at the base so we could take the car and go as we pleased to explore new areas, quaint little shops or large department stores all over Augsburg, which was quite a large city. That was the life!

It was fun trying to communicate with the Germans, especially when we shopped, and shop we did! At one point, I realized my hair was getting straight and shaggy. I really needed a perm, so we looked around for a beauty shop. Of course, we couldn't find anyone who spoke English, so one day we just picked a shop and went in. I picked up a magazine of different hairstyles and decided on one I liked, showed a young lady the picture, made a snipping motion with my fingers to communicate that I wanted a haircut, pointed to some perm rods and sat down. Somehow, I trusted her, thinking it would be a neat adventure to see what would really happen. She did a wonderful job! It turned out great and it only cost me $3.25. Wow!

The guys had Saturdays off (unless an alert was called), so we would take off to a different area of Germany to sightsee. We usually took in movies several times each week for 25-cents at the Infantry Kaserne next to the mess hall on the post. Or we frequented some of the other theaters owned by the U.S. The meals we ate out were inexpensive and always very good. Frequently, we ate at a German cafe that featured pizza; that was a treat as well.

One weekend, we all decided to travel to Chiemsee and the Berchtesgaden recreation area, the U.S. Armed Forces Recreation Center in Bavaria, known at that time as the convention site of Europe. There were 13 different tours to choose from with varying events available, four hotels and four movie theaters, as well as 12 different sports activities offered. There were church services for all faiths provided as well. We chose to tour Obersalzberg, the former mountain retreat of Adolf Hitler. His headquarters cost around $2 million dollars to build in 1938. This area included barracks for SS Troops, Hotel Platterhof, where Hitler's party delegates stayed (known as Gen. Walker Hotel when it was owned by the U.S. Military), the Hotel zum Turken, the homes of Bormann and Goering, Hitler's closest associates, and of course, Hitler's own house, the Berghof.

On April 25, 1945, The Royal Air Force had bombed this area and later on May 5, the SS troops set fire to Hitler's house. In April 1952, the Bavarian government decided to blow up all the buildings because they didn't want any shrines to be erected in Hitler's honor. They did leave his Tea House as it was and gave it to the German Alpine Club, who used it as a restaurant. Our tour scheduled us to see the Tea House, which is called Eagle's Nest, built high on a mountain, 5,000 feet above sea level. It took 3,000 men 17 months to build it, and on April 20, 1937, it was presented to Adolph Hitler for his 50th birthday. Mussolini, Hitler's friend from Italy, gave a marble fireplace as his gift. Needless to say, the 6-room home was lavish and cost around $7 million. It was used as a tea house and for conferences during the five times Hitler was there.

The road leading up to Eagle's Nest is four miles long. We couldn't help but be frightened as we looked out our tour bus windows. All we could see was the steep mountainside and the deep valley below. The last 4,000 feet we rode in an elevator after we walked through a brass tunnel. We had a beautiful view from Eagle's Nest. From there, we saw the Danube River far below, Salzburg, Austria, and Konigsee, which is a beautiful lake. Inside the house, we saw all the original furniture of the Tea House. Hitler's live-in girlfriend, Eva Braun, had her own living room, lavishly decorated.

We also saw the homes of Bormann and Goering. Another weekend, we chose to tour the salt mines at Berchtesgaden, Chiemsee. We were given funny-looking uniforms to wear, consisting of black trousers and black coats with leather belts that came low in the back and funny black hats for the guys. We girls received the same coats and belts, although we got to wear white, draw-string trousers, and our hats were larger with white trim. A small train with a full-length, brown leather cushion to sit on carried us deep into the mine. We hung on to each other so we wouldn't lose our balance and fall off as the little train ran swiftly down deep into the mine with 11 other people hanging on behind us.

We had the fun of sliding down slick, wooden slides to get to another part of the mine. This explained the purpose of the leather belts, to protect our fannies from the friction. We were surprised at how the salt was mined and all got a little box of different salt samples. They even took a photo of our little group.

Another weekend, we toured one of King Ludwig's three castles in the Chiemsee area. It was built on an Island in the Chiemsee Lake in approximately 1885. This one, Herrenchiemsee, was styled after Versailles, King Louis XIV's castle in France, since King Ludwig idolized King Louis. We rode on a cabin cruiser to get to the castle. After the tour, we enjoyed our lunch at the Chiemsee Lake Hotel and rented small paddle boats to try out on the lake after we browsed around the recreation center. The boats turned out to be loads of fun for the four of us. We girls laughed till we cried, as our guys had trouble peddling the proper way, causing the little boats to turn around in small circles on that huge lake, with the German guide shouting and waving at us from the shore.

Marv decided it was time to use some of the leave time he had saved up before I came to Germany. We chose to take a 10-day bus tour to Italy from May 2nd through the 11th. We began our tour with Ludwig, our cheerful German bus driver, leaving from the Munich bahnhof (railroad station), traveling south to Garmisch, where we picked up the tour guide Ruth. As we passed through the Inn Valley in Austria, we saw many large meadows with lots of shacks for storing hay and equipment. Shepherds tended their flocks, and we passed through numerous covered bridges, some of which were quite narrow. We enjoyed the scenic murals on the outsides of the homes, apparently an Austrian tradition.

Seeing the snow-capped Swiss Alps made it obvious we were in Switzerland. Because of our bus driver's skill in maneuvering the narrow, hairpin turns, the drive proved to be quite exciting, especially when he had to back up the long bus to make the turns. We gasped and squealed imagining tumbling over the edge and down the steep mountainside, much to the driver's amusement. Passing through Maloja Pass was definitely the most beautiful of all Switzerland. The mountains were covered with snow, and the lake at the summit glistened in the sunlight. The sky was brilliant blue and the white clouds hugged the mountain crest.

We arrived in Milan, Italy, in the evening, which was quite different from the high mountains we had just left. The hills in Milan were covered with acres of vineyards. We visited the huge Cathedral of St. Mary's and the gallery of Victor Emmanuel II. Genoa, the home of Christopher Columbus, was a beautiful city next to the Mediterranean Sea. We were fascinated by the large ships and the many fishing and sailboats. Across the highway stood the NATO building, which explained the numerous American cars parked there. As we left Genoa, we saw groves of orange and lemon trees with their bright fruit ripening in the warm sunshine. In the background were hills covered with thousands of olive trees along the Italian Riviera as well as a medieval castle.

On Sunday, we attended Mass at the Cathedral in Pisa, all in Latin so it was quite familiar. After breakfast, we joined the guided tour of the Leaning Tower and Baptistery. The Tower leaned after only two stories were built due to a faulty foundation on soft soil, so it was abandoned for many years until later when builders added the remaining six stories. From top to bottom, the tower leans 10 feet. The Baptistery, beautiful inside, was especially interesting because of the acoustics. The shapes of the interior dome and the exterior roof work together to create a chamber that produced beautiful tones when someone hummed a few notes.

We arrived in Rome late in the afternoon. After dinner, we took a guided tour by night. The neon lights made the famous buildings look beautiful. We especially enjoyed seeing the bright lights and the Trevi Fountain, where the movie Three Coins in a Fountain had been filmed four years before. The next day, we saw many famous landmarks. However, St. Peter's Basilica was the most impressive, because of its wonderful proportions, the amazing harmony of color and decoration in the gold and glittering mosaics and different colored marbles and statues. It is next to impossible to describe this church, which is the largest in the world. There were so many famous works of art in the 6-acre area, including the Pieta by Michelangelo.

After walking through St. Peter's, we waited in the square for Pope Pius XII to appear at his window, which he did at 12:19, to bless the crowd; he stayed only about seven minutes. We were quite far away, but could see him clearly through our binoculars. Being of Catholic heritage, this experience was one of the highlights of our trip.

As we continued our drive along the Mediterranean Sea, we saw the Appian Way and passed the Monte Cassino. After lunch at Naples, we toured a cameo factory and continued on to Pompeii, which is noted for its famous Mt. Vesuvius eruption. The volcanic eruption completely covered the city in the 4th century.

We were excited to sail to the Isle of Capri the next day in a cabin cruiser. We then boarded a canoe to go inside the Blue Grotto. This is an opening in the rocks where the water is a gorgeous shade of blue. Its brilliance and color are caused by light streaming in through the opening and shining through the seawater. The reflection lit up the cave. As we put our hands into the water, they glowed. When we returned from the Grotto, we walked along narrow paths to view gardens and tiny shops on the Island. The gardens in Sorrento were gorgeous as well.

In Assisi, we toured the church where St. Francis' tomb is located, and we learned more about his life. We saw Florence, which is known for its linen and straw products, and Padua, where St. Anthony lived. At Venice, we were fascinated with the "streetcar" we rode, a ferry that motored up and down the canal "streets". Venice is also known for its glass, so we toured glass factories. After stopping at Innsbruck, Austria, we arrived back at Munich, after traveling 3,000 miles in 10 days, with the weather being perfect every day. We were tired but happy that we had taken this tour.

About six weeks later, the four of us decided to take a tour together to France, Holland and Belgium where the World's Fair was being held. We left on July 10 for a 5-day tour, arriving at Brussels about 9 p.m. The next morning, at the fair, we were most fascinated with the enormous, magnificent Atomium monument, which symbolized the Atomic Age, at the front entrance of the fair and bought a guide book to help us find our way around the 460 acres of exhibits. We didn't hesitate to ride on one of the many cable cars and get a close-up view of the spheres of the Atomium, which were 69 feet in diameter and 335 feet high.

We saw many nations' exhibits, but of special interest was the huge Russian Pavilion, which emphasized power with their arrays of large machinery and enormous bronze statues, including one of the late ruler,

Vladimir Lenin. Of course, their satellite, the "Sputnik," was displayed, during this period of the Cold War. I especially enjoyed French Morocco's pavilion, which displayed a huge portrait of Princess Grace and her family. We met back at our bus at 8 p.m. to take us to dinner and our hotel. On Saturday, we rode around the city of Brussels on a guided tour, including Brussels Square, built in the 16th century, the Metro Goldwyn Mayer Building, Arc de Triomphe, built for the first World's Fair in 1880, and many other sights. After dark, the fellows got some neat photos of the city's lights and visited some remaining displays and the huge amusement park while Phyl and I lounged at the hotel.

The next day, our bus drove us to Holland, where we were captivated by the numerous thatched roofs, working windmills, and the way the farmers divided their pastures by way of canals in place of fences for their many heads of Holstein cows. Holland is definitely a dairy nation. Arriving at Amsterdam in time to tour the city through the canals and harbor on a large cabin cruiser was a highlight. We saw many points of interest in the city, including a large flower market, seven bridges in a row and the last windmill to be seen in the city of Amsterdam. Later we had some time to shop at the little souvenir shops. Of course, we bought decorated wooden shoes for the guys and small sizes for our future children.

The next day, our first stop was Sorbonne, France. As we traveled, we noticed that the farmers lived in small villages, rather than near their land. Their fields were small and the crops were poor at that time. During our guided tour in Paris, we saw Place Charles de Gaulle (also known as Star Square) with twelve large avenues meeting in this square. The Arc de Triomphe is located here. The Tomb of the Unknown Soldier, erected in honor of the French killed during the World War I, was here as well. The Eiffel Tower, built in 1887 for the World's Fair, was impressive.

We ladies especially liked Fashion Street, the Champs Elysees, with its 18 cinemas and shops. There I purchased a gorgeous, sequined evening bag. We saw beautiful clothes and accessories, which, of course, were very expensive, as well as the wares in the many perfume shops. We wondered how many movie stars and celebrities had walked the same sidewalks.

After viewing the art at Le Louvre, our bus took us to see the huge and lavish King Louis XIV's Palace of Versailles. We took in the Folies Bergere, where we saw colorful costumes in a play done in the French language. Homeward bound the next day, we were happy because we had a good time once again.

In mid-September 1958, Marv had to pack and leave Germany by ship bound for the good ole' U.S.A. I stayed behind with Merv and Phyllis because my plane reservations had been scheduled for a week later. I was glad they were there for me and could drive me the 40 miles to Munich where I caught the flight back to New York's Idlewild Airport.

A problem awaited me when I arrived in New York, however. I found that no reservation had been made for me from New York to Omaha via Chicago, as my ticket stated. I panicked and prayed my begging prayers again. Wilma and Paul were due at the Omaha Airport to meet my flight, and now I definitely would not arrive on time. There was no way I could contact them because they had no telephone.

I began to cry. God answered! The lady at the ticket counter felt so sorry for me; she told me to hurry. All the porters rushed around and I didn't know what else to do. I should have prayed for help, but instead I carried my 40-pound luggage myself. Bad mistake! I noticed I started spotting blood after that. I had suspected I may be pregnant so I was concerned and worried about the baby I may have been carrying for about six weeks.

When I finally arrived in Omaha, sure enough, Wilma and Paul had been waiting for a long while. It was so good to see them again, and I was glad they decided to wait or I would have had another crisis. But God, in His goodness, answered another prayer. They dropped me off at Marv's parents' home, where I awaited Marv's return from the New York harbor where his ship docked a week later. That weekend, I was really concerned about my baby, so I shared my concern with Marv's mother after praying many times that if I was pregnant, I would not miscarry. Again, God was faithful. We were blessed to find that a young doctor had office hours in Hooper on Saturdays. With instructions to stay in bed for a few days, he confirmed that I would be having little Kathy in May. That was exciting news, yet scary as well, as I hoped and prayed for her safety.

At last, my beloved came home to Hooper, thinking he would be free. We were disappointed to find that he was not. His orders stated he had to report to Fort Riley, Kansas, to finish the last days until the two years were up. All he did was sit around waiting with nothing to do before receiving his honorable discharge, while I waited for him in the comfort of his parents' home. Once he had his discharge papers safely in his hands, with his military obligation fulfilled, we could start anew with a baby on the way.

After Marv got home, we found an apartment in Fremont, and he began making the rounds to get a job. It was discouraging because there were few jobs available. He applied at the Geo. A. Hormel meat packing plant in Fremont but they were not hiring. He was hired at Campbell Soup Co. for night hours, which was quite boring, however, it brought in the paycheck for our necessities. The bank officials offered me a teller's position but by this time I had morning sickness each day, so I declined the job offer. I couldn't very well be sick while waiting on customers. I passed my days setting up homemaking again and sewing maternity clothes on my portable sewing machine.

CHAPTER 13

FIRST HOME

*"He gives the barren woman a home,
making her the joyous mother of children."*

Psalm 113:9 RSV

As soon as his honorable discharge from the U.S. Army was finalized at Ft. Riley, Marv found work for the summer as a hired hand on a farm near the small town of Scribner, Nebraska, about 20 miles northwest of Fremont. We moved to the farmer's old house after he and his wife built a new home on a different farm they owned. After we settled in, it was soon time for our first baby to arrive. Due to be born on April 30, I had been praying for a May Day baby, and God answered my prayer. Kathleen Elizabeth arrived on May 1, 1959, weighing in at 7 lbs. 1 oz. We were thrilled to have a lovely little girl. We chose her name right after we were married, because we always liked the name Kathy.

Oh, you never saw a prouder father than Marv. He came bouncing in to see me and told me all about his little girl in the hospital nursery, who, of course, was the "best lookin' kid" there, as if I had not yet seen and examined her thoroughly. Later, while we were gazing at our tiny offspring in the nursery, he startled another new father with his statement, "Did you see the stamp on her butt, 'Made in Germany'?" Marv's joke, of course, was that she had been conceived in Germany so she would carry a stamp to show it. I will never forget the look on the other father's face as he stared at us. We both snickered.

We were blessed to have Kathy sleep well from the start. She was sleeping 12 to 14 hours when she was just 6 weeks old. Our doctor said, "You'd better enjoy her; your next baby won't do that." The doctor's prediction came true.

Because of being the youngest in our family, I never had much of a chance to babysit or learn about babies. I was not prepared to be a mother so I was nervous! I was overly protective and too devoted, but Kathy thrived in spite of me. I prayed for myself and the baby because I was so afraid I would harm her in some way. Everything seemed to be a crisis with me. I sure didn't have the abundant life that the Bible promises we can have.

The following September, Marv received a call from the Geo. A. Hormel Co. in Fremont, offering him a job at the meat packing plant. Though the work was difficult, the salary was good. It didn't take us long to save the money to put a down payment on a small, starter home in Fremont, which was still in the process of being built. We had a "working agreement" to do the painting ourselves, for which the realtor deducted $500. We really liked our little home because it was much more convenient than the rental we had been living in.

Soon after, Karen Anne arrived on October 6, 1960, at 7 lbs. 8 oz. Marv again came bouncing into my hospital room announcing that, "She's the best-lookin' kid in the nursery." He sure loved his little girls. Though I worried about how I would take care of another little one, with Kathy still so small, it was wonderful to have a little girl for Kathy to play with as Karen grew. Karen had the problem of projectile vomiting so she couldn't keep enough in her stomach to sleep longer than two hours at a time. We were pretty frazzled then, but she grew out of that by the age of seven months.

Soon, I became pregnant again. This pregnancy was difficult because my hips were in constant pain from my fourth month on. My doctor explained that I was having my babies too close together, therefore my muscles were too weak to carry the baby high enough. I was carrying him low, which caused him to lie between my pelvic bones, spreading them too far apart. It felt like my hips were broken. I was in constant, severe pain, especially when I had to move in and out of a chair or bed. At night, when I had to go to the bathroom, Marv carried me and sat me on the toilet.

Kenneth Gerard arrived on May 12, 1962, at 8 lbs. 4 oz. Marv and I were both pleased that he looked so healthy and chubby, and we were delighted to have a little boy after having two sweet girls, and of course, to pass on our family name. The word was out again; his daddy said, "He's the best-lookin' kid in the nursery!" After Ken was born, my hips didn't go back into place like I thought they would. I prayed, "Lord, I don't mind having more babies, if it's Your will, but I can't take care of anymore little ones at this time. Can You wait for five years or so 'til my muscles are stronger?"

Ken was an average baby to care for and we soon saw that he had different interests than the girls. I giggled one day when I heard Ken as a toddler crawling on the floor with a toy car, making "vroom vroom" sounds. I was shocked because neither Marv nor I had taught him that or even made those noises in front of him. I thought they sounded so cute and realized then that the Lord really does put instincts in little people. I was certainly busy by then, having two small ones in diapers. Kathy had just turned three years old; I was overwhelmed with the work of caring for them.

Right after Ken was born, I bought a new Singer sewing machine. I loved that machine and had so much fun sewing. It became an emotional outlet and therapy for me. That summer, I started learning how to can foods as well. It was really important to Marv for me to do this, and Marv's mother shared vegetables from her garden. We also bought many lugs of fruit.

While I was busy canning in the basement, Kathy wanted to play with the other kids on the block. We had a hard time keeping her out of the street, so I longed to be out in the country to raise my children. As little as she was, Kathy started picking up wrong values from the neighbor kids, stomping her little foot in anger at me, saying, "Why can't I go in the street? All the other kids do." I became increasingly concerned, worrying how we could raise our children to become good people. Many times, I would just stand at the front window and cry when I watched for Kathy outdoors. I was fearful she would be hit by a speeding car. The neighbor's teenager would barrel around the corner, his tires squealing and brakes screeching into his parents' drive, directly across the street from our home. I just knew he would never be able to stop in time to see any small child in the street.

Eventually, I met some of the neighbor ladies, one of whom came over quite often for coffee. One day, my new friend, Marilyn Speicher, observed me yelling at little Kathy. She said, "Elsie, you are too hard on her. You need to see one of the priests and get some help." I realized I really was harsh, but didn't know how to stop, so I made an appointment with one of the younger priests, who was very kind. After I told him my story about Kathy not obeying me by staying out of the streets, he said, "Elsie, your little girl still has a short attention span. At her age, she doesn't remember you telling her to stay out of the street. She is not being disobedient." I was so grateful for his wisdom.

Another lady who lived across the street, Jolene Braasch, was always sweet and kind. Her three girls were good friends to Kathy and Karen. I realized that I just had to help Kathy cross the street to their home or have their girls come to our home. Marv built a picket fence around our backyard, which helped greatly, although one little boy in the neighborhood kept opening the gate, leaving it open for our little toddler, Karen, to escape. I prayed for our girls' safety, and I prayed for a farm for us.

In the meantime, we kept looking at newspaper ads. Marv hated living in the city as much as I did. During the winter he sat in our house, becoming discouraged when he couldn't drive out to his parents' farm and help his dad. He was determined to live on a farm again and made it his goal to buy one so that he could retire from Hormel one day. He would say, "I want to own a farm to retire on by the time we get old. I don't want to work at Hormel all my life."

That goal became our dream, although at the time I thought it was impossible. As I got more desperate, my faith grew. I got to thinking that if I could be a better mother, surely it would be the Lord's will for us and since it was His will, He could grant our wish. In our desperation, we prayed daily to find a farm to buy or lease. Everywhere we inquired, though, the land owner would not agree to rent their farm to us unless Marv quit his job at Hormel. This was financially risky, as there was always the chance of crop failure. About the time Kathy was almost five, we contacted two spinster ladies who were selling their farm. They originally wanted a down payment of $20,000, but all we had been able to save was $2,000. Though the house was very old, we really wanted that farm because it was located only six miles from Fremont and Marv's work. We continued to pray about it, but Marv said one night, "Forget it! There's no way we can get that farm."

I kept thinking, "Well, if it would be God's will and if we prayed hard enough, I don't see why God wouldn't answer our prayers." So I kept praying for Him to lower the down payment so that somehow we could buy that farm. I bargained with God, telling Him that I knew I could be a better mother if I didn't have to worry about those dangerous city streets. I added that our little ones would have better values if they weren't influenced by some of the rougher children in our neighborhood.

In the meantime, we visited the sellers. We hit it off beautifully. The two sisters, in their 80's, liked us very much, and they were impressed with Marv's job in the shipping department at Hormel. They were willing to lower the down payment for us because they felt we would be able to make the payments on time, unlike the young couple currently living there.

We gave the sisters a check for $2,000 in earnest money and signed the contract to come up with the rest of the cash by March 1, the usual time to make transactions for farms. Oh, how we agonized over that. We prayed and prayed for enough money by that date. After Marv's dad offered to give us $1,000 to reimburse him for the years Marv helped him on their farm without pay, we were still short $1,000. On February 24, the day before we were to move, we prayed again for an answer. Finally the realtor asked, "Do you have any life insurance?" Marv thought perhaps we could borrow $1,000 from that policy, and that's just what we did. Now we were getting close to the deadline. God worked it out for us in a beautiful way, answering our fervent prayers.

We moved to that small 160-acre farm on February 25, 1964. I will never forget the shock of seeing the inside of that old, tumbledown house. It had snowed the night before we moved. The woodwork on the bottom of the back door was extremely worn. The newly fallen snow sifted under the kitchen door, through the narrow slit under the door frame. "Oh, that's nice," I thought a little sarcastically, "snow in my kitchen," though I didn't really care very much. I was just so thrilled that I would now have a place to raise my children away from the dangers of living on a busy street.

During the few months of chilly weather left that winter, we were really cold. There was no furnace (no central heat), but there was an oil burner in the middle of the front room. The kitchen was actually a lean-to with very little cabinet space. Against a wall without a window were a few built-in cabinets, painted white, with a large rectangular sink. We had to cram our electric stove and the refrigerator opposite the stove in a small space against the lean-to wall.

After we placed the trash burner, a tiny wood stove with two lids, in front of the chimney, there was little room left for the kitchen table and chairs. Marv fired up that stove with dried corn cobs and wood, so that the heat buckled the wall-covering behind the stove pipe. However, the heat couldn't circulate to the rest of the rooms very well. Of course, the fire would go out at night, which caused the kitchen to be cold in the mornings. When I invited guests for a meal, I needed to set up a card table near the china cabinet so I could get to the stove. My Bavarian china and matching crystal that Marv had selected and shipped home to me from Germany stayed packed away in the walk-in attic. I needed the same corner to hold the hot pots of food I had already cooked until the rest of the meal could be served. Those had to be placed on the floor under the card table.

It was amazing to me how healthy my kids were during that first winter. Since the kitchen was so cold, the water pipes started freezing up, and the potatoes under the sink had frost damage. My feet were so cold, I had to wear my heavy leather snow boots in the house. The children would go into the living room for their toys and race into the dining room by the stove to warm their hands. They played right in front of that stove. None of them got colds or infections that year. When summer finally came, the house was uncomfortably warm. Marv got weary from not sleeping well in our hot home that summer, so he announced one day after work, "I ordered a furnace with central air-conditioning today." I said, "What?" He repeated himself and I said, "Oh!" I thought, "Wow, he must have been really miserable," but I rejoiced that we wouldn't have to be so cold in the winter and would have cooler bedrooms in the summer.

To begin farming, Marv brought the tractor that he had bought new while he was a teenager. He scrounged around for other needed farm machinery and figured out how to make a planter for his soy beans. He found some International 2-row corn planters in a junk yard and put them together by extending the frames and bolting them together to make a 4-row, soy-bean planter. He used that for several years before he bought a used planter.

At harvest time, he bought a used pull-type combine for his tractor, and then later, he progressed to a used self-propelled combine. Finally, the fourth year, he got a new 15-foot header for the combine to harvest the beans. Meanwhile, he used a 2-row corn picker for three to four years before he got a combine and a brand new 4-row detachable picker, which also had a 15-foot header that he put on for harvesting the soy beans as well as the corn. He used that same old machine until he was 74 years old.

When the weather warmed, the children played happily together on the farm. I loved the freedom of instilling values that we believed in along with the quiet and privacy.

In the springtime, the day after Kathy's 5th birthday, when Marv was working in the field nearest the road, a Catholic priest, Father Trausch, the Pastor of St. James' Catholic Church in the little town of Mead, stopped by to say hello. Marv was just finishing for the day. Father Trausch wanted to meet me and the children, so Marv invited him to our home. He was such a gentle, kind man; he reminded me of Jesus. He talked so sweetly to our little ones. I can still remember his attention to Kathy as she showed him her magnetic alphabet board with its colorful plastic letters and numbers to make words. She made the word "dog" for him.

He showed her how to reverse the letters and asked, "What does that spell?" She sounded out "God." He was so pleased to show her that, and she felt special as well. I invited him to share our supper but he refused, saying, "My housekeeper will have supper waiting for me." I offered him fresh peas that I had picked. He also declined, explaining, "My housekeeper is really good at stretching our food so we always seem to have enough." From then on, we attended and became members of this little Catholic church, located seven miles south of our farm.

Soon, Father Trausch asked our neighbor lady, Georgia Feist, to give me a ride to the women's group, The Ladies Altar Sodality. Georgia and her sister, Kay Morris, became good friends through the following years, along with our dear neighbor, Leona Nelson, an elderly lady who was sweet and kind, especially to our children. She always had cookie treats for our youngsters and loved to call baby Kevin her "little mannie." Many in our neighborhood came regularly to buy our fresh eggs.

That spring, some of the other young neighbor women called to invite me to their homes for coffee. It was then that our children met the other little people in our neighborhood, including the Winkelmans, the Irishes, and later when Kevin was older, the Ondracek family. Our children made strong friendships with these children, as I reciprocated with the coffees. All of these women certainly were nice, and we arranged to take turns babysitting when we needed to go shopping.

I planted a large garden, buying almost every type of vegetable seed I could find. It took a lot of time to weed the garden, and then pick and process all the vegetables before they were ready to be frozen or filled into the jars I processed in the large pressure cooker. I found it certainly was much harder to can food in this inconvenient house. Our small home in the city had a large basement in which I did my canning while I had the little ones to look after. This 100-plus-year-old house had an outside entrance to a tiny, dark cellar with open wooden steps. Along one wall were built-in shelves for canning jars. The small cemented area had only room enough to hold the water heater, our large 22-foot chest freezer, and the furnace. There was a small pathway space to set a few buckets of supplies, so I had to do all my canning and freezing in the little lean-to kitchen upstairs.

Marv's parents' farm had been sold right after we bought our farm, so his dad, John, would come frequently from their little retirement home in Hooper to help Marv with the farm work. Consequently, besides large suppers for Marv, I had to come up with large farmer meals at noon for Marv's dad, plus sandwiches or at least rolls and coffee around 3 p.m. Marv's dad was so appreciative of my efforts and was always kind to me. If there was something he could not eat, he would tell me in a gentle way and I would avoid serving it from then on.

Though I felt blessed that we had running water and electricity, the bathroom adjoining the front dining room had no cabinets whatsoever, so I bought a narrow, white steel cabinet, which held our washcloths, hand towels and toiletries. The large towels were stored either on top of the large hamper standing by the bathroom sink when clean or hung over the free-standing tub to dry after being used. When soiled, they were stored in the hamper, waiting for laundry day.

Next to the bathroom was a closet that became my tiny utility room with a trap door leading to the cellar. I had to cram our Maytag wringer washer in there, right on top of the closed trap door, along with two galvanized wash tubs held up on a double stand with hoses attached for draining the rinse water. Each time I had to rinse the soap-laden clothes in the second tub, I had to jump up to sit on the closed washer lid in order to reach the first tub, swing the wringer over the center of both tubs and dig in the water to rinse the load of clothes the second time. The room was just too small. Of course, with no drain or sink, I had to carry out all of the drained water each time I did the laundry.

The room did have two shelves to hold laundry soap and other cleaning supplies, with simple, hot and cold faucets underneath. On the opposite wall, clothes hooks were lined up along the wall, held up with strong boards. The window panes in these tiny rooms were all rotted. The window frame in the bathroom would barely hold the glass pane in it any longer. The occupants before us had painted over the varnished woodwork, which had chipped off, so each spring I had to clutter on more layers of paint to cover the unsightly woodwork. I did a lot of painting and went to work on my precious Singer, sewing fluffy, ruffled print curtains in different pastels to cover up all those unsightly windows, making them cheerful looking again.

One warm spring day, I had been washing the bathroom windows inside and out. After finishing, I had to stop quickly for some reason, and forgot to put the storm window back on. Later, I was horrified to find hundreds (or so it seemed) of dirty, buzzing flies all over the bathroom. They had come in through the window pane that had separated from the rotted window frame.

I didn't know whether to cry or laugh at my dilemma, but I was just grateful that I had a storm window to fit tightly on that old window. There was quite a pile of dead flies in the dustpan later after I used some fly spray. I did think, "Oh, my, I surely chose a disgusting situation by wanting to live out on a farm, didn't I?"

We only had two tiny closets in our home, one upstairs near the walk-in attic and one downstairs in our bedroom. The girls' room upstairs had no closet, so we bought two small, steel wardrobe closets for them. When winter clothes were used, the heavy coats took up most of the closet space. After we were able to remove our propane heating stove, our dining room with its seven doors held our oak dining room table and matching chairs, and we bought a divan-type couch to set against the double front windows. We carpeted the living room, and I bought new draperies. I dyed the sectional sofas with spray dye and used our occasional chairs we had purchased when we were first married. Our master bedroom was small, but all of our furniture fit in there nicely.

Besides housework, I still tried to keep up my sewing projects. Had I had more storage, I would have fared much better. I had to pick up, fold and put away all my sewing equipment and ironing board each time guests came. It took me several hours to put everything into our tiny bedroom closet; it all had to fit like a puzzle or it would all come tumbling down.

CHAPTER 14

HOGS AND CHICKENS

In the spring after we moved to the farm, Marv informed me that we needed to start raising hogs, that we would be able to make more money for our farm payments if we did. Oh, how I hated to hear that! I knew without his saying it that I would have to take care of them. I didn't know the first thing about pigs, being raised with four big brothers to do those farm jobs. I began to feel panicky, but didn't want to admit my doubt because I was afraid Marv and his family would think I was lazy. I had heard my dad say that often enough to me. I didn't want anyone else thinking that, so I reluctantly agreed.

At that time, Marv was still working late hours in the Hormel shipping department and usually got home from work at 9:30 at night, so guess who had to take care of those sows and babies? Boy, did I get an initiation when I had to take over that job. Never in my life did I get any training with a hog or little pigs. But I had no choice because they had to be fed and their pens cleaned, and we didn't have anyone else to do it while Marv was gone to work.

Somehow, I learned to deal with them. Since we did not have any conveniences at that time, the sows that had not yet delivered had to be fed outdoors separately on concrete; they ate from a long wooden trough. I tried to sneak quietly over the fence, avoiding contact with the dreaded electric fence, to reach the trough before they heard or saw me. No matter how sneakily I trod, struggling to climb over that fence with two 5-gallon buckets, three-fourths full of feed, one sow would hear or see me and jump up and come running toward me, grunting loudly all the way to beat the others to the trough. Then, of course, the stampede would begin as the loud grunts woke all the rest. Many a time, they almost knocked me down as they pushed and shoved to be the first to the trough for the biggest share of grain.

I saw why Adam of old named them hogs. They always thought the feed was better where the other hog was eating, so they quickly backed up with their mouths dropping ground feed and rushed to an empty space, shoving and squealing as they fought to get their share. I had to be careful not to get my feet stomped on or get knocked over as they frantically switched places. I was sure I wouldn't live through these famished frenzies and prayed for protection. God saved me from their sharp hooves.

In the heated barn when it was time to farrow, Marv built separate pens for the sows to have their babies. During labor and delivery, they were cantankerous from the pain and fiercely protective of their babies after they were born. They did not like me getting near their baby pigs, so the loud roaring of angry, defensive mothers began. I was terrified and they knew it. I would retreat about three feet, either heading for the barn door or jump up on the fence. Often, I cried while praying desperate prayers the entire time. Occasionally, when I tried to kick their butts, I was reminded that they weighed much more than I did. Whoa, my foot felt like I had kicked a concrete wall!

When farrowing, we had to check them regularly to see if they had any trouble delivering their piglets. Somehow, the Lord had the emergencies come while Marv was home. He'd have to be the hog "mid-husband" (midwife) and reach in and pull out those stuck little pigs to save the mama hog, or the sow could die as well.

One bitter cold winter afternoon, I remembered again to heed Marv's instructions and check the barn often to see if any babies needed to be placed closer to their mothers or if any mother was having trouble delivering. My, what a frightening sight I found! One of the heat lamps used to keep the baby pigs warm had fallen down on the straw and thick smoke was flowing right near the babies. I certainly thanked the Lord for nudging me to go to the barn at that precise time. The barn would have caught fire very soon, otherwise. After that, I kept a careful watch on those lamps.

I remember spending up to four hours a day with those hogs. The kids were still preschoolers, so I worried about them burning the house down or getting hurt in other ways. I used to let them watch afternoon cartoons to keep them occupied. I could always see their little profiles sitting before the TV each time I trudged to the house and looked through the tall kitchen window to check on them.

Of course by that time we were raising chickens for laying eggs and for butchering. Our first batch of hens was laying so I carried buckets of feed and water to them and gathered their eggs. We had a good outlet for all the eggs, as Marv took them to work to his fellow employees in the shipping department. On some days, when I was short on eggs to fill the orders, I actually walked out to the chicken barn to wait until some hens would lay their eggs. Yes, sometimes the tame hens plopped one in my hand. Now that's what we called a fresh egg!

If we didn't pick the eggs up several times a day, some bored hens would start scratching in the nests instead of on the straw-laden concrete floor. Then, of course, the eggs would break. The hens soon found out that the eggs tasted good, so we usually found a nest or more full of messy eggs to wash. The eggs left were sticky with smeared egg yolks, along with dried-on straw, not to mention all the cracks under the yolky mess. Those eggs needed to be soaked clean a long time. If they were cracked, which they usually were, the eggs were tossed to the cats or hogs.

I still remember one sweet lady who had lived on a farm before retirement who always teased me when she called to place her order. She asked if cracked eggs were cheaper. I said to her one day, "Yes, if they are clean before we wash them." She always said, "Well, crack me a few clean ones, would you?" Then we'd have a good laugh.

Chapter 15

Parenting

The September after our move to the farm, it was time for Kathy to start kindergarten. We lived almost a mile from a lovely little country school, District #119, where 18 to 30 children in Kindergarten to 8th grade were taught by two teachers. It was quite a new school, and the neighbors' children were all good kids. The children who attended that small school later enrolled at various high schools in the area. Kathy's teacher was young and good to her students. She sent a message after two weeks that Kathy often arrived at school crying. I was surprised because she liked school and was eager to go each day.

I asked her, "Why do you cry when I drop you off every morning?" She answered, "I'm afraid the big kids are going to be naughty to me." I said, "Are they?" She said, "No, but I'm still afraid of them."

I told her that if she wanted me to I would walk to the front door of the school with her. After that, she seemed brave enough to run into school by herself and realized that these children would not harm her; she had no more problems the rest of the year.

A year later, Karen started kindergarten, and that was hard on her. Because her birthday was so late, October 6, I had wanted to keep her home another year, but her little friend, Kris, who was born about two weeks before Karen, planned to go. Her mother insisted the girls would be fine, so Karen wanted to attend school with her. The school board members maintained that the kindergarten class should attend all day for three days a week rather than half days for five days. Karen would get so tired, she'd zonk out during their noon rest time.

This was stressful for Ken as well, since he was so close to Karen; he was lonely without her. This situation set the stage for a serious mistake I made in judgment with Ken, which I still regret after these many years.

"Fathers, do not provoke your children to anger, but bring them up in discipline and instruction of the Lord."

Ephesians 6:4 RSV

A wounded little boy

This is painful for me to write, but I feel it's important for you to know that sometimes a spiritual enemy called Satan or one of his demons can give us thoughts we think are our own – negative thoughts meant to destroy us. Had I known the Holy Spirit's voice back then, I would have recognized what He wanted me to do and I would have taken the time to take care of something so important, no matter what.

It was one of those days when I was swamped with work. Marv's dad had come late that morning, which did not give me time to prepare the noon meal. Kathy and Karen were at school and Marv was at work. I was rushing around when I noticed that Ken was whiney, angry and really out of sorts. I couldn't seem to please him; I asked him what was wrong but he didn't answer. He just didn't want to do anything I suggested and he fussed around.

The thought crossed my mind that he probably needed attention since this was the first week of school for Karen. I thought, "I suppose he misses Karen. I sure don't have time to go play with him now though." I told him to go play by himself. He probably felt rejected. He started screaming and making a scene. I got angry and told him to stop. He threw himself on the floor, kicking and screaming. I thought, "This must be a temper tantrum like I heard about other kids having."

I had never had one of my kids do that before, so I didn't know what to do. As I stood there trying to figure out what to do, I received a thought, "Pick him up and hold him." I was afraid he would hurt me with his kicking so I just stood there; he acted worse. Another thought came, "You need to ignore him; he just wants attention."

My mind flashed back to an article I had read months before in the Parents magazine, instructing mothers to always ignore a tantrum because the children are just trying to get attention. I couldn't waste time listening to Ken right then because I had to fix the meal. I couldn't stand his loud screaming, so I jerked him up to get his attention and yelled several times, "Stop it! Stop it!"

Somehow, he flew away from my hands and he hit his head against the door frame. He screamed. I got so scared that I had hurt him, but I dragged him into the bedroom, threw him on the bed and spanked him, saying, "You can come out when you stop your bawling."

Now, here comes the really hard part. For an hour, he pleaded with me, "It's bleeding, Mom, it's bleeding!" But I was convinced that I should not go to him or I would spoil him and have worse trouble with him; I let him cry. When he finally calmed down and I had the dinner made for my father-in-law, Ken seemed different. He had an angry hard look on his face. I began doubting myself, thinking perhaps I should tell him I was sorry.

A thought came again, "He's sad because of Karen." Another thought came, "You can't tell him you're sorry or he'll think he was right to act so naughty." From that day on, my little boy was rebellious and filled with pain. I knew it was because of what I did to him when he needed my comfort so much. He was only four years old, after all. Of course he needed my attention! He was sad and needed me to understand.

My father had been extremely strict with his discipline, with many scoldings and put downs, which I'm sure he felt was needed. I thought that my siblings and I had turned out all right, so this was probably the way to handle one's children, like my father handled his. If I had only apologized to Ken, perhaps he could have gotten over it, but, no, I thought if I once punished him for something, I should not backtrack and say I was sorry. What a deceived and messed-up mother I was!

I never realized until years later why I heard two voices: one was the Holy Spirit speaking and one was a demon. But not knowing the Lord like I do now, I didn't realize the difference back then. I have shed so many tears through the years since 1966, and I am crying as I write this just thinking of the pain Ken went through. He has forgiven me and I have forgiven myself, though I have not forgotten. I still feel sorrow for my little boy who was convinced his mother did not love him and, I believe, carried anger at the injustice of it all during all of his childhood.

CHAPTER 16

GROWING FAMILY, GROWING ANXIETY

About a year later, God sent us another little baby boy, Kevin John, born on January 2, 1967 at 6 lbs. 14 oz. We were so happy to have another little boy. Though there was an age difference of four and a half years, we thought it was special that Ken now had a little brother. Once more, Kevin's daddy exclaimed to me and to everyone who would listen, "He's the best lookin' kid in the nursery!" Kevin slept well in our chilly bedroom that winter, taking up residence the first few months in the tiny, antique crib my uncle had made for me when I was a baby. Kevin was easy to care for, and, by this time, the girls were old enough to really enjoy him, and so did Ken.

As our children were more involved in school and I had another baby to care for in my overextended schedule, I became more emotionally troubled. I interfered often with our children's behavior, expecting excellence from them as well as from the teachers. Often I kept Marv up late in bed, talking and complaining to him until all hours about our children's latest problems, whether with academics or socializing. I talked about my burdens too.

When he exclaimed, "I can't listen to you anymore. I've got to get to sleep so I can work tomorrow," I started going to my dear friend, Sharon Randell, who by this time had moved to our neighborhood with her husband, Gene, and their two little ones. Sharon stayed up half the night while Gene worked the night shift, 11 to 7, as a supervisor at his job. She was patient with me, counseling me or just listening. I really feel that her dear friendship kept me from having a total mental breakdown. In the meantime, I prayed so much for our children that they could learn well in their various situations and handle their social lives, but most of all that they would become good adults and have good Catholic values.

Because of Marv's difficult schedule of long hours at Hormel, and all the farm responsibilities, we had little time to see each other and hardly ever had time to go out for fun. Our neighbors organized card parties at our local school and brought snacks with coffee. I learned to play the card game Pitch with different couples while all of the children played on the school grounds until dark. Marv could never attend. He always worked late. Since microwaves did not exist, I left supper in the oven for him and he would be asleep when I returned home with the children. I really missed him at the school socials and never felt like going without him. I felt it was important for the kids to socialize with the other school children, but I always felt more sadness in my heart than joy.

When my name was placed on a committee for the Mothers' Sodality at St. James Church, it became a burden to get there on time. I had to make sure to clean up the house for the babysitter, and hurry to make a dessert for the meeting before I picked up the kids from school. Then I oversaw their homework, rolled up my hair in curlers, and was sure to cover my head with a shower cap over those curlers before doing the stinky hog chores.

In between, I made supper for the children, making sure there was supper in the oven for Marv when he got home from work. Then I'd get cleaned and changed for the meeting, trying to smell like a lady after being in the stinky barn. I was exhausted and hungry by the time I got there, not getting a chance to eat any supper. Because it was so stressful to get to those meetings on time, I decided not to attend very often until my children were older. I only went when I was required to serve dessert.

One evening, after having a terrible time with the sows in the barn, one of the outspoken ladies, whose farmer husband was always there for her, driving her everywhere, and whose two children were already adults, said sarcastically to me in front of everyone, "Elsie, you need a gold star for showing up tonight."

I got upset and yelled, "You bet I deserve a gold star for coming, after all I went through: cleaning the house for the sitter, doing all the hog chores, rushing around to get supper and the dessert, picking up the sitter and getting ready. You bet I deserve a gold star!" Everyone got quiet, but after the meal was served, several ladies came to me saying that she had offended them as well with the same remark, and that I shouldn't take it personally because she was always unkind.

It did help me feel better at the time, but it really was hard to have so much to do with Marv gone so much. When I needed to have some fun time alone with him, the schedule was usually in the way. It didn't seem worth it anymore, once I went through that stress, to go out. We were not able to drop our children off at their grandparents' for an evening out because of distance, and it was hard to find a local sitter. It helped some in the daytime, when several of us neighbors took turns watching children for each other, but what Marv and I both really needed was a "date" with each other to have fun again. Lacking those times together really took its toll on my emotions and our marriage.

Besides going over to Sharon's late at night, my only therapy became staying up late when all was quiet and creating items with my sewing machine. It became a habit with me to stay up till 2 a.m. to sew. I felt the stress drain away as I created something from fabric in peace and quiet. I never realized at the time that four hours of sleep from 2 till 6 just wasn't enough, so I was tired all of the time. My patience wore thin because my workload with the growing children and more responsibilities became more than I could bear. I became anxious and yelled at the kids frequently, putting them down if they didn't obey quickly or act perfectly. I became paranoid about people gossiping or thinking poorly of me. So, I tried to do more to make a good impression, meanwhile hating myself because I couldn't say "no" to people, when I was already so overworked.

I knew in my heart I was harming our children, but I didn't know how to stop. I begged God to help me be a better mother; I knew there was something terribly wrong with me and searched for an answer.

One day, after a rainfall, when I returned home from grocery shopping, I carried a case of canned peas down the cellar steps, which were wet and slippery. With no railing to hang onto, the heel of one of my shoes slipped off the edge of a step and down I went with the cans of peas. With no way to brace myself, my fanny hit the sharp edge of the wooden step. The pain from the fall was so great, I felt like fainting. I saw what seemed like hundreds of pieces of crystal before my eyes. I sat there a while and could barely make it back upstairs, so weak from the pain.

After X-rays, our family doctor stated that I had indeed broken my tail bone. And since he could not put that area in a cast, all he could do was give me pain pills. I had to continue to drive the children to school because Marv was always at work. Several times, I felt weak and faint from the pain while driving, so I'd stop the car, get out and lean on the hood for a minute or so before continuing to drive. It took a long time to heal, so I used a lot of pain medication. Soon after, I learned that I was pregnant.

About this time, my dad found out he had leukemia. He didn't suffer long and died at age 78, the morning of December 6, 1971. The timing was hard, so close to Christmas. I grieved because I felt I had wasted my teen years by not having a close relationship with him. I cherished a special letter he wrote from the veteran's hospital a few years before in answer to my long letter of apology for the pain I caused during those turbulent teen years when he seemed overly strict and unfair to me. Apparently, he forgave me because his letter in answer to me was very loving.

I was the last one to see him alive when Marv and I visited him at an Omaha hospital the night before he died. I could see then that he didn't have long to live. He was so thin and pale, his skin looking yellow. He was nauseous that afternoon, so we didn't stay long. I regret that we didn't say some kind of goodbye, but I thought we would see him again. I didn't know the Lord at the time, so I was at a loss for words to comfort my dad.

The mortuary experience was hard because I did not want to see him as he looked at the hospital. I wanted to remember him as he was before he got sick. I was seated next to the casket, but I couldn't bring myself to look. I could see out of my peripheral vision that he seemed to have healthy coloring, so finally I got the nerve to peek. I was amazed. The mortician had done such good work at preparing him, he looked healthy and 10 years younger. He looked as if he were asleep. This greatly comforted me; now I could imagine him happy in heaven.

A few days after the funeral, when his siblings were at school, Kevin, who was almost five, wanted to put up the Christmas tree. I was so depressed, I couldn't get myself to do anything with the decorations I had brought out. I kept putting Kevin off, saying I was sad about Grandpa dying. Kevin said, "Why are you so sad if Grandpa is in heaven?" I said that I missed him.

Later I found Kevin trying to put the string of lights on the bottom branches of the tree by himself. I came to my senses and thought, "That poor little boy is not grieving, so it is unfair to him to deny him the joy of decorating." I was surprised how much better I felt. I was actually able to function after that and provide a nice Christmas for my family. It was also good that our extended family gathered together the weekend after Christmas at my brother's home. It helped us all get through the holidays. Of course, it was hard on my mother to live alone now. (Ten years before, they had moved into West Point in a little home on the west end of town.) She stated later that those were the hardest years of her life.

When I found out I was pregnant, I gladly accepted having another baby, knowing it must be God's will. I had an uneventful pregnancy, which was a blessing. However, I was worried that the baby might have birth defects from the pain pills I had taken after my painful fall. I prayed every day that God would somehow protect this little one I was carrying.

Kristeen Lynne was born healthy and strong on July 15, 1972 at 7 lbs. 12 oz., one month after Marv's dad died of lymphoma on June 15. Marv's dad, like mine, didn't know he was dying, not having any prior symptoms, except for a lump he found under one of his ears a few weeks before. He saw his doctor, who recommended surgery. We visited him at the hospital the night before; he was jovial and at peace, thinking this wasn't serious. He went into a coma during the surgery and never woke up. He died four days later. His death was even harder on me than my own father's death because Marv's dad had always been so kind and understanding. Marv's mother was devastated, but plunged herself into cleaning homes for some of her elderly friends. This work became her therapy.

Though it was hard losing both our dads within six months, our little baby brought so much joy and helped soothe our grieving. All of her siblings thought she was so beautiful and special. Even Kevin, now five and a half, enjoyed his little sister. One more time, her proud daddy exclaimed to me and to everyone who would listen, "She's the best lookin' kid in the nursery!"

Marvin's parents, John Popken and Julia Neels
Married June 6, 1932

Elsie's parents, John Luebbert and Elizabeth Hagedorn
Married May 25, 1921

Marvin and his sister, Betty

Elsie and her siblings, 1936
Back – Casper
Front – Leo, Fred, Bernard, Elsie, Wilma

Elsie with her best friend, Virginia Grovijohn

Our wedding, May 16, 1956

Marvin & Elsie, Augsburg, Germany, Summer 1958

Marvin & Elsie with Kathy, Karen & Ken, Christmas 1963

The Farm – 1965

The Farm – 1990's

Kathy
Born May 1, 1959

Karen
Born October 6, 1960

Ken
Born May 12, 1962

Kevin
Born January 2, 1967

Kristy
Born July 15, 1972

Marvin & Elsie with their children, 1986

Cliff & Kathy Grant
Married March 1, 1996

Bob & Karen Birdwell
Married April 20, 1985

Ken & Helen Popken
Married March 1997

Kevin & Zoryana Popken
Married November 9, 1996

Casey & Kristeen Mitchell
Married May 12, 2012

Marvin & Elsie Popken, 50th Wedding Anniversary, 2006

CHAPTER 17

HE GIVES AND HE TAKES AWAY

"Your compassion is great, O Lord;
preserve my life according to Your laws."

Psalm 119:156 NIV

When Kristy was only 7 months old, I had to have surgery on several cysts in my throat. I was frightened of possible cancer. I prayed a lot that somehow the Lord would spare me from death because of my young children. I didn't know what would happen to them if I died. Marv had to continue to work at Hormel because the income from the farm basically paid for the farm expenses; we had no other family to care for the children.

The surgery took place on February 12, 1973, and I was greatly relieved when I learned the growths were benign cysts, not cancer. One cyst was so large, the surgeon had to remove part of my thyroid. That really took its toll, but I was thrilled with the news; being grateful to the Lord for sparing me from the dreaded disease of cancer.

In a few weeks, while driving to my appointment with the surgeon on a blustery cold day, I had a blow-out on a car tire and had to walk for help in that damp cold wind. Eventually, a kind man stopped to help me. I developed a severe cough from being outside for so long. By the time I returned home, I had pulled my chest muscles from the coughing and the long incision at the base of my neck tore open. I only had fitful sleeps, night after night. Nothing, not even the strongest cough syrup prescribed by our doctor, would touch that cough, which lasted day after day for a long time.

Each afternoon, my faithful friend Sharon came over to pick up Kristy to care for her so I could lie down before the older children arrived home from school. When another friend, Lee Brinkman, found out about my severe cough, she came over with her husband, Len, to tell us about using special all-natural vitamins from a company named Neo-Life. We decided to purchase them and were amazed at how much help we all received. Months later, though, when I reported to Lee that the cough was not better, she asked how many vitamin A's I was taking. I told her one and she exclaimed, "Oh, Elsie, you need to be taking about 12 each day."

I was happily surprised after only a week of taking 12 vitamin A's, along with other multiple vitamins, that the cough I had for over six months finally went away. A benefit received from all of these health problems was that we all got on a good nutritional program.

Once I got over the lingering cough, I noticed ten different health improvements in all, including the fact that I had more patience. Because I physically felt better, I was no longer so nervous. I did, however, still have the emotional problems and discovered that I had hypoglycemia (low blood sugar).

Lee taught me so much about nutrition; it was like entering a whole new world. I started shopping at health food stores and began baking whole wheat bread, omitting bleached flour and white sugar whenever I could. I struggled to learn how to bake that bread and it took a while for my family to adapt to our diet changes, but we all noticed that I rarely had to take them to the doctor.

As we gave up more white sugar and bleached flour, we ate less fast-food and prepared foods, and ate more vegetables and fruits and other nutritious foods. We also took natural vitamins rather than drugstore brands or prescriptions. Our older children became healthier and seldom got sick. Much later, I realized we had not taken most of them to a doctor for ten years.

After I recuperated, my work schedule was fuller than ever. Though I still needed to get away alone with Marv, it seemed hopeless. We could eat out after Mass on Sundays, but by the time I chopped up all the food for the two little ones at the restaurant my food would be cold. And when I tried to eat my cold food our toddler Kristy would get fussy and Kevin would walk or even run with her right in the restaurant. I soon learned it was easier to stop trying to eat my cold meal and better to take the children home. That discouraged me because I had so needed the dining out experience. We'd just have to wait until the children got older.

It was about this time that Marv's foreman, Dick Larsen, had asked his wife, Audrey, to drive out to our farm to pick up their egg order. They had a little boy, Kevin, who was only two months younger than our Kevin. They became good friends. The older boys, Eric and Ken, also enjoyed playing together. Their daughter, Beth, was younger than Karen, but she enjoyed our older girls' attention. Audrey and I always had coffee together as the children played. As I got to know this lovely woman, I admired her so much and enjoyed spending time with her. She had real class, in my estimation. She seemed to know how to do everything regarding homemaking and she had other talents too. She never gossiped or griped, and she was always kind and cheerful. She became such an inspiration; I found myself wanting to be just like her.

I thought, "There's just something about her, such a beautiful lady inside and out." Many times, I stopped by her home in Fremont to drop off eggs and have coffee. She talked about church and God freely, and I always felt comfortable visiting with her. Then the day came when the fellows at Hormel stopped buying our eggs. The feed cost had risen substantially and it now cost us 54 cents a dozen to produce them, so we were forced to raise our price from 50 cents a dozen to 65 cents a dozen. Without the egg sales, I no longer saw Audrey regularly. I missed seeing her, but we both became increasingly busy with our growing families.

When Kristy was almost two, on July 3, 1974, we got a shocking phone call from Marv's sister, Betty. Kathy took the call and was distressed when she called her dad to the phone. Betty told Marv that his mom had just died of a heart attack. Her next-door neighbor found her lying behind the lawn mower with the engine still running. He called the doctor, but it was too late. Two young boys reported later that they had walked past on the way home from school and they saw her clutching her chest as she was pushing the lawnmower. Apparently, she had the chest pains but kept on going. Of course, we were flooded with shock and grief.

Two weeks before she died, we had our last visit with her. She joyfully told us about a beautiful dream she had had that week. She told us, "I had a dream about Grandpa. I was on a real pretty path and he walked slowly toward me. As he came over to me, he smiled and held my hand a little, and then he turned around and walked away again. I want to go soon, too, to be with him in heaven."

She was so joyful; I had never seen her that happy. She bubbled with joy. That day, she had been so sweet and kind; we felt so loved. It seemed almost like a divine love. Now that she was gone, we felt sad that we couldn't enjoy her anymore.

After the funeral and luncheon for the people attending, we were invited to Betty and Richard's home for more fellowship and to comfort one another. That day, for the first time, our children all formed a strong bond with their cousins. Comments were made years later how the Lord's grace overflowed that day to comfort all of us upon Julia's death. We also found that she had made her arrangements with the parish priest for her funeral. We realized she sensed her upcoming death would be soon. Apparently, she had committed her life to Jesus before she had her beautiful dream. We knew from all we learned of the circumstances before her sudden death that God certainly answered her prayerful desire to go to heaven to join Marvin's dad, her beloved Johnny.

CHAPTER 18

WORKING TOGETHER

As the children got older, Marv and I expected them to help out. As soon as I thought they could do the work, they each were assigned their jobs and chores. I taught them early to do dishes. Our kitchen was inconvenient with one large sink, so I placed two plastic dish-pans side by side. Somehow the old, dark-green linoleum would get really wet, but I wanted the children to have the responsibility of having to help, so didn't mind the spilled water.

They griped and complained that one or the other was working less, but I knew this was good for them. I fashioned a list of chores, and then made a name slot so we could rotate the jobs from week to week. I hung the list on a nail in the kitchen. They didn't complain as much after that.

Each spring, I continued to plant a large garden of vegetables. I always expected the kids to help me as soon as they were old enough. Besides helping sow the seeds, they had to help harvest the veggies from the garden, and help prepare them for the freezer or canning jars. These occasions would always bring out groans of "Do we have to?"

"Walking beans" was a dreaded job for all of us each summer. But it had to be done. In order to get better prices at the market, we needed to have clean soybeans to sell. Clean beans had very few weed seeds and volunteer corn in the loads we delivered to the grain company in Fremont. Of course, the days were always hottest when we would all receive a sharpened hoe or corn knife from Dad Popken, as he smilingly handed them out to all who could swing a tool.

"Okay, time to walk beans," he chimed, and we all groaned inwardly while quickly shooting up a short prayer for rain that would cancel Dad's plans. He always assigned us two or four rows (whatever he thought we could handle) so we'd start out our rows side by side, but soon one or several of us would lag behind. Our tools of the trade were sharpened corn knives or sharpened garden hoes to cut the weeds down without damaging the soybean plants.

In the meantime, Kevin, being a toddler, sat at the end of the rows with a little straw hat in the hot sun and played with an assortment of cars and miniature farm machinery. He was such a good boy, never complaining. We always moved him to a new spot, making sure he had a cold drink when we finished our assigned rows.

Marv always encouraged us to keep going. Faster than the rest of us, he would get far ahead and then walk back to meet us, chopping weeds for us as we met. Then we'd drink from the water jug and begin our next set of rows. All of our muscles got so sore, and blisters formed on our hands. We felt we would drop for sure from the heat and sweat, but it was fulfilling when we looked back at the end of a hard day to see the beautiful weed-free fields, seeing what we had accomplished together. Many times, Marv drove us in the pickup into town to the Dairy Queen for a cold treat to cool us off. In those days, the kids would ride in the back, wind blowing in their faces. The children still mention that happy memory of going to the Dairy Queen after our hard days in the field, even though we were all sweaty and filthy dirty.

Though we had good family times while we worked together, I was still unhappy and took a lot of my frustration and anxiety out on our children. After their bed times, the regrets would come. "Why, God, can't I be a better mother? Look at them. They look like angels; their faces are so sweet and innocent. I was so harsh with them today, Lord. They had such scared looks on their faces. I don't want them to be scared of their own mother. They didn't mean to make such a mess. I don't know what's wrong with me. I wish I could be more patient with them, Lord. They try so hard to please me."

I whispered those thoughts many times when all of my young ones were sound asleep. I would always walk out of their rooms and cry. It seemed to me I was always angry about something and I continually asked God to help me become a better mother.

As they grew older, I got more demanding, expecting them to obey instantly. If company was coming, woe to them. They had better get all of their work done so the house would be uncluttered. "What will the people think of us? They'll think we're a bunch of slobs. Hurry up with that! Get going, NOW!" were some of my many stern orders. On and on it would go. The more I yelled and screamed, the slower they moved, and the more guilt I felt. I was afraid to apologize. My crazy thinking was that they would get mixed signals if I apologized to them too often. They might think I didn't really mean what I said in the first place.

If the weather was nice when the pressure got too great, I rushed out the back door to the grove of tall elm trees with its border of beautiful evergreens. I'd think, "I just have to get away for a breather, or I might kill 'em. I can't take this anymore." Woe to anyone who followed me. I always warned them, "Don't follow me! I'm going to talk to God," and I did!

Always, I sat on a big, fallen log and sobbed, telling God all of my concerns and problems, crying out to Him to do something. I'd ask Him to help us get all the work done and pray that the kids would obey me. And I asked would He please, please forgive me for being so cross and mean. I never heard Him talk back to me, but I always felt better and calmer. For a time, I talked more kindly to the children – until the next pressure-filled circumstance.

Sometimes in desperation, I would tell Marv, "I don't know what to do. I'm afraid one of these days I might kill one or even all of 'em." He always said, "No, you wouldn't do that. You love them." I wasn't so sure.

All the work and responsibilities became more overwhelming. Many times I stayed up all night long, never even going to bed so that the house would be clean and the food a feast when company came, just so no one could talk about us. My motives were all wrong. All I ever worried about was whether the guests would spread unkind words against me.

I expected perfection from the children whether in work around the house, academics, manners, being appropriately dressed, or being polite to everyone they encountered. Almost always, I'd be on their case about something. In other words, I wanted perfect children who would not embarrass me or make me look bad. I was filled with extreme pride and fear of people rejecting me.

Chapter 19

Happier Days

Thank God for the ordinary days, where I didn't have to perform to receive love. I allowed my children to do a lot of fun things when I was relaxed, even if it required more work for cleanup. I have a snapshot of Ken as a toddler in training pants with his big sisters, who were five and four. The three got into a deep mud puddle in front of the old car shed, which we called the outdoor garage. Then they put muddy hand prints all over the white painted shed door. Ken, being only a little over two, sat down in the mud puddle in his little white underwear and the girls followed his lead. When I checked on them, they were almost unrecognizable from all the mud. I laughed when I took their picture. Later, I placed Ken in the bathtub with his then-brown training pants and soaked him clean. I didn't care because I knew they had had great fun.

I baked lots of cookies and other goodies for them so they could have happy memories of hot cookies and milk after their school days. Always, I tried to send nutritious lunches, along with just the right amount of small treats in their lunch buckets, which were the tin ones with different childhood themes painted on them. Every Easter, I made a big deal of coloring eggs and sewing each child a brand-new outfit, even for my little boys when they were preschoolers. They were all totally coordinated. Always, I was so thrilled with the results of my efforts. I felt fulfilled and good about myself then. Sewing late at night had become my mental therapy for years. I absolutely loved to sew and create. I had the proof of a finished garment that said I could "do something right."

I had the children's classmates and chums over to play often because I wanted the children to be balanced in work and play. But if I had to entertain any adults the next weekend, I turned into the mean mother, ordering them around to perform. No playing for them at those times until they had their work done! I'd be mad the whole time we were getting ready for company.

My perfectionism always took over, even with birthday cakes. I wanted each cake to be special for that child's day so they could store up happy memories. As they turned older, the girls wished for frosting flowers rather than the simpler cut-up animal shapes, so I bought new cake pans and cake decorating books, and I ordered from a mail order catalog all the necessary decorator tips, frosting bags, ornaments, and accessories. Then I set out trying to learn how to do the cakes myself. Oh, did I hate that! I had to practice and practice to get the frosting just right. I practiced making hundreds of frosting flowers till I was so sick of the whole procedure I wanted to throw the whole gooey mess out along with the darn frosting tips and food colors. I was so frustrated, but determined that my children would have a few happy memories from their childhood instead of only bad days. When they were small, I planned small parties and games for each child, always having them help in the planning.

I remembered with sadness that we didn't have decorated cakes for our birthdays when my siblings and I were young, not because our dear mother didn't care, but because they were so short on money and she was so overworked, not having any modern conveniences.

Before we had the creek straightened for purposes of land conservation, our older three children spent many hot afternoons sliding down a mud slide in the creek that flowed from a deep spring of continuous clear, cold water. I had the kids dress in their oldest worn-out summer togs and led them to a smooth, steep slope along a shady creek bank without branches or tree roots sticking out of the soil.

Sometimes, when it was a little too dry, we'd pour extra water dipped from the warm shallow pool of water below onto the bank path. We flattened it down with our bare feet. Then they could really fly down on their wet behinds. Soon they'd be whizzing down that slippery mud bank, splashing into the warm pool of water, which became browner with each trip down. Eventually they were totally covered with mud, squealing with delight as they hit that warm water. I didn't care how filthy they got. I was as delighted as they were because they were making memories and so was I. Times like these reminded me of some of my own carefree summers, playing in our creek with my siblings.

Since I loved to sew and could easily visualize projects, I made creations from scraps of fabrics left from previous items or even old clothes cut apart and saved for just such plans. Or I used various fabrics from our many fabric stores, which abounded in those days. Each Halloween, I sewed unusual costumes, which always, without fail, brought a prize from the elementary school parties. Somehow, I managed to think up ideas to make the kid's their requested creations each year. Besides the usual ones – bunny, cat, monkey, pumpkin, clown, Native American, or princess – they had a Julius Caesar, Lone Ranger, Yoda from Star Wars, and many more. My creative juices flowed freely then, and it was a happy exciting challenge bringing the ideas into existence. When I kept busy creating, some of the pressure of work or performing for others eased up.

One of those creations was a "Cousin It" costume from "The Addams Family," a weekly TV series popular during the early '70s. That costume took me days to make. I painstakingly washed all the beige twine saved from our hog feed burlap sacks, untangling dozens of the long, thick strings. Then I sewed them one by one to a sort of tunic I had fashioned with a separate, loose hood, to put on Kathy's head, covering her face. It was tough going and I was concerned that I would plug up my beloved Singer sewing machine, but I was determined she would have her costume. She really did resemble the character "Cousin It!"

When the girls were old enough to stay alone for an hour or so, I drove the boys with one or two of their classmates, Steve Irish or Troy Moerker, to a fishing hole that Troy's mother told me about. It was located near a farm, about three miles away. Since the pond was not very deep, I felt it safe to have the boys sit on the bank with a picnic lunch and fish to their hearts' content. All the fish the 12-year-olds and Kevin, only 8, ever caught were small, but they enjoyed those little adventures on hot summer days.

All of our children had their share of playing with pets. We had chickens from day one and they all loved to hold the adorable little puff balls while they were still cute – the first week of life. Cats and kittens were in abundance, as well as favorite dogs, pet bunnies, and little pet piggies, along with a pony for Ken, named Flicka, and her baby, Queenie. We had a chicken named Henrietta that Kristy retrieved from our Siberian Husky Vanya's mouth as a tiny chick. Henrietta thought she was human and let us pet her. Then she'd cock her head and respond favorably with her hen talk. Ken's favorite animal was our beautiful German shepherd named Duchess. She was an intelligent and loyal dog. Although protective of all our children, she was a constant special companion for Ken as he grew up roaming the fields and creeks during his youth, setting traps for various wild animals.

The boys built forts that somehow shrunk in size as they became adults. One was abandoned immediately when our young builder-owner, Ken, found a large bull snake curled up enjoying the cool dirt floor one hot summer day. To this day, we see a few boards left standing among the trees. Another fort was standing in our grove of trees (known much later by our grandsons as the forest) until a tornado hit our farm several years ago. It was a unique little fort, built from scrap wood rejected by the carpenters when our new home was built when Kevin was 10 and Ken, 15.

Kevin placed small windows on two sides. To provide lighting, he connected a single light bulb to a long extension cord hanging under the rafters. He put carpeting on the floor and added a discarded but intact bathroom cabinet, useful for its mirror and shelving. He dug a hole under the tiny creation for its basement. He used a galvanized ladder left from a torn-down windmill, which he placed on one side to reach a lookout on the perfectly shingled asbestos roof. An ancient rusty tractor seat was nailed to the roof for a lookout to spy on possible enemies: wild or tame animals, girls snooping around, or just suspicious spies in the neighborhood. Kevin had secret meetings with the members of K.C. Raiders (the initials of Kevin and

Chris Randell) with our other neighbors, the Adams brothers, in their boys' club. Little sisters and friends' sisters were definitely not allowed.

Winter days provided more fun as I reminisced about the winter adventures I had as a child, sledding and playing games in the snow. We taught our children how to enjoy winter too. Snow always seemed to abound when they were small. We had many winter holidays from school when our roads were impassable for days. If Marv had the day off from Hormel, he pulled the children on their wooden sleds behind the tractor all over the icy trails. The kids loved that!

CHAPTER 20

4-H DAYS

Getting ready for 4-H fairs offer vivid memories. I wanted to be sure my daughters received the proper training to become good homemakers and felt the only way they would have the patience to learn domestic skills was to provide them with incentives.

The desirable Purple Ribbon (the top ribbon award) would be a good incentive to get them to put forth a lot of effort. In the meantime, I presumed, the domestic skills would follow. Oh, the struggles to get the quality the home-ec judges expected in order to receive that almighty ribbon! I went to many sewing classes to learn to teach proper sewing methods. I learned to bake the hard way in my early years, by trial and error, always taking notes on failures or successes in my experiments, making recipes over and over, trying all kinds of different ingredients so I could teach the children properly.

For several years, we belonged to a neighborhood 4-H club. The group's leader insisted I teach cooking and baking if I wanted our children to be in their club. I felt overwhelmed because I was still experimenting on baking recipes myself, so I had very little confidence in helping all the girls. That filled me with anxiety, guilt, and depression. I was so much better qualified to teach sewing. Baking seemed to be more chance than skill.

It seemed easier to have the meetings at my home where I had equipment to demonstrate and teach, but it took its toll. Marv was getting irritated because I spent so much time cleaning and getting our old house ready for the meetings that I neglected the garden vegetables when they were ready to can. I was so worn out from the stress and pressure. The girls did not always listen or understand my instructions, so they were not as successful as we had all hoped. Eventually, I started a new club for 10 girls, most of whom were younger, appointing myself as their leader. The older girls chose a name for our club, "Mod Squad," after a popular TV series at the time. Eventually, I had 15 girls of all ages, with me as the sole leader.

Though it was rewarding, it was a lot of stress and worry as I had to figure out the judging standards. Some judges were strict and others more lenient. Some understood clearly that the little ones didn't yet have their coordination fully developed, while others were used to judging work from college-aged girls. It was easier to evaluate my own daughters, because I knew how far I could push them. I wanted so badly for all the girls to develop confidence in their abilities that many times I found I was more concerned about the others than I was my own daughters.

I never cheated by doing the creative work for my girls because I felt that would defeat the purpose of learning domestic skills. Besides, I felt the Lord couldn't bless us if I sinned in that way. The girls and I still laugh at the many times we had to stay up all night before "fair entry day" to complete everything. We each took turns nodding off for a while in the sewing room even as I sat on a stool, waiting to advise on the next step of whatever they were completing.

I remember one time I was nodding off while standing at the ironing board, pressing some pattern pieces so they would be easier for the girls to work with. Usually during those all-nighters, we got punchy and giggled a lot before those projects were ready. The projects were successful, because my three adult girls are now good homemakers and are grateful for their experiences. Kathy and Karen both found the area they wanted to excel in, which gave them confidence in their career choices. All three girls earned the right to model the clothes they sewed at the State Fair Dress Revue, which was a great honor and gave them more self-confidence. Both Kathy and Karen did demonstrations at State Fair, Kathy in First Aid and Karen in Baking. Karen also made a pie and chocolate cake for the Open Class Judging at the State Fair.

During her high school days, Kathy won a contest by submitting an essay for the Hugh O'Brian Youth Leadership organization. When Karen was a junior, she entered a Junior Miss Pageant, held in our county. Though she won 3rd place instead of the top honor, she won Miss Congeniality, which was a thrill for her as well as for me because I knew that Karen had gained confidence after being a shy little girl for so long.

In the meantime, the boys, in their own 4-H club with a kindly older gentleman at Fremont, enjoyed their projects as well and learned so much. Ken's projects were woodworking and rope. Ken displayed different knots on a beautifully finished wood board for competition and was pleased with his ribbon placement at the county fair. One year, Ken chose a project in woodworking that was really too advanced for him, but he did very good work at age 10. I believe his woodworking project in 4-H caused him to wholly enjoy his projects in his high school shop classes. One project was a beautiful gun cabinet that still holds his guns.

Kevin had a special breed of colored chickens that were raised as a 4-H project, as well as a rabbit project and hog project for the fair. We all enjoyed those tiny, colorful banty hens and chicks as well as the beautiful bunnies of all colors and sizes. On county fair entry days, we had to load so much into our old pickup with the hogs and crates of chickens and rabbits tied to the tail gate. We laughed at the sight we must have been as we drove into the fairgrounds with our odd assortment of animals, overloading the pickup bed, much like the Beverly Hillbillies.

Kevin also tried his hand in woodworking, which carried on to a high school shop class. As an adult, he now enjoys remodeling his 100–year-old home, completing a different project each winter season when his lawn season has ended. We are amazed at the beautiful work he has accomplished.

Kristy excelled in the arts for her 4-H projects, though she also won top ribbons at sewing and modeling her garments at State Fair as she learned to sew and bake. She fashioned numerous items for her dollhouse from the time she was a little girl; that creativity blossomed during her 4-H experiences. These ideas progressed as she graduated from high school and chose studio art as her major in college.

Chapter 21

Harder Farm Work

In the meantime, the hogs were with us all year round. Marv needed the help, but his main goal was to teach his children to accept responsibility and learn to work hard. Ken began helping me with the hogs when he turned 12 and Kevin helped later. They often commented, "Dad must lay awake nights thinking of ways to make us work." He always laughed and agreed. "Hard work never killed anyone" was his favorite reply.

I thought my hog education had been completed by then. To make it easier for Ken and me, Marv decided to install farrowing crates in the barn. These are steel pens with room for the babies to sleep on both sides of the mother. Heat lamps hanging on one side of the mother entice the babies to walk away from her after they have nursed and go to sleep under those lamps to keep warm during cold weather. This prevented many deaths from the mother unknowingly lying on them, crushing them to death, especially when she is giving birth and so miserable.

When we let them out twice a day for exercise, we opened the back of the crate and let them walk out on the concrete outdoors so we could feed them on that platform. That worked better than me running with the feed buckets to beat them to the troughs. While the sows ate, I washed out and put fresh water in the round galvanized pans and put baby pig feed pellets in separate pans for the babies to learn to eat solid food.

Some of the sows, however, were cantankerous enough to stall before going in with their babies after they had their dinner. I'd get so frustrated! When they spoke their low grunt, the babies all woke up and the whole barn would be filled with the sounds of squealing pigs – usually more than 100, depending on the number of sows that had farrowed. So I would open the gate as the mother stood in front of her stall, and then she would carefully step over her babes. There was always one sow who wasn't interested in going in, so she'd back up or move away. Then all the pigs would scramble out to chase after the mothers and get mixed up with the others as I opened the gate. Oh, I got so mad!

Somehow I survived all that, having to chase and catch all the little pigs and throw them in with the right moms. We could usually tell which the right mother was if we watched them or went with the trial and error method, but it was so time-consuming. If I had scheduled a babysitter to watch our children so I could attend a church meeting or card parties with my friends, I'd feel sorry for myself and beg the Lord to help me get those sows in.

I didn't much like the vaccinating or the castrating of the little pigs. They would be so frightened and the loud squealing in our ears would be hard to deal with. I felt really sorry for them, though, so I didn't blame them. Once when I was pregnant, I was to hold the pig "just so" so Marv could castrate the small males, and then spray them with disinfectant to prevent infection. My abdomen was so heavy with child that I couldn't find a comfortable place to set the pigs. My big belly being in the way caused one of the pigs to slip just as Marv began the cut, and he sliced his finger but good. That was the last time he asked me to hold the pigs. From then on, he held them upside down between his knees with their little behinds facing him to do the dastardly deed. I was okay with that idea.

Childhood mishaps and concerns

We had a frightening experience when Kathy was seven. After she had been happily playing all afternoon with her cousins at their home, she told us her ankle hurt when we arrived home. We couldn't see any redness or swelling, so we gave her children's aspirin for the pain. The next morning the pain was so much worse that she would not let us touch her ankle or even go near it. We dropped the other children off at the neighbor's and took her to our doctor, who took blood tests and decided to hospitalize her for observation.

In the meantime, the tests showed she could have any of the serious chronic diseases like cancer, rheumatic fever, or some infectious disease. However, our doctor kept thinking it could be fibrositis, which was explained as inflammation in her fibrous tissues in an area where she had possibly received an injury. He decided to treat her for the inflammation while waiting on the final test results. We were so afraid that it was serious and could be fatal, yet prayed and hoped that our doctor was right. Many people criticized him for waiting while he gave her antibiotics but he was right. Soon, the pain and inflammation subsided and she was dismissed four days later. How grateful we were to the Lord for answering our prayers for our precious young daughter.

When Kevin was a baby, he needed his second series of DPT shots. I noticed he had a dry cough so I called our doctor for advice. He suggested we wait on the shot if he still had symptoms, but the next day when I called, the nurse in charge told me, "Oh, that won't hurt anything – just bring him in." The night of his shots he was so sick with a high fever. I was up with him most of the night, giving him liquid aspirin as often as I dared and trying to comfort him with wet washcloths and holding him with his bottle as he slept fitfully.

At 4 a.m. he cried even harder so I took him to the bathroom light. Apparently he was hallucinating because, as he looked at me in the dim light, he screamed loudly and began jerking backward, almost falling out of my arms. I saw then as his eyes rolled backward and his tongue rolled under that he was having a convulsion. I called the doctor, who suggested we place him in cool water, and then bring him to the hospital. His temperature had shot up to 104 degrees so we laid Kevin in the water. The doctor explained that a convulsion is like a valve, releasing pressure off the brain when the temperature gets too high. He was admitted to the hospital and was there for three days while the staff worked to bring his temperature down. I cried and cried because I was terrified he had brain damage and blamed myself for taking him in for the shots. He checked out fine after the fever dropped. How thankful we were that God answered our prayers and our little guy was all right again.

When Kevin was four, he was waiting at the end of the soybean field, playing with his little cars in the fine dirt, as we faithfully walked beans. As Kathy got nearer to the end row where Kevin was playing, he hollered to Kathy, "Here's one, Kathy," while I hollered to her, "Be careful you don't hurt Kevin."

Kathy was careful to chop the weed. But as she brought her corn knife back up, Kevin stood up and the blade sliced his eyebrow as he walked into her knife. He screamed, and Kathy sobbed, "I'm so sorry, I'm so sorry!" as the blood flowed into his eye and down his face. Marv and I ran to them as fast as we could, and Marv carried Kevin to the pickup. Kathy was 12 then, so we dropped the older children off at home and rushed to the hospital with a clean washcloth to compress the bleeding. The other three children were devastated about their dear little brother, wailing, "He's going to die!" I tried to calm them, saying, "Oh no, he won't die, but we have to take him to the hospital for the doctor to fix it now. Just pray that the doctor can get there soon. He will be all right!"

Kevin was brave when our doctor attended him. We felt sorry for our little boy, but we were so grateful the knife missed his eye. We never scolded Kathy because we knew she had been careful, that it was an accident. Again, we thanked God the knife didn't injure Kevin's eye. His scar still remains as a reminder of God's protection.

The Lord gives all of us an inborn discernment, according to 2 Corinthians 5:11. One Saturday in summer, when Ken was about 12, he was stung by a wasp on his wrist. He came to the house for me to treat the painful sting. The next morning, it was still quite swollen and painful as we headed off to Sunday mass at St. James. During Mass, I looked down and saw two red streaks running up his arm. Scared, I thought he must have blood poisoning. I couldn't wait for Mass to be over and told Marv as we walked out, "Marv, we've got to get Ken to the hospital right away. Look at his arm.

It looks terrible!"

When our doctor saw it, he exclaimed, "It's a good thing you brought him in. The bee must have stung him in the vein and he's got blood poisoning. He could have died, had you not come." Our doctor gave him a Cortisone shot. How we thanked the Lord that I recognized what was wrong just in time.

High school

As our older children were finishing elementary grades at our country school, we needed to decide where they should go for high school. We decided to send them to Bishop Neumann Catholic High in Wahoo, 15 miles away. It would be difficult for me to drive them that far, especially in the winter months. So, we asked our priest from Mead Catholic Church, Father Rauth, to give Kathy rides to school. He drove there daily as he was the high school guidance counselor. When Karen entered high school the following year, the school board was able to arrange for a school bus to pick them up at Mead. I still drove them back and forth the seven miles to meet the bus, besides getting the younger children to their elementary school. Eventually, we bought a nice, used Ford for the girls to drive to Neumann because of their extracurricular activities.

Funny farm incidents

It seemed the funny incidents usually happened when I was "great with child." One spring day, I was driving some hogs, mothers-in-waiting, off the concrete so I could let the nursing mothers out of the barn to eat. Below the gate was deep, soupy mud, from water that drained off the concrete. One cantankerous sow didn't follow my instructions and tried to dodge me so she could stay in the yard, so I lumbered toward her as quickly as my 8-month pregnant body could move.

When I hit the slick mud, I slid right off the concrete into a deep puddle of muddy water, and there I was, on my hands and knees, my swollen belly hanging right smack dab in that deep puddle of filthy watery mud, mixed with you know what. Ugh! Boy, I was really mad. I told Marv that I would no longer do his chores until we had the entire yard cemented. He got it done quickly, as soon as the weather warmed, which made things much easier.

Ken came out of the house to help just as I fell into that yucky mud mixed with manure. I heard him say, "Oh, you poor thing." I felt better when he expressed his sympathy because I certainly was in the middle of a pity party at the time, and madder than a wet hen.

Another time, after a refreshing summer rain, Marv had to move a sow to the shed to be bred. Since she was in a romantic mood, Marv thought we could just lead her down to the pens with only a rope tied on one of her hind legs. He asked me to come and hold on to the rope, while he hurried ahead to open the gate. I had my doubts this would work, but I agreed. We were halfway down a knoll where it was really slippery with mud.

At that point, the sow decided to rush to her "lover" and took off running. I was so clumsy, again, heavy with child, and I got the giggles at the ridiculous sight I must have been. I laughed as the sow pulled me down the knoll in the mud, with me sliding behind her, hanging on to the rope for dear life, skidding all the way. I was surprised that I didn't slide down that slippery slope on my butt in my round form as I hung on. I still smile thinking about that silly scene.

There were times that we needed all of our children to help with the monthly pig drive, the task of chasing around 30 half-grown pigs from the barn to the open shed where they were put on a different diet. These drives were required before we built the hog finishing unit for the weaned pigs.

We were amazed each time we tried to drive the pigs that there was always one that would "dare us" to drive it to where Marv decided it should go. That stubborn clever pig would turn around, stand very still, watch us closely, and wait for one of us to put down our guard so it could quickly sneak through the line to get where he/she wanted to go. Suddenly, it would quickly bolt between two of us, trying to make its getaway, and then the chase was on.

As soon as the person standing nearby started running wildly to head the pig back to the group, other pigs turned around rapidly, following the fleeing pig. We all had to run them back and forth until they got tired, and then they walked placidly to our planned destination. We always knew each time there would be one who stubbornly refused to be driven, so it was a matter of who outran whom. Those pig drives could be quite exhausting, humorous as well, but we the people always won out!

CHAPTER 22

TO BUILD OR NOT TO BUILD

With very few cabinets and closets in our 100-plus-year-old farmhouse, as well as our bedrooms being crowded, we knew we had to make some changes. We had put off building a house or remodeling because we didn't want to lose the farm from overextending our finances. Though we had quite a bit of money in our savings account for the house project, I knew Marv would be devastated if we were foreclosed on, because he loved farming and he worked so hard for it. I didn't want to lose it either, because we all loved living here, so we prayed that God would stop us if we were not supposed to remodel or build.

We called a contractor to show us how we could enclose the old, open-front porch for a bedroom for young Kristy, who still, at age four, slept in a crib in Kathy and Karen's room. The contractor laughed at us, saying, "You need to build a new house. This one doesn't even have a foundation. You would never get done remodeling it. There is too much to work on. Build yourselves a new home."

Marv told me to draw up on paper what I wanted. "Don't make it too small," he said. "We will be stuck with it the rest of our days on the farm. We can't build a larger one if this is too small. If we were in town, we could just move to a larger house." I drew up the plans and we took them to an architect. I was encouraged as I thought about having an easier home to clean with lots of storage as well as bedrooms for everyone.

After I completed the plans, the rains stopped and our crops yielded little because of the drought. We knew we had our answer from the Lord, which was, "Wait." Marv said, "We better wait on building the house. What if we keep having dry years? We need to put in an irrigation system instead of the house." I was disappointed but I knew he was right.

Irrigation

Because we endured those dry summers with little rain, which cut down on our crop yields, Marv realized he needed to drill an irrigation well. This would be our first experience watering our crops at will with a hand-moved pipes system. Since Marv was still driving each day to work at Hormel, poor Ken got the brunt of moving the water pipes each morning and evening. It was a horrible job for him. He lost a lot of weight as he entered his freshman year in high school.

The system consisted of 30-foot-long, 4-inch diameter aluminum pipes, which connected to each other, resulting in 60 feet of pipe. Moving the length of those pipes across 30 rows of corn required four people to carry the pipes, which were connected to mainline pipes lying across one end of the field. The first set of 4-inch pipes was connected to an 8-inch mainline pipe. Each time, the mainline coupler had to be moved to the next set so it matched up to the 4-inch sprinkler pipes. The guys had to slog through six inches of oozing mud to return for the next set to move across.

The 4-foot-tall corn was not a problem, but soon the corn grew to 12 feet. Then each worker had to use a pitchfork with the middle tine cut off to lift the pipes above the tall corn, while simultaneously running across to lay the pipes down in the right row. Once there, they attached the set of pipes to the next set. This was a strenuous operation because they had to run as fast as they could maneuver yet not sink into the sludge. Of course, they would be totally covered with mud. Each guy lost a few tennis shoes in the ooze during their summer careers.

This summer job for the older teens paid well but was tough to commit to because they needed to arrive twice a day. Friday nights of socializing with their friends took its toll. Many Saturday mornings they never bothered to call me, choosing instead to stay in their cozy beds. By the time I realized our help was not coming (we had no help for the days while Marv was at work), Ken was the only lad I had and Kevin was too young. I couldn't do it either, so Marv and I were discouraged. After repeated frustrations with the "no shows" for three dry summers, causing the rest of the corn to dry up without the much-needed water or rain each year, Marv had had it. One steaming hot Saturday, he came home from work announcing, "That's it! No more of this. We can't depend on those kids, so next year I'm getting a center pivot system." And he did.

Meanwhile, when the soybeans needed irrigating before the season was over that year, Karen and I were asked to help. "You can go on the end, and then it won't be so hard," it was explained to us. I almost looked forward to this adventure and got out my ol' tennis shoes, thinking I would do just fine. I could just visualize Ken saying with pride, "Way to go, Mom." Though her shoes were sucked off by the sticky mud, Karen did quite well, but after only a few rows of running through the deep mud and jumping across the 2.5-foot beans, I soon tired. As I tried to jump over more bean rows, the guys literally dragged me across the field on one end of that set of pipes. I laughed so hard, I couldn't catch up as I stumbled and tangled myself up in those bean rows. All I did was hold up the pipes, not carrying them forward, as I giggled. Finally, they got that field finished with me lagging behind. For some reason I was never invited to help irrigate again!

Before we made the change from the hand-moved pipe system to the center-pivot system, I injured two discs in my back. Ken and I needed to disconnect the large, 8-inch mainline pipes to move them to a different area in the field. I did not realize that I needed to jiggle the rubber-sealed pipes to get them apart. The rubber seals formed a powerful suction to keep the pipes together during the tremendous pressure from the large flow of water coursing through them.

I ignorantly pulled the pipe straight back as hard as I could and felt a pop in my lower back. Instantly, I had tremendous pain. From then on, I had constant severe pain, especially at night. After I explained what happened, Marv told me I should have jiggled the pipes apart because of the suction, like Ken did. Ken didn't tell me because he thought I knew. I decided to go to a chiropractor, who helped, and each time I went, the pain was relieved. But, as soon as I was working around the kitchen, if I just turned to one side, it would pop out again and the pain returned. Somehow the pain level went down by these continued chiropractic adjustments so I figured I could stop going to him. Though tolerable, my back was in constant pain for over a year.

Because so many center-pivot systems were ordered by other farmers, a pivot crew arrived during the following cold winter to set up the pivot system in the center of the field. Marv still had challenges to overcome, such as guiding the system safely through our creeks. First, he threw lots of crushed rock in the paths where the wheels would cross, but they sank too deep or washed away. Then he tried wooden pallets, but most of them were crushed as the heavy system went over them, so that failed as well. Some also washed away during heavy rainfalls.

Finally, Marv ordered custom-made, welded pivot bridges for the pivot wheels to cross safely to the other side of the creeks. We were all so happy to finally have an irrigation system that worked so well!

CHAPTER 23

NEW HEART AND NEW HOME

"But if from there you seek the Lord your God,
you will find him if you seek him
with all your heart and with all your soul."

Deuteronomy 4:29 NIV

As my workload increased and my responsibilities grew, I got more and more overwhelmed and miserable. Most nights, I didn't get enough sleep and the pressure mounted. Marv and I had even less time to spend together. Because of the long hours and work, we couldn't get away by ourselves as we needed. All we did was work, work, and work.

As I became more desperate, I took out my fear, worry and depression on Marv and the children to the point of verbal abuse, which filled me with guilt, shame, and more fear. I repented and apologized to them and to the Lord over everything I did wrong, but I still couldn't seem to change, no matter how hard I tried. I continued to pray desperate prayers for God to change me, to make me a better wife and mother. I felt so hopeless, wondering what the meaning really was to my life. I remember crying from hopelessness almost every Sunday as I sat in church during the Mass.

One Sunday, before the annual Lenten observance was to begin, we saw a notice in our weekly Parish bulletin stating that the nuns who taught at Neumann High School were going to have a "Life in the Spirit Seminar" for six weeks. I really wanted to go, because I wanted to learn more about the new ministry going on, "Charismatic Renewal." The nuns held the seminar at their convent home. Marv agreed to go with me. Seeing only women at the meeting didn't seem to bother him. All he could think about was eating out at one of our favorite restaurants after the meetings.

Well, I was so hungry for the things of God, that I couldn't get enough. The nuns were kind and loving and so were the Catholic women who attended. Each time we returned home, I was full of joy. I couldn't understand what really happened at the meetings; however, I didn't really care – I just wanted that joy. One of the nuns (and Kathy's art teacher), Sister Paula, shared that someone from Fremont had written a letter to her. The group had prayed two weeks prior for her little boy who had cancer and he had been healed. The doctor couldn't find any cancer and told his mother, "The cancer is gone."

When Sister Paula read the woman's story, I was thrilled and excited. I almost jumped off my chair. I exclaimed, "That was a miracle. Wouldn't it be wonderful if Jesus still lived on the earth and we could see His miracles?"

Sister Paula answered, "Yes, though Jesus is in heaven with His Father, the Holy Spirit is doing the same work as Jesus did when He was on earth." I said, "Oh, He does?" She said, "Yes, He's never stopped. He still heals people all over the world." I replied, "Really? Why, that's amazing!"

Boy, no one could keep me away after that. Each week I marveled at what I heard and Marv continued to look forward to eating out afterwards. One particular time, Sister Paula sang a wonderful melody in an unusual language. When she finished, I told her, "That was just beautiful. What language was that?" She said, "I was singing in the Spirit. That was the gift of tongues. The Holy Spirit hasn't gone away – He's still giving people that gift." "Really?" I said. I sure wanted that gift too.

At the next meeting, we were the only ones there with the nuns. I got to talking about my childhood burdens, and Sister Paula picked up that I had a few things wrong. I asked that evening if I could receive the gift of tongues. Sister told me, "Well, I can tell you have resentment in your heart. It's unforgiveness against one of your brothers. You don't realize it, but you have a problem there." She said, "You just pray. The Holy Spirit will help you forgive. When you have forgiven your brother, then you can have that experience too."

On the way home, I was on cloud nine, yet I struggled with forgiving my mean big brother. We were never able to visit those sweet nuns again. They had to move the meetings to the convent in a town farther away, too far for us. I prayed almost daily for four more years that I would forgive my brother.

Our new home

In January of 1976, we seemed to have peace that the time was right to build. We were able to start the construction of a brick veneer ranch-style 14-room home with 5 bedrooms, 3 bathrooms and tons of cabinets and closet space. Our oldest, Kathy, was a junior in high school and Kristy was still in preschool. We hired a contractor who agreed on our price. Work started on our home in May.

Because our contractor worked full-time at another job, he had only one man working on the house most of the time, except in the summer when the contractor's son came each day to help. One day, Kevin, age 9, was walking around the construction site, snatching up bits of scrap lumber to work on his tiny fort. Just then the young man threw a 2 x 4 board down to the ground, hitting Kevin in the head. Kathy, 17, was babysitting but she had no way to contact me while I shopped for groceries.

I got home about an hour later and Kathy rushed out to tell me what had happened. I immediately took Kevin to the hospital where the nurses followed our doctor's instructions to keep him on a gurney so they could observe him to see whether the concussion had caused any brain damage. As he lay sleeping in the emergency room all afternoon, I prayed diligently that he would be all right. I felt such guilt for not being there to take him in sooner. After about three hours, Kevin woke up and seemed to be all right. He was released with instructions to watch him closely to see if any serious symptoms showed up. He was alright, and again we were grateful for answered prayers.

CHAPTER 24

ETERNAL LIFE

"Jesus answered him, 'Truly, truly, I say to you,
unless one is born anew,
he cannot see the kingdom of God.'"

John 3:3 RSV

When the house was nearly completed, in February of 1977, we realized we could not decorate it in time for Kathy's graduation on May 22. We hired a painter, Tom Ryan, to stain and varnish all the woodwork in the 4,000-square-foot house while Marv and I did the painting. Mr. Ryan said we could save money if I would stain all of the insides of the cabinets while he worked on the rest, so I agreed to do it.

Whenever Tom and I were working in the same room, we would talk. He was older than I, and reminded me a lot of some of my older brothers. He had been raised a strong Catholic just as I had been and he had even attended a Catholic monastery when he was young. I noticed he talked about God and Jesus a lot, and I was interested in hearing his opinions because I could tell he was a good man and that I could trust him. Day after day, he told me stories about the Lord. He told me a lot about his family, but especially how the Lord had changed him after he repented and gave his life to Jesus. That certainly piqued my interest.

"You will seek me and find me when you seek me with all your heart."

Jeremiah 29:13 NIV

One day, as Tom was coming close to finishing the staining and varnishing of the woodwork, I wanted to hear more about his commitment to Christ and felt I needed some spiritual advice. After he answered more questions and shared with me more wonderful things the Lord had done for him, I confided, "All these years, I've tried to be obedient. I've prayed a lot and gone to church faithfully, but something is missing. I have so many blessings. Why can't I be happy? I don't understand what's wrong with me. I am doing everything the Catholic Church tells me to do, yet I am still so miserable. I am so hard on my children; I feel I am abusing them and I am so ashamed. I seem to do everything wrong. Everything seems to turn out badly. I just can't seem to change, and some days I just can't take it. I just want to die."

Tom answered, "Elsie, it's not the Catholic Church or any other denomination. You can't earn this. All you have to do is ask Jesus Christ into your heart and to take over your life, and you'll have your joy. He will change you from within."

I replied, "Is that all? That's easy. I'll be glad to give Him my life. I've made such a mess out of it anyway."

In an instant, without my even saying anything more, I felt tremendous joy and peace. I didn't know yet that I was born again. All I knew was that I felt so different – so overwhelmed with pure joy. Much of the fear I had felt most of my life was instantly gone. I knew something wonderful had happened to me but I wasn't sure what. Never in my life had I felt so much happiness and peace. Once again, I had hope.

I have learned since then that even though Catholics have confessed their sins many times to a Catholic priest, those who are willing to give their hearts and lives to the Lord are instructed to say a sinner's prayer. They need to confess again that they are sinners, sincerely asking the Lord for forgiveness for all their past sins. Jesus wants to forgive us and give meaning to our lives by coming into our spirits as well as bring glory to Himself. In turn, Jesus wants us to lead others to Him, telling them about Him as well as follow His example by living holy lives. Then we need to disciple and teach them, of course. Jesus wants to take us all to heaven when we die.

God uses His laws, the Ten Commandments, to make us conscious of sin so we become convicted of our need for salvation. Eventually those who come to true repentance make a spiritual U-turn in their lives, which is necessary. Many people are sorry for the consequences of their sin, but not sin itself. Second Corinthians 7:10 states, "Godly sorrow brings repentance that leads to salvation and leaves no regret, but worldly sorrow brings death." Jesus said, "I tell you, no, but unless you repent, you will all likewise perish." (Luke 13:5 NASB).

The Lord surely saw my heart of repentance. For years, I was so anxious to change for the better. I remember confessing to Him every time I thought I had sinned, sometimes over and over. Each time I committed a sin, I was so afraid that I might have committed a serious sin and will go to hell. I was terrified of hell. I always wanted to do better and hoped to be perfect so I could go to heaven and be with God. No matter how hard I tried to be perfect, I found that I could never be good enough, that I was still breaking one or more of the Ten Commandments.

I worried almost all the time. That fear and worry worsened after I married and had our children. God surely must have honored my sincerity in repenting and my desperation in wanting Jesus to take over my life because there was instant change in my heart. Tom explained to me that I was now "born again" and that meant that I would go to heaven as soon as I died, not even going to Purgatory as we were taught. He said that I needed to talk to Jesus each day and continue to have a personal relationship with Him. I thought that was wonderful. The day was March 17, 1977.

Tom finished his work in our newly built home about a week later. During that time, he instructed me, talking a lot about how to walk with Jesus, explaining that it was more important to follow all of His instructions, day by day, rather than being concerned with keeping all of the Ten Commandments. He told me about Galatians 2:16, "A man is not justified by works of the law [Commandments] but through faith in Christ Jesus," (ESV) and Ephesians 2:8-9, "For by grace you have been saved through faith and that not of yourselves, it is the gift of God; not as a result of works, so that no one may boast." (NASB).

I was so at peace and happy to do anything I needed to do to please the Lord and to keep the wonderful feelings I had. Tom said, "You're a new creation now. You have Jesus in your spirit permanently. He's taken over your life." Tom wanted me to listen to a local Christian radio station in order to learn more about Jesus. "You need the Word of God besides the Sacraments," he said. "That's how He teaches you. You can't grow without the Bible."

He talked about grace also. Galatians 2:21 states, "I do not set aside the grace of God, for if righteousness could be gained through the law [Commandments], Christ died for nothing!" (NIV). He told me which teachers and evangelists I should listen to and the times they were on the radio. He suggested Kenneth E. Hagin and Kenneth Copeland. I took notes on everything Tom said so I wouldn't forget. He told me I needed to get into a good Bible study. He said that he would pray for me each day so that I would find the right one and that I needed to pray each day as well and read my Bible, telling me that it would be better to read from the New Testament rather than from the Old because the New Testament was easier to understand and spoke about Jesus' teaching.

The last thing he told me before he left was, "Now, you have an enemy, the devil. We all do, and now he is really mad at you. He hates you and will do anything to stop you. He will attack you and even try to kill you, but don't worry. God is stronger than the devil. God is in control. Hang on to Him. He will protect you."

I didn't worry too much since I believed God would protect me. I did everything Tom told me as best I could. I was amazed at the preacher named

Rev. Kenneth E. Hagin, as well as Kenneth Copeland. I was so impressed with how they seemed to know what God was telling them, the strong faith they had, how joyful they seemed, how beautifully they prayed and how much they knew about God and the Bible. I also learned why I suddenly had so much peace and joy. Romans 5:1 states, "Therefore, since we have been justified through faith, we have peace with God through our Lord Jesus Christ." (NIV).

CHAPTER 25

WALKING WITH GOD

"He lifted me out of the slimy pit, out of the mud and mire;
He set my feet on a rock and gave me a firm place to stand."

Psalm 40:2 NIV

Two days after I made my commitment to the Lord, I sensed the Lord was telling me not to watch the soap operas I had watched every day, whenever I could, for years. I said, "What?" and noticed the voice again. It was actually a thought that seemed like a voice – it was so clear.

I argued and said, "I just want to see how it ends."

The next thought that came was, "If you watch that, you'll be in sin."

I said, "Okay," and turned off the TV. The next day, He said the same thing in my thoughts as I switched it on. Once again, I decided to obey. I was surprised that I was never tempted to watch the soaps after that. Good thing I gave that up because I just didn't have time for that stuff anyway, especially since it was a sinful thing to Jesus.

Graduation

Since Kathy would be graduating from high school soon, I needed to hustle to help Marv finish painting the house, get ready for a large reception to celebrate her special day, and sew a prom dress for Karen. Though I was quite stressed with all the work I had to do, I noticed I had a real peace, and I didn't get so terribly nervous trying to get the house ready with all the preparations for her graduation. The cake I baked and decorated in white daisies, Kathy's favorite flowers. It seemed to go well, as did all of the other special preparations I made. The girls helped me after school and most of the arrangements fell into place.

We moved over to the new home the day before graduation. The morning of the big day, we had a catastrophe: a huge downpour of rain. The newly dug soil caused brown muddy water to pour in through the basement window wells all over our basement kitchen. We hadn't brought over mops or buckets yet from the old house, so Ken went scurrying over to the old house to get everything he could find to clean up the flooded, muddy basement floor. We worked fast and hard and got everything cleaned up in time to leave for the graduation ceremony, with the party following immediately afterwards. I could tell I didn't get as panicked as I would have during other seasons of my life. We all had a great time with our relatives and friends at the ceremony and reception.

During the summer, I listened to Christian teachers on the radio and prayed a lot, and I learned to praise and thank the Lord more often. Even so, I didn't say much to my family or friends about my newfound faith, because I didn't know how to explain my experience very well. I didn't really understand yet what had happened to me; I just knew that I had such peace and inner joy. I was more patient with the children, with Marv as well, and they all noticed that I had changed in many ways. I checked around for a Catholic Bible study, but the small parish at Mead where we were members did not offer one, nor did the large Fremont parish. I was disappointed and didn't know what to do, so I just kept listening to Kenneth E. Hagin and Kenneth Copeland on the radio.

I was so surprised at the good things these Bible teachers shared, and I learned many new truths from the Bible. For instance, I had never been taught that we can all have strong faith by studying the Scriptures. Eventually by listening to other teachers and pastors, I realized that God is actually speaking to us, not just to the people He talked with or about when He lived on earth and at the time the Scriptures were written. I learned that confession is not only confession of our sins but also speaking the words of the Bible for situations in our lives.

I realized I was a very negative woman when Tom mentioned it to me one day and as he was instructing me. I had been complaining about something and he said to me, "Now that's a negative confession. You must not talk that way because you will get what you say." At first, I was puzzled, but I learned what he meant after listening to the daily teachings on the radio. One of the Scriptures, "He who guards his mouth and his tongue guards his soul from troubles," (Proverbs 21:23 NASB) makes it clear.

It took a long time to overcome my bad habit of talking negatively because I had been into self–pity, as well as whining and complaining, for so long. But through the years, I've learned to watch the words I speak about the situations in my daily life, though I still blow it now and then. When I do, I quickly say, "I break the curse of my words in the name of Jesus and I ask You, Father God, to forgive me for speaking doubt and unbelief." I realized that talking that way is a sin. His Word states in Romans 14:23, "Everything that does not come from faith is sin," (NIV) and Hebrews 11:6: "Without faith it is impossible to please God." (NIV).

Leaving our nest

Our summer was really swamped with getting ready for Kathy's last year in 4-H. She chose a hard project, a 4-piece wool suit, and even sewed a coordinating blouse. I had taken tailoring lessons with a home-ec teacher in Fremont, so that I could teach the Mod Squad 4-H girls. Karen, too, had several different projects she was working on, so we didn't get much sleep. I couldn't do any of the work for them, of course, but had to stay up to guide them each step of the way. Their projects turned out very well, thanks to our great God who answered our prayers. The girls received the desired first place Purple Ribbons!

It was really hard to see Kathy move out in August to begin her freshman year of college at the University of Nebraska at Lincoln. I knew our lives would never really be the same. I had a hard time not crying, but I didn't want to make it harder for her to leave home. I did have a good cry afterward, but I consoled myself that I still had the other children at home and that Kathy was only 50 miles away. I missed her so much, so I was glad that she called us often. She enjoyed her classes, preparing for her major in Home Economics, and made lots of friends. I also learned gradually how to pray more effectively for her and the other concerns I had. I got used to her being gone, and as I kept busy with the other children, and I handled the separation quite well.

Search for a Bible study

When September arrived, I tried to find a day care center for 5-year-old Kristy so she could play with other children. She was alone at home so much and I wanted her to mingle with other children so she would adjust better to Kindergarten the following year. As I inquired of different friends, I learned of a lady, LaVeeda Anderson, who had a large group of children at her day care. I had met her once before and liked her, knowing she was attentive to the children. When I called her, she said that she was filled to capacity but told me about another woman who could take Kristy. I enrolled Kristy in a different preschool class and she went with her dear little friend, Ruthie.

By October, Mrs. Anderson told me about a Bible study she enjoyed. I found out she was a born-again Christian, which really piqued my interest. I was concerned, though, because it was not a Catholic group. Then in March, a few months later, Tom Ryan called me. He told me something rather shocking. He said, "I have been praying for you to find a Bible study. The Lord showed me that there is one but you didn't join."

I told him there were no Catholic Bible studies available. I had heard of only one, and the ladies seem to be born again, but not Catholic. He said immediately, "Now, that's the one. You go to that one."

"Anyone who runs ahead and does not continue in the teaching of Christ does not have God; whoever continues in the teaching has both the Father and the Son."

2 John 1:9 NIV

Since I trusted Tom, I checked with LaVeeda. In November of 1977, I went with her to the home of the teacher, Sharon Steinbach, where about a dozen ladies attended. What a wonderful teacher Sharon was! All of the ladies were so kind and nice. When they prayed together, I was almost overwhelmed with the beauty of their loving prayers. I noticed they had so much love for each other. I had never been around a group of ladies who did not gossip, criticize others, or repeat someone's problems, who responded in so much love when burdens or problems were shared. They seemed so holy to me. I remember thinking of a statement I had heard somewhere, "See those Christians, how they love one another."

Always, Sharon would suggest praying in agreement for the ladies who needed prayer. "Again I say to you that if two of you agree on earth about anything that they may ask, it will be done for them by My Father who is in heaven. For where two or three have gathered together in My name, I am there in their midst." (Matthew 18:19-20 NASB). Soon, they started praying for me each week, patting my shoulder in kindness. I was so touched; I ended up crying every time they prayed for me. As I read the Bible to complete our assignments, I found something good in the Word every time. "May my lips overflow with praise, for you teach me your decrees… for all Your commands are righteous." (Psalm 119:171-172 NIV).

Sharon played her piano for a time of worship each week. The music and words of the songs were so beautiful. You could tell in the sincerity of their singing they all loved Jesus so much. The Scriptures in Psalm 119 was surely fulfilled with the fellowship of that group of ladies. We followed a booklet, "Life, God's Way," written by Nancy Murdoch. It was a short course in basic Christianity and was well-balanced teaching. I learned so much. I had never known God's love so much as when I learned about His promises. I couldn't seem to get enough.

Each week, I brought Kristy along, and she played nicely with Sharon's young boy, Kurt. It was good exposure for her as well. I knew I needed to come to learn more of Christ's teachings so I attended week after week. I couldn't bear to miss.

As I continued to attend the Bible study, Sharon talked more about the baptism of the Holy Spirit, according to Acts 2. As she explained the gift of tongues, which is our heavenly language and evidence that we have the Baptism of the Holy Spirit, I realized that it was the same experience the nun had talked about in the meetings at the convent more than four years earlier. I remembered the tremendous joy I had felt each time we returned home from those Sunday night meetings. As I listened with continued interest, I wanted that gift very much but didn't feel worthy.

Sharon explained that our spirits are praying directly to the Lord when we pray in tongues, so there was much more power. She explained, when we pray in our own English language, we are praying with our minds' understanding, which the apostle Paul explains in his writings. I realized these ladies seemed to be closer to the Lord than anyone I had ever known or heard of. They also seemed to have more power and inspiration when they prayed. The more I observed, the more I wanted the Holy Spirit to give me that gift. I went home, crying every time because I wanted to be like those ladies.

In the meantime, the ladies talked about a Christian ladies' group that met in Fremont regularly. "Women's Aglow Fellowship" met once a month to listen to a guest speaker and enjoy breakfast and fellowship together. It sounded wonderful, but I was afraid. Since they were not a Catholic group, perhaps they would teach or talk against the Catholic Church. I definitely felt I should not get involved. All my life, I was taught to be careful so as not to listen to false teaching or I could lose my Catholic faith and go to hell.

I did not respond for months, but finally I realized it would be safe to attend and sit quietly just to check them out. If they dared say one thing against the Catholic Church, I decided, I was outta there and would never return.

By April of 1978, I found myself doubting that anything different really happened to me. I got depressed because all I wanted was to be born again. I didn't realize it was the devil putting those thoughts in my mind. Those ladies at the Bible study were so loving. I wanted so much to change and be like them. I admired Sharon so much. She never put anyone down but lovingly corrected them with the Word of God. She never said anything negative against my beliefs and teachings of the Catholic Church, but continued to explain exactly what the Word of God stated. She was such a good representative of Jesus. I started praying to have the Lord show me if I was really born again. I told Jesus that's all I really wanted.

CHAPTER 26

RADICAL FOR JESUS

"Now this is eternal life: that they know you, the only true God, and Jesus Christ, whom you have sent."

John 17:3 NIV

One Saturday, I happened to think of the brother who had hurt me when I was young. Suddenly, I noticed I had an intense love for him as well and no longer cared about the hurt. I knew then that the strong love I felt for him was like the love Jesus has for all of us. I suddenly realized I really had forgiven him for the years of pain he had caused me. I never knew one could love someone so much. It must have been a divine love. Suddenly, for everyone I had held a grudge against in the past, I felt tremendous love as I thought of them. I just didn't care anymore about what they had done or said to me. I was so thrilled, because I finally "knew that I knew" I really was born again. I cried from pure joy and thanked the Lord over and over for showing me that; I literally danced in the laundry room as I sorted the dirty clothes.

"I'm born again! I'm born again!" I shouted.

Just then, our older son, Ken, who was almost 16, came upstairs from his basement bedroom. When he saw me crying, he said "What's the matter, Mom?"

I said, "Oh, Ken, it's all right. I am so happy because I just heard from Jesus. He loves me so much and He really loves you too."

Then I explained what Jesus had shown me – that I had forgiven my brother. For four years I had prayed that I could forgive him. Now I knew beyond a shadow of a doubt that I already had forgiven. I cried even more from joy.

Ken was so surprised at my new joyful loving attitude and was interested in knowing what happened to me. Ken later shared that he had felt like he actually hated me and thought about all the trouble he could get into just to get even with me, but since he couldn't get away from the farm until he was old enough to drive, he had no chance to do much wrong. Suddenly, he saw me as a different person. He couldn't get over how much love I had. I had been so mean. "Mom is so different now," he and all his siblings thought.

One of the first things the Lord showed me when I made the commitment to Him was, "All you have to do with Ken is to love him. I will do the rest." I was so thrilled because that certainly would be much easier than the discipline I thought he needed. I really did love him as much as I did his siblings. I was so glad to be able to make up for the terrible mistake I made with him when he was a little 4-year-old boy. Whenever we had some time, after school or on Saturdays when Marv was at work, he and I sat on the front porch steps together, and I'd brag about Jesus. Ken always listened to everything I had to say. I just couldn't keep quiet about my wonderful Jesus.

Soon, I was busy getting ready for Karen's graduation and reception. Her heart's desire was an elaborate cake with ivy leaves all over it. I practiced with those and they turned out well. Karen loved her gift of love from me Everything went well and we had a wonderful time.

"He put a new song in my mouth, a hymn of praise to our God.
Many will see and fear the Lord and put their trust in him."

Psalm 40:3 NIV

Later in June, I noticed that Ken had a different attitude toward Kevin and Kristy. He seemed so at peace and was so kind to them. He had been so hurt because of my harsh treatment that he thought I didn't love him. He thought we loved Kevin more than him so he was unkind to Kevin quite often. He was usually good to Kristy, but he seemed even sweeter to her now. The next day, I noticed the same thing, so I asked him,

"Ken, did you have an experience with the Lord or something?"

He said, "Yeah, Mom, the other night I was reading the Bible you gave me when I got confirmed and I told the Lord, 'God, make me like Mom. I want you too, God.' I got so happy, I almost cried." He also said, "I'm not going to drink either when I go out."

He told me later he wanted the same love that I had. He knew that rather than being crabby and controlling, I was now loving and kind; he wanted that love too. Oh, what a glorious day that was! I knew God had supernaturally saved him. I could tell, because of his wonderful, new attitude and I was just thrilled. I knew he was going to be all right and my songs of worship to the Lord were even more enjoyable and meaningful to me then.

That summer, I got radical and told everyone I saw about Jesus, how wonderful He was, how much He loved them and how happy I was to have Him in my life. I was so thrilled, I just couldn't keep my mouth shut. I wanted everyone to know. My constant excitement about Jesus embarrassed Marv.

He told me one day, "I wish you'd shut up about Jesus. People must think you're nuts."

I said, "Well, I won't say anymore to any of your friends since it embarrasses you, but I gotta tell the rest. I just can't shut up about Jesus. He's so wonderful and has done so much for me."

I kept telling 'em and telling 'em while continuing to listen to Christian radio, getting more and more fired up.

Around this time, I heard an evangelist, Don Stewart, from Arizona preaching on the radio. One day, he talked about the Bible story in Acts 16:25-31, about Paul and Silas who were singing in prison after being beaten. The Lord sent an earthquake, which caused the doors of the prison to open and the prisoners' chains fell off. When the jailer saw what happened, he knew he was in big trouble, so he decided to kill himself. Paul stopped him and assured him they and the other prisoners were still there.

The jailer then fell down before Paul and Silas in fear and brought them out, saying to them, "Men, what must I do to be saved?" And they answered him: "Believe in the Lord Jesus, and you will be saved – you and your household." (verse 31 NIV).

The evangelist then said that we should pray and believe that our families would all be saved, and they would be if we prayed and believed that for them. He said if we wrote to ask him, he would send a piece of red cord to place in our Bibles to remind us to pray that Scripture for our families each day. I got excited and thought, "Oh, I can do that," so I wrote to him and received the red satin cord. I placed it between the pages of Acts 16 of my Bible and prayed each day for my family and thanked the Lord for "me and my whole household" being saved. One by one, the children all saw what happened to me. They thought, "Whatever happened to Mom, I want that too." The Catholic faith had become so much more enjoyable. The Masses were more beautiful. Everything had more meaning.

Another salvation

A month later, on Kristy's 6th birthday, I was talking to her about Jesus and asked her if she would like to ask Jesus into her heart. She said, "Yes, Mom!"

I told her, "Okay, just go into your bedroom and ask Him to come into your heart." A little while later, she came out smiling and told me she had Jesus in her heart. I could really tell too because she was so full of joy. Each day, she shared what Jesus was telling her. It was so much fun to share about Jesus with her because she was so innocent and open to hearing everything about Him.

CHAPTER 27

STRAIGHTENED TEETH IN JESUS' NAME

When Kristy's permanent front teeth came in, one top tooth was so twisted, her lip would catch on it, which was bothersome to her. I felt sorry for her and decided to lay my hands on her closed mouth each night before she went to sleep. I prayed, "Lord, we ask You to straighten Kristy's teeth while she's asleep. We ask it in Jesus' Name and thank You for it. Amen."

Months later I noticed her teeth looking straighter. Six months after we started praying, when our dentist saw her mouth, he gasped and said, "Oh, my gosh! Your teeth are straight. I was going to tell your dad that he needed to take you to an orthodontist to have braces."

Kristy was able to tell him that God straightened them. Since then, two other dentists have told Kristy that she has the straightest teeth they have ever seen. When God does something, He does it perfectly. Praise the Lord!

Soon, Kristy started having visions – apparently having the spiritual gift of discerning of spirits, which means she could see angels and demons in the spirit realm. One day, she came out of her bedroom and told me that she saw Jesus. I was really excited and asked her to tell me about it. She said she saw herself and Jesus riding bareback, side by side in a large field filled with daisies that stretched out really far. Jesus was laughing as He bounced along on His horse. He had His head back with His mouth wide open because He was laughing so hard. She said it was so much fun watching as He spent time with her.

He would come to her quite often in her bedroom to teach her things about prayer and for whom He wanted her to pray. One day, several years later, I was rather down about something, and she and I were talking. Then she said, "Mom, there are two angels standing beside you. They must be your guardian angels. They are quite tall and large. They are talking to each other and laughing."

She saw they were quite relaxed, talking and smiling as they stood by me. Soon Marv called me to help him chase some sows into the barn. I went out and the angels followed. Kristy said, "They just hung around you, laughing and talking as they watched while you and Dad finished your work with the sows."

The next salvation

In August 1978, the Lord worked on Karen's heart. She was open to hearing things about the Lord, which encouraged me. I was so glad that I could talk to her about the Lord, which I so enjoyed doing. The following month she was preparing to go to college. She chose a program in Commercial Horticulture at the University of Nebraska School of Technical Agriculture. The school year started in late September. Before she left, an evangelist from Springfield, Missouri, Duane Friend, was scheduled to come to Fremont with his sons for four days of preaching and teaching.

I attended the first night's performance. I loved the worship music, and the preaching was convicting. The next night I convinced Karen to go with me. I told her, "The young men sing beautifully and one is really good-looking." That did it! She went with me the evening of September 17 and her reaction was surprising during the altar call. When the evangelist invited everyone who wanted to repent of their sins and ask Jesus into their lives to come to the stage for prayer, she literally ran up to pray the sinner's prayer with others because she felt empty, depressed and cynical after trying so hard to be good all her life. I asked her later why she ran up, rather than walk. She said she felt the Holy Spirit literally tugging at her and she couldn't wait to go. She felt such a load of guilt fall off her back; she truly changed from then on. The key Scripture for her was Ephesians 2:8-9, "For it is by grace that you are saved, not a result of works, it is a gift from God, lest any man should boast." (ESV).

Salvation for all

The last day for the Duane Friend Ministries to sing and preach was on a Sunday afternoon. I wanted to go badly and convinced Marv, Kevin and Ken to come with us. Of course, Kristy went as well. I asked Ken ahead of time if he would walk up front with Kevin to encourage him if Kevin indicated a desire to commit his life to Christ. Ken agreed.

Marv was not interested, insisting on sitting in the back. I was annoyed with his attitude but I couldn't very well sit apart from him. He kept looking around, and didn't seem to be listening to one word the preacher said. I was so disappointed and wondered why I even had invited him along. I could hardly concentrate on the words, but noticed Duane began describing hell. He made it clear that people would go to hell if they didn't repent of their sins and give their lives to Jesus. When people started getting up out of their seats, I got up for Kevin to get past me; I sensed he wanted to go forward. Ken got up right behind him. I could hardly believe my eyes when Marv got up as well and brushed past me to follow Ken and Kevin. While I was happy that he responded, I feared that he was not sincere and nothing would change in his spirit. I asked the Lord to please show me if he was sincere; I needed to know if he really was accepting Christ. Karen, seated elsewhere with her friend Kris, came running over to me when she saw her father and brothers go up. We hugged and sobbed in each other's arms. After Marv and Kevin spoke with counselors, Marv came back. As he drew near to me, all he said to me was, "It's real." In that statement, God showed me Marv had been saved. In tears, I hugged him and said, "I'm so glad. You won't be sorry."

Ken confirmed that Kevin had been sincere as well, though Kevin wasn't sure what had just happened to him.

A week after our commitments, I called Kathy at college, telling her about our new lives in Christ. She said she had already asked Jesus into her heart and life as well. So, every one of us had found salvation in Jesus Christ and were born again according to John 3:3: "Jesus answered [Nicodemus] and said to him, 'Truly, truly, I say to you, unless one is born again he cannot see the kingdom of God.'" (NASB). God had answered my fervent summer prayers. Each one of my family had committed their lives to Jesus and were saved for eternity, all in five months. How I rejoiced and thanked the Lord as I prayed each morning!

Miracle upon miracle

As she prepared for college that summer, Karen called the bank to check her savings account balance. She had been concerned because she was still $200 short of her goal to begin college after we had already paid her tuition. I prayed that God would help us get the extra finances. Lo and behold, the balance in her account showed the extra $200 that none of us had deposited in that account. I called the bank to make sure that money had not been deposited by mistake, perhaps being someone else's money. Once again, we raved about God's great goodness! All this excitement and blessings helped me greatly to get through having another child go off to college.

The man who briefly counseled Marv and Kevin when they made their commitments to the Lord explained what their decision to commit to Christ and give up sin really meant. He also mentioned some Bible studies where Marv could attend and learn more. After harvest time, when he had more time, Marv agreed to go to a study at the home of a long-time friend, Bob Newkirk, who had been a strong Christian for years. His wife, Mary, was a sweet kind lady. Bob had wonderful teaching and we faithfully attended all winter. Ken even attended with us for a time. There were just a few of us at first and the fellowship was wonderful.

The Sunday after Christmas 1978, we were invited to Leo and Lorraine's home for our annual family Christmas party. Just before we went home, I wanted to tell them a little about knowing the Lord. Leo was interested in all

Marv and I had to say. He suddenly exclaimed, "That's just what the Mennonites say! One of them works with me, and he is always talking about the Lord too." A few days later, on New Year's Day, Leo called me and asked which Bible he should buy. We talked for a while as I told him which translation I liked. After listening to him, I knew that he had given his life to the Lord. Soon after, Lorraine talked about Jesus, too. They were attending all of the meetings and fellowships they could, and they joined the Full Gospel Business Men's meetings in West Point as the dear Mennonite man had encouraged them to do.

Soon after, I ran into Audrey Larson at the Fremont Mall. I had not seen her in several years. As we talked, I told her that I now had a personal relationship with Jesus. She exclaimed, "Elsie, that's wonderful! I have been praying for you for the last six years."

"So that's it!" I said. "Thank you so much for praying for me. I always wondered why you were so sweet and special." How grateful I was that she was so faithful to pray and never gave up on me.

In the meantime, I started attending the Women's Aglow Fellowship. I felt uncomfortable the first time. When they began the worship music, I thought, "Now what do I do?" I noticed every lady raised her hands in the air while having their eyes closed. I didn't see how I could do that, but since their eyes were closed, I figured I could keep my hands down. I felt nervous until I peeked over at the head table. I saw one lady weeping, tears running down her cheeks, while she said, "I love You, Jesus. I love You, Jesus."

When I saw that, I thought, "Why, there's nothing wrong with this group. They just love Jesus like the ladies at Sharon's Bible study. It's okay for me to be here."

Besides attending the Bible study at Newkirk's with Marv, I attended the Aglow meetings regularly. I never wanted to miss. At the December meeting, it had been decided that we could bring our husbands as guests. Most men were at their jobs; however, several couples came. The fellows were asked to stand up and give their testimonies (stories) of how they met the Lord.

One happy fellow stood up. As he finished speaking, he mentioned that they were members of the Catholic Church in Fremont. My ears perked up. After we were dismissed, I hurried over to introduce myself to Ken and Jackie Hartman. We were compatible right from the start and formed a close friendship from that day on. Soon after we met, I invited them to our home for fellowship. They brought their teen-aged daughter, Michele, and her younger brothers, Mark and Mike. Michele and our son, Ken, became close friends and dated for quite some time until they both went their separate ways to different colleges. As families, together we attended Catholic charismatic meetings, Christian fellowships, prayer meetings, Full Gospel Business Men's Fellowship meetings, and Aglow breakfasts whenever we could. We were excited to hear testimonies and teachings, along with healings and prayer, and whatever message the speakers would bring to us. We were all hungry to hear more about the Word of God and learned something wherever we went.

During one of the Aglow breakfast meetings, the guest speaker invited anyone up for prayer who wanted the Baptism of the Holy Spirit. I almost ran up to the front. They prayed for me and I received a few words in a spiritual language; however, I got confused and thought I probably was repeating some of the words they prayed. I struggled with that for months. Eventually, I received the wonderful gift of tongues in my bedroom after I continued to ask the Holy Spirit to give me my spiritual language. That gift has been wonderful for me through the years.

And it turned out to be the beginning of seeing many more miracles in our family – and the truly amazing power of God!

CHAPTER 28

GOD'S HEALING POWER

"They will lay hands on the sick, and they will recover."

Mark 16:18 ESV

At an Aglow meeting, the speaker told us that God wanted to heal those of us who were in pain. She pointed to people and mentioned what disease they had, and they were all healed. She specifically called out backaches. I certainly had a backache!

Remembering the slipped discs in my back and how much pain they caused, I went up to the speaker. When I explained to her what was wrong, she laid her hands on my back and prayed. As her hand moved down and touched the injured area, she said, "There it is." She continued, "Well, you're healed. You can now do anything you couldn't do before."

Before then I could not touch my toes without terrible pain, but I reached down and did just that. Then suddenly the pain started again. "Something is terribly wrong," I told her. "My back hurts worse than ever!"

"Just tell the devil no. Resist him with the Word of God; he will go away. You are healed and a doctor will confirm it." She repeated, "A doctor will confirm it."

I went home with my backache once again and kept thinking about what she had said, even though I didn't really understand. Then I found the Scripture, "The thief comes only to steal and kill and destroy; I came that they may have life, and have it abundantly." (John 10:10 NASB). So I kept saying, "No, I am healed and a doctor will confirm it." Five days later, I noticed very little pain. I went to a doctor who specialized in bone injuries of backs, knees, and hips. He took X-rays of my whole back. When he looked at the film, he declared, "I can't find anything wrong with your back."

When I returned home, the pain never bothered me again. I was so excited and thankful, and I felt so loved by God that I said, "Someday, You're going to heal my hip, too, aren't You, Lord?" referring to the old hip injury from the time I had been pregnant with Ken, 17 years earlier.

The pain from that injury never really went away after Ken's birth. It would feel like a catch in my pelvic bone area, especially when I bent over to scrub floors. At times, it would leave almost right away, but other times, I would be limping along with my hip out of place for several days. I had a hard time sleeping at night because of the pain. Each time I tried to get up after I scrubbed our floors on my hands and knees, I stumbled around awhile before I could straighten up. Eventually, it would pop back enough so that I could move. I had accepted the injury as being permanent. Not anymore, and I praised Jesus every time I thought of it.

"I am the Lord, who heals you."

Exodus 15:26 NIV

I kept attending Women's Aglow prayer breakfasts, and each time I cried with joy when the women got up and shared their stories. One day I whispered to the Lord, "Whenever You're ready, I'm ready, Lord."

One day at a prayer breakfast, about three months later, I felt impressed that He wanted to do something with me. We had a delightful speaker from Kansas. Before she began her message, she said, "While I was in prayer about the message the Lord wants me to share with you today, I heard Him say that I should pray for a lady who has a problem with her left hip."

I sat there and thought, "Gee, it's neat she heard that."

She mentioned it again and added, "I can certainly be wrong, but I really think He was saying a left hip, not a right one but a left one."

I suddenly realized I had a problem with that left side, so I raised my hand. She exclaimed, "Come on up here. The Lord wants to heal you." I hurried up to her, and as she prayed, her hand got warm. Where she was touching me became hot. As soon as I got home that day, I quickly pretended that I was scrubbing the floor on my hands and knees to test for the pain. Sure enough, I bounced right up and the pain was gone. Oh, what joy, just thinking how much He loved me! The hip pain never came back and neither did the pain in my lower back.

More and more, I listened to Christian radio. One of the programs was hosted by a minister who had the gift of counseling people. People called in with their burdens, emotional problems, or questions. He'd pray after he advised them. I could tell he was getting inspiration and answers from the Holy Spirit. Sometimes his wife joined him and would provide answers as well.

One day, a young mother called in telling him that she didn't understand why she would get so angry at her little girls, who were such good children. Yet she would get so angry at the least little things they did wrong. She didn't want to be that way but could not seem to change or treat them well. That really piqued my interest because that was my problem too, so I listened closely. The minister asked her how her relationship was with her dad. She answered, "Oh, it's okay."

Apparently, the minister was hearing from the Holy Spirit because he stayed with that train of thought. She answered with irritation, "I could never do anything right for my father, no matter how hard I tried to please him."

The minister stated, "There's your problem. You felt anger at the injustice of it all, that your dad was never satisfied with your performance, no matter what. You thought you had to be perfect, which you couldn't be. When your little ones do similar things, it reminds you of the incidents with your dad and you get angry all over again. You are not angry at your little girls but at the memory of painful times of your childhood."

When it appeared she understood, he prayed a beautiful prayer for her and her little girls. I was almost in shock. I saw immediately why I had been so hard on my kids. It was for the same reason. I could never seem to please my dad. Our children were really quite good, but still I was never satisfied. I thought they should be perfect. At night, I watched them sleeping like angels, looking so innocent. Then I'd cry because I had been so hard on them. I didn't know enough to apologize for fear of losing control as a parent and possibly having them go wild as teenagers. I always prayed to be a better mother, but I just couldn't change. When I heard the minister explain the situation to that young woman, I saw that his words were for me as well.

I repeated the prayer as the minister prayed on the radio, and I did change. God gave me the understanding to know when discipline was needed and the grace to have patience when we were all having a bad day. Oh, it was glorious to be set free from that anger! I was so grateful to be able to be a more loving mother with our younger children. I just wish I had known sooner so I would not have been so hard on the older three. I also forgave my dad for his mistakes with me, knowing that he couldn't help it either. He and my mom did the best they could with what they knew and were taught.

CHAPTER 29

DIVINE APPOINTMENTS

"Then you will call upon Me and come and pray to Me, and I will listen to you."

Jeremiah 29:12 NASB

Because of the good Bible teaching I had received, I wanted to spend time each day with the Lord in worship and prayer. I had the most success when Kristy began kindergarten. Kevin was still in elementary school and Marv still worked at Hormel's. Each morning at 10:30, I would drop everything and go to my bedroom for my appointment with God. Somehow, His presence would be there right away, and Jesus and I would have glorious times together. Those were the days when He answered my prayers in remarkable ways. One time in particular, Marv said we needed rain. I asked, "How much?" He answered, "We could use two inches."

I said, "Okay, I'll pray." When I met with the Lord, I asked Him to meet our needs and send us two inches of rain. That very night we got a gentle two inches of rain without any wind or storm. I was quite surprised at first. However, Jesus and I had become such good friends by then. Even our priest noticed that when I prayed, things happened; he told people at our church about it. Perhaps it was because I kept my commitment to go to meet with the Lord in our bedroom each day, even if I was in the middle of doing dishes. Jesus always "showed up" as well, probably because of my appointment with Him.

But, sad to say, as time went on, I got busy with other things. I didn't always go in at 10:30, but I did go in and talk to Him at different times of the day. Though I still had time alone with Him each day, and He is still so faithful to answer our prayers, it was not quite the same. Bits and pieces of time were just not the same. I noticed when I don't look at the clock and just rest in His presence, just enjoying Him as my dear Friend, then I seem to trust more in His love. My simple trust then brings faith. My worship for Him at that time is so sweet and sincere that I often weep. That's when He speaks to me and I can really hear Him talking to me in my mind. I know then that He will take care of me, no matter what.

"At the acceptable time I listened to you,
and on the day of salvation I helped you.
Behold, now is the acceptable time;
behold, now is the day of salvation."

2 Corinthians 6:2 NASB

My mother was quite lonely without Dad, so about every two months she would come to see us. She always spent a week or two. One day, she agreed to go to a Bible study at Sharon's with me. I was surprised that only one other lady, a senior, was at Sharon's home that day, and she left early. So Sharon was alone with Mom and me. I asked Sharon if she would explain the story of salvation to my mother. Sharon immediately said, "Mrs. Luebbert, if you were standing under the cross when Jesus was hanging on it, what would happen to you?"

Mom said, "Oh, I would get blood on me."

Sharon said, "That's right, and that blood cleanses you from all your sins. Would you like Jesus to come into your heart today?"

Mom said, "Yes, I would."

Sharon said, "Well, you pray and tell Him you are sorry for all your sins and give your heart to Jesus."

Mom started praying softly to herself. I said, "Mom, the Bible says that we need to acknowledge Jesus to other people so that He will acknowledge us before God, His Father in heaven. So, you need to say your prayer out loud."

She said, "Okay! Dear Jesus, please forgive me of all my sins and come into my heart so I can go to heaven to be with You. Me and my whole family." It was such a sweet prayer.

Sharon talked to us about reading the Bible and how to walk with the Lord, and soon we left. Of course, I was thrilled, but when I took Mom home I started to doubt that she had been sincere. (I didn't realize that those were thoughts from the devil.) I prayed then, asking the Lord to tell me whether Mom was sincere and really born again. I remembered that she still had emotional pain and sorrow at the way her father had abused her and her siblings when they were young. Almost every time she came to spend time with me, she would talk about her youth. She would end up saying, "I wonder what the Lord said to him when he died and came up to Him?"

I told the Lord I would know she was born again if she had forgiven her dad. So when she visited the next time, sure enough, she talked about many of the times her father had mistreated her and her siblings.

I thought, "Oh, no, here we go again." But this time the conversation ended differently. Her last statement was, "I wonder what was wrong with him."

I was so thrilled, because I immediately saw a different attitude. I knew she had forgiven her father; she had changed and truly was born again and would go to heaven when she died. She was 80 years old. She had not read the Bible much before she got saved. But after her death, my sister and I were getting her things ready for an auction and we found a Jerusalem Bible and another version she had been reading. What a blessing that was to know!

An officer with Women's Aglow fellowship

The Lord did a surprising thing with me that year. I knew the officers of the local Women's Aglow board but now I was introduced to some of the state officers, Mary Ward, Marge Clements, Vernie Marquette, Twila Birdwell, and Myrtle Asper. Because the acting recording secretary had moved away, our Fremont chapter needed a new corresponding secretary. When the state officers told me that God was choosing me to take her place and had given my name to them all, I was stunned. "Who, me?"

I felt so inferior to all of the ladies. I didn't see how I could do it, yet I was so honored to think that little ol' me was chosen by God Himself. The Fremont ladies set up a meeting where I would be trained for the responsibility of contacting speakers and arranging the meetings, motels, and meals for our guest speakers. The spiritual training, which was powerful and offered with such love, was much more important than the job itself. Myrtle, the teacher, kindly told us in such a sweet way how serious it was to serve the Lord in this way and that we must never gossip or criticize or ever be in disunity over any decisions, even in tiny matters. If we didn't or couldn't agree on decisions after praying to hear from the Lord, we needed to be honest and say so, so we all could pray again to make certain that everyone heard the Lord accurately. They wanted to make sure the Lord was in charge of every detail of the ministry.

I was in awe and felt so privileged to be a part of that godly group of ladies. The lady whose place I took gave me lots of names with phone numbers to contact about becoming our speakers. As I continued to be active in the group, I was also privileged to attend the fellowship meetings at different cities as well as the yearly weekend retreats. The speakers were all godly women who operated in the gifts of the Holy Spirit and seemed to accurately hear from and be led by the Lord. I still wept during those meetings – not sure why I was crying but knowing that the Lord was healing my heart from past wounds and hurts. I remember being embarrassed, but I couldn't stop crying. The leaders knew the Holy Spirit was doing a wonderful work within me. They were always kind and caring and would let me weep while they ministered to others, many of whom wept as well.

The presence of the Lord was powerful, sometimes causing us to be "slain in the Spirit" whenever the leaders gently placed their hands on us as they prayed beautiful loving prayers. I couldn't remain standing when the power of God overcame me. There was never any pain, just a gentle impression on my body, as though someone gently touched my back. We rested while the Holy Spirit did His work in us. I was never afraid because I knew the Lord was doing a great work in me and I always felt joy and peace when His work was finished.

Another healing miracle

At one of the Fremont meetings, we invited a special guest, a charismatic nun from South Dakota. The ladies from out of town as well as the Fremont officers gathered with our guest of honor at our farm home for supper. The Fremont ladies graciously brought their delicious foods for a potluck. I felt so honored to have a lovely Spirit-filled nun, Sister Frances Clare, come to our home.

The day before the event, I went to get rice for a dish I was going to serve. First, I picked up 13-year-old Kevin and 8-year-old Kristy from school. In the car, I said to Kevin, "You hop out with your things. I will run over to Mary's to pick up the rice." He said, "Wait, Mom, I'll drop off my stuff and go along."

When he opened the back door to our station wagon, I said, "Kevin, wait until I stop the car!" Kevin fell out of the open door, catching his left foot under the wheel of the slowly moving car. I saw him limping to the garage and knew something serious had happened. When he took off his tennis shoe and sock, I saw that the heel of his foot was bruised and discolored, and it bore deep imprints of the stones and marks from the tire tread. One of the stones caused a dark purple mark below his ankle bone. Because he was in so much pain, I began to make plans to take him to the hospital, saying, "Kevin, we have to get you to the hospital."

Kevin said, "It's not broken, Mom. Besides, Dad is waiting for me to haul corn." Since Ken was gone, it fell to Kevin to drive the tractor and pull the wagon full of combined corn to a grain storage bin where the corn was unloaded. I thought, "Well, our Lord will have to take care of it then."

I laid my hands on his foot, reminding God that He had promised to take care of all our needs "according to His riches in glory in Christ Jesus" and asked Him to take away Kevin's pain and to heal his foot. Fifteen minutes later, Kevin was driving the tractor without a problem. Hundreds of pounds had passed over that young boy's foot and yet, several days later, the bruised area showed only a little discoloration and the ankle pain was gone! I was confused, however, because he talked about the calf of his leg still hurting.

Sister Frances Clare prayed for him as well, yet that ache persisted. A day later, I questioned the Lord and He kept saying, "Muscle, muscle."

When I prayed for Kevin's calf muscle to be healed, the pain went away also. I wondered why the Lord didn't heal Kevin when Sister Frances Clare prayed. I believe it may have been that He wanted me to learn to hear His instructions. I also believe that God gave me a gift of faith when I prayed for Kevin instead of taking him to the hospital when the accident happened.

The Aglow experience that stands out to me the most is a retreat we attended at Kearney when our own Twila Birdwell led the worship. She held the office of State Treasurer and she knew how to lead us all into worship and into God's presence. This was not because she had a gorgeous voice or an expensive instrument, but because of her deep pure love for the Lord. At one point in our time of worship, it became quiet. There was such pure joy, I wanted to stay there forever. The Lord's presence was so strong that we literally felt we were in a cloud of His glory. Although I don't know how long we worshiped, it seemed like a short time. None of us wanted to distract others or be distracted; our time with Him was too sacred. As I kept my eyes closed, I felt like I was in heaven. When our District Leader, Etta Schafer, felt led to speak again, she told us that she believed we had entered the very throne room of God.

She also stated that after our glorious time with Him, we would never forget this experience and would probably never really be satisfied again in any worship. That has been true for me. From then on, I felt such awe of Him, His strong presence, and such deep reverence and love for Him during worship at a public gathering. Times of worship have never quite been the same except for my times in our bedroom with the Lord. I have noticed that I weep easily when I am able to worship as long as I want to because of my love for Him and His wonderful loving words to me in the quiet of our bedroom when it's just Him and me.

CHAPTER 30

FAMILY CHANGES AND INCREASED TRUST

Ken graduated from high school in 1980. All our relatives and friends attended the reception we had for him. This time, after having some experience with graduation receptions, I was able to get the preparations ready more efficiently, including the decorated cakes in Ken's favorite colors of blue and white. I stayed calm and was able to enjoy the time with everyone. At the graduation, I received the neat surprise of having another of my brothers tell me he received Jesus as his Lord and Savior. My brother, Ben, told Jackie Hartman how God had answered my prayer in a beautiful way for him by giving him a miracle when his farm was being sold. After that, he wanted Jesus to take over his life because he felt so loved by the Lord.

A few months before, Ben's landlord had passed away, so the farm he and his family rented was being sold. On the day of the sale, I was praying in my bedroom for him when a nearly audible voice said, "You need to call him and tell him you have forgiven him for the hurt he caused you."

I thought, "He won't be in the house at this time."

The voice said, "Call him anyway." So I went to the phone and dialed. He didn't answer the first four rings. I started arguing with the voice and said, "See, I knew he wouldn't be in the house," even though by this time I knew the Holy Spirit had told me that I needed to call my brother.

When Ben answered the phone and we had time to talk, my brother told me, "Remember when you were so nervous and scared, you got sick to your stomach a lot? I always thought you were just trying to get attention, but today I am so upset about the farm being sold that I feel sick to my stomach too, so I know you couldn't help it then."

He continued, "Remember when our cousin Marie came to take care of us while Mom was in the hospital? She told me one day, 'How can you be so cruel to your little sisters?' I didn't even know I was being cruel to you."

I told him that I had forgiven him several years ago, when I asked Jesus to take over my life, and I just didn't care about those hurts anymore. Then I tried to encourage him in the crisis of his farm being sold. Though I didn't know why, I told him that if God closed a door in his life, He would open a window of opportunity for him, and that is just what the Lord did in a very unusual way.

Ben was able to stay on the farm until he retired because a farmer wanted the 40 acres that my brother was buying. The man insisted on trading his 60 acres for the 40 acres, because the man wanted to build a home on that acreage for his adult son. They arranged the land exchange, and my brother and his wife continued to live on their farm until retirement. Years later, when they eventually sold the farm, they got a much better price. From then on, Ben wanted to serve the Lord because he felt so loved by God.

"For He will give His angels charge concerning you to guard you in all your ways. They will bear you up in their hands, that you do not strike your foot against a stone."

Psalm 91:11-12 NASB

One evening, I was listening to the news while preparing supper. Kristy walked by the TV when an announcement came on that a known pedophile had been arrested. As a TV camera flashed on the man's photograph and his old, beat-up looking van, Kristy shouted, "That's him, that's him!"

I said, "Kristy, what are you talking about?"

She answered, "That's the man who tried to pick us up. That's the same van he drove."

When the weather turned warm, I encouraged the children to walk the one mile from their country elementary school to home. I was very strict and warned them never to walk alone and never ever to get into a car with anyone they did not know. If someone got persistent, I told them to start running into the fields to get away. That road had always concerned me because it was a direct route from one of the main highways leading out of Omaha.

When Kristy was in the second grade and Kevin was in eighth, they were walking home from school one afternoon with their neighbor friends Scott and Julie Adams. Kevin and Scott's older brothers walked a distance behind the girls. A man in an old van stopped to give the smaller kids a ride. They all said, "No!"

He said in an impatient voice, "Aw, come on." Again, they refused. Then, as he looked straight at Kristy, he started opening the van door to get out. Kristy knew he wanted to grab her. Just then, the older boys, Kevin, David, and Tom came up. As they got close, David yelled out, "Hey, you heard them. They don't want to go with you." The man slammed his door, gunned his motor, and drove off.

I was shocked that Kristy had never told me of that incident, but she had forgotten all about it. I realized it was the Lord who had erased the fearful memory from them all. No one, not even Kevin, said anything about it. God must have been protecting them from nightmares or a lifetime of fear. I knew, of course, that the Lord had prevented a terrible tragedy. I knew that even if the kids had started running, surely an adult would have been able to catch them. That day, our Lord had a perfect solution for the potential danger Kristy and the other children were in.

As our children became active in attending different ministries and conferences, we were all eager to attend the interdenominational gatherings at the Civic Auditorium in Omaha to celebrate Jesus '79. The Charismatic Movement was active in the Catholic Church at the time. One Catholic priest, Father John Bertolucci, an instructor at the University of Steubenville in Steubenville, Ohio, was the main speaker. He gave his testimony about his encounter with Jesus and was such a powerful speaker! What a thrill it was to see so many nuns and priests taking part in this wonderful occasion where the unity and love between so many different denominations took place.

Marvin had a unique experience there. While we all worshipped together, at one point, we were encouraged to pray. Marv suddenly realized he was speaking out some strange, unfamiliar words. At first it scared him, he said, but then he realized it must have been the gift of tongues.

The service was so glorious, we rejoiced all the way home. I felt closer to Marv than ever before now that he could pray in tongues as I did. The Omaha people organized two more ecumenical services to bring glory to the Lord: Jesus '80 and Jesus '81. Those, too, were such joy-filled experiences; we wished it could have gone on longer. It was so encouraging to see thousands of people from so many different denominations loving Jesus. Strangers became family at those occasions.

"Delight yourself in the Lord; and He will give you the desires of your heart."

Psalm 37:4 NASB

Karen's college graduation

In May of 1980, Karen graduated with her Associate Degree in Horticulture at UNL. Marv, Kristy, and I drove five hours to her graduation. I had a desire to give her a surprise reception at 2 in the afternoon on the day we returned home, to honor her for her accomplishment. Though I had made mints and sheet cakes, had the napkins engraved and the house quite clean, I still had to work hard the night before to make tiny pink rosebuds to decorate her sheet cakes. I knew I had to get most of the preparations finished before we left early the next morning.

The day before, a tornado touched down several miles west of our farm.

The wind was terrific and branches flew everywhere. When the power went out, I continued to work on the frosting. In the dim lighting, I got too much pink color in the frosting, making it too bright. I was so disappointed, I could have cried. I so much wanted to have light pink roses to match the small, fresh sweetheart rose bouquet that sat in a dainty, porcelain Victorian vase I had ordered for Karen at a local greenhouse.

Karen received her degree outdoors in a park, on a warm, sunshiny, spring afternoon. We enjoyed the long drive home, chatting all the way about her plans and experiences. I was so grateful that Marv's boss allowed him to take the Saturday off to go to Karen's ceremony. I had arranged with Karen's best friend, Kris, to pick Karen up the next morning, to go shopping, and then to have lunch together so that I could work on her reception. Karen was busy unpacking her college paraphernalia that morning, which took quite long. I was in a rush, but it seemed to me she was poking around. I tried to stay calm as I worked on the party.

While she was still home, I made an excuse to go to Fremont to pick up the flowers and other supplies. When I stopped at the greenhouse, I was overwhelmed with joy and I started to cry. The small roses were exactly the same shade of pink as the roses on her cake! When Kristy and I came home, Karen was still there so I unloaded all of the bottles of cold punch outdoors behind the barn so she wouldn't see them!

I was getting panicky, so I almost told her about the surprise, thinking, "What in the world am I doing? Now I'll never get done in time. I need to tell her." But I still had such a strong desire to surprise her. Kristy was still too young to be of much help, so I almost panicked, all the while praying to the Lord to help me get it all done.

Finally, Karen went off with Kris. I told Kristy she needed to go outdoors to pick up all the small sticks and branches that were littered all over the lawn from the windstorm. I didn't expect her to get much accomplished because at her age, not yet six, she usually got distracted. I was amazed at how efficient that little girl was. She did so well that in less than 40 minutes our large lawn looked wonderful. While she picked up sticks, I set out everything I needed for the serving table. Then we both literally ran down to the basement to take the sheet cakes out of the freezer. Kristy carefully placed the little roses in the center of each slice of cake.

As I rushed back upstairs with the cakes, I literally ran to complete each job. At one point, I distinctly remember a clear voice instructing me as I was rushing back down the basement stairs to get rid of some equipment I was finished with. "Wait, go back and pick up those other things that need to go down there. You will save a trip down." I felt like I was in a daze, yet a voice I knew was the Holy Spirit's gave me step-by-step instructions. All the while I prayed, "Lord, what next?"

When I looked at the clock, it was already 20 minutes till two. I panicked again, telling the Lord, "God, they will be coming any minute and I don't even have the table set up." Just at that moment a car drove up. I stressed out again, "Why, God? Not yet." But in walked three smiling faces, Jackie Hartman with her daughters, Michele and Patti, who asked me what they could do. I told them they could set up the serving table, using their own judgment, pointing to the dining room where I had the sparkling table service and serving pieces sitting with the cakes, mints, nuts, and punch. The minute they finished, the doorbell rang with the first guest arriving.

Whew! Just in time! Everything was ready and looked beautiful, thanks to my dear friends. I was in awe of how the Holy Spirit had directed every step. How I thanked Him!

Kris arrived with Karen after all of the guests were seated. As the famous word "Surprise!" was exclaimed by all, Karen looked like she was going to cry. A few minutes later, she caught me alone and quietly said as she gave me a big hug, "Mom, thank you so much. All my life I have wanted a surprise party. This means so much to me, Mom."

Then I knew why I had felt such a strong desire to surprise her and how God wanted to bless her with the desire of her heart as He states in His word: "Delight yourself in the Lord; and He will give you the desires of your heart." (Psalm 37:4 NASB). Then I was the one who almost cried as I thought of how the Holy Spirit had organized everything, despite all of the challenges I experienced. He wants to show us how much He loves us when He makes those dreams come true. I learned to trust Him much more that day because He demonstrated so beautifully His love for us.

Kathy, who was beginning her senior year at the University of Nebraska, moved out of the dorm and into an apartment with Karen as Karen started her work in sales at Danielson Floral Company. The Lord brought young Christians into the girls' lives to learn from and fellowship with. Kathy continued her coursework in Home Economics, including student teaching, and worked part-time at the Student Union.

Pastor Robert Birdwell was the Pastor of Christian Life Fellowship in Lincoln. His wife, Twila, was a state officer in Women's Aglow Fellowship. Karen was eager to know more about the Scriptures so she attended the Catholic Masses on Saturday nights and Christian Life Fellowship on Sunday mornings for the Bible teaching. After a few months, she asked me one day, "Would it be all right if I stopped going to the Mass and just went to the Birdwell's church from now on?"

I thought for a minute and answered, "Karen, if you are sure you are hearing from God, it's okay with me. You will certainly go through persecution when the Catholics find out. This will be quite a scandal to them. Just be absolutely sure this is of God. Then it will be alright. He will get you through it. I know Twila and Pastor Bob so well from Women's Aglow Fellowship; she and her pastor husband are wonderful godly people. I am sure your dad will be all right with it too." Karen didn't tell me at that time that when she met their son, Bob Birdwell, she knew that someday he would be her husband.

Another one off to college

In the fall of 1980, Ken left for the University of Nebraska, majoring in agronomy. I had a hard time adjusting to having another child leave the nest but it helped that he came home frequently for visits. I enjoyed cooking for him as he had a healthy appetite and always appreciated mom's home cooking.

We grew close by sharing all the things we had experienced with God. Like most public colleges, the University of Nebraska had many secular or atheist professors who negatively impacted the faith of some of the students toward God. Ken was a light in that dark world as he testified about his own experiences. He attended three campus groups at the same time, including Baptist Student Union, Campus Crusade for Christ, and Maranatha Ministries. These groups had many outreaches to the unsaved, including a trip to Daytona Beach, Florida, to share the gospel with college students on spring break. He also had a great roommate named Sid Ready who was also a dedicated Christian. Together they had Bible studies in their dorm room for other students.

During his college days when Ken visited Tulsa, Oklahoma, he met a Rhema Bible College student by the name of Ken Schroeder who would later return to his hometown of Omaha and start a church. Ken started attending this church and later became the youth pastor. He would ride his motorcycle from Lincoln on weekends while attending college and ministered to street kids. He remembers wearing a snowmobile suit and driving his motorcycle in subzero temperatures on ice and snow to go to Omaha for youth ministry. Once he fell asleep on the motorcycle and woke up some miles later but he had not fallen down or crashed even though driving on ice and snow.

Most of the kids he ministered to were from broken homes, and without a father; they seemed to gravitate to Ken, a form of stability and comfort in their world. Parents noticed the positive change in their children. One father named Lee Huelle who had a Christian radio station wanted to raise support for Ken because of the positive change he saw in his own boys as a result of Ken's ministry to youth.

Ken did his best to teach biblical principles to live by. Once he brought the children to the farm for a hayride. On another occasion, he planned a canoe trip for them to some islands in the Platte River by Fremont. There he had war games where they made dust bombs, from limestone dust tied in tissues. The boys had a great time and begged to do this again.

The two Kens enjoyed each other and became good friends. Soon Ken and Kevin started attending Ken Schroeder's new church in Omaha, Word Outreach Center. Eventually, I wanted to hear the good teaching as well. Kristy and I would attend Saturday evening Mass with Marv. On Sunday mornings, she and I attended Word Outreach Center.

I was so excited about the preaching, much of which came originally from Kenneth Hagin, who I continued to listen to daily on the radio. Marv was not yet ready to join us but didn't mind us driving there each Sunday for services.

Chapter 31

Our Silver Anniversary

The following spring, in 1981, Marvin and I decided to have an open house for our silver wedding anniversary. We decided to schedule it from 7 till 9 p.m. on Saturday evening on our actual anniversary date, May 16. I didn't know how I could ever get the work done by myself. Our girls, both at Lincoln, couldn't help me because Kathy was taking finals before her graduation and Karen was busy with her job. The loving ladies from my Bible study offered to help, so I bought all the sandwich fixings for the ladies to take to their homes and make. They also offered to man the serving tables all evening.

On the big night, after having pizza for supper, Marv and I were still making sandwiches, when two couples came an hour early!

We all needed to get dressed and I never did get my hair done right because of our early guests. All evening, I felt like a "sheep dog" and I sure looked like it, which all the photos prove. Now, many years later, I can laugh at the photos, but at the time I was quite embarrassed.

Light rain fell the entire evening and the 173 people who came couldn't help but track mud all over our home. We were so blessed that our young parish priest, Father James Schrader, came to witness us renewing our vows and added loving words to us. We added our Christian witness by having Kristy give copies of the story of our commitments to the Lord to all our guests. To add to our blessings, Sharon Steinbach's children, who had formed a Christian band with their friends, came to sing gorgeous worship songs in our honor.

At midnight, after the last guests left, our children blessed us with a motel room they had reserved for the night, with all expenses paid. Our instructions were that we could not return home until Sunday afternoon. What a good rest we had! We slept late for the first time in months and attended a late Mass.

What a lovely surprise awaited us when we returned home. I couldn't believe it when I saw the clean house. There was no sign that so many people had trudged through our home the night before with muddy shoes. I had been concerned that the carpets would be stained but they were so clean and everything was back in order. I felt so loved, and I realized once again that

God inspired our children to take care of it all. He wanted to bless us once again. He is so good!

Kathy's college graduation

Shortly after our anniversary celebration, Kathy graduated from UNL with a bachelor's degree in Home Economics. I gave her a reception at our home the following Saturday and invited her dear friends from college as well as all of the neighborhood ladies and their daughters. Daisies were her favorite flower, so they graced the cakes and décor.

Kathy liked everything and was so happy to see all her friends as well as neighbor ladies and others she hadn't seen in a long time. That summer she continued working part-time in Fremont, while she looked for full-time work in her major. In July, she packed her worldly belongings and moved to Russell, Kansas, to work in her first job, as the County Extension 4-H Agent. We were very proud of her, but sad to see her moving so far away.

Another healing

The summer Kristy was 12, we were shopping for sandals for her, and as she tried them on, I noticed she seemed to be stepping wrong. The saleslady exclaimed, "Look, she has a crooked foot. You need to take her to a doctor to get corrective shoes."

I was so surprised that neither Marv nor I had noticed it before. Was it a birth defect? As Kristy and I talked about it, we both remembered that she used to have trouble running at school. As she got into the intermediate grades, that foot always hurt when she ran very far. She mentioned it a few times but I didn't think to have a professional check it out. Back then, I hadn't seen any bruises or injuries. Now I thought it strange that we hadn't noticed that her foot was turned inward at her arch.

I felt guilty, but I had an idea. An evangelist, Reverend R.W. Shambach, was coming to Omaha in a few weeks for a weekend tent revival. His ministry planned to pitch a large tent on open grounds. I had listened to him regularly on our Christian radio station and heard his stories about people being healed supernaturally when he prayed for them. I told Kristy we would take her there. "Perhaps the Lord will heal you," I said. Sure enough, when he finished his message, he said he wanted to pray for all the children in the audience. He had the children walk up on stage with a parent or guardian, and then he had them pass in front of him as he sat on a chair, so that he could lay his hands on them and bless them.

I was so excited. I said, "Here's your chance, Kristy." I was so sure the Lord would touch her. As Rev. Shambach touched Kristy's head, she said she felt "electricity" in her foot. I rejoiced with her but didn't say any more.

That night I didn't notice any difference in her foot, but the next morning, I could see that her foot was straight. I said, "Kristy, look at your foot." She saw immediately that her foot was straight. She put on her flip flops and squealed with delight. We both thanked the Lord and danced around, praising Him. How grateful we were that she would be able to run normally and wouldn't have to wear uncomfortable shoes, perhaps for years, to try to get her foot to grow straight. Perhaps the Lord did not have us notice her crooked foot before so that later He could heal it for her supernaturally!

CHAPTER 32

THE GIFT OF HOSPITALITY

That year, Jackie Hartman was chosen by the Lord to be the president of our Fremont chapter of Women's Aglow Fellowship. Eventually my other close friend, Marianne Roberts, served on the Aglow Board as well. Those were glorious days. Because we officers needed to be at the events, we women drove together to attend out of town retreats. I remember riding home with a carload of ladies for several hours late one night after the final seminar. We were so happy, we heartily sang our favorite worship songs. The driver suddenly realized she was driving 80 miles an hour where the speed limit was only 55. Apparently, the more joyfully we sang, the more she stepped on the gas pedal! We assumed that the Holy Spirit was snickering at us and prevented us from receiving a speeding ticket, or worse, experiencing an accident.

Whenever guest speakers would come to Fremont, I was privileged to host them at our home, one or more nights. They were such kind ladies and I learned so much about walking with the Lord just by being around them. I always considered it a privilege and honor to serve good meals and make their stay restful and peaceful in our quiet country home. It was a lot of work, but I did so enjoy doing anything I could to make them comfortable.

The guests I had several times were Mary Ward of Lincoln, Nebraska's Aglow President, and Etta Schafer, District Representative of Women's Aglow and her husband Ben from Topeka. Several times I was privileged to have two ladies from California stay with us as well who were delightful to have around. They told me I had the gift of hospitality and they noticed I was a detailed person. One pastor's wife, Lorna Sherwood, became my mentor and ministered to me often. She said she noticed that I would remember details of different people's likes and dislikes. Here I had been criticizing myself for being so detailed, but she said I should not despise that gift, which was from the Lord.

She added that the Lord is a detailed God in the way He pays attention to tiny details in flowers and in all of His creation. She stated that He created me to be detailed for a special reason, which was a surprise to me. She added that I always remember who wants their coffee black or with cream or sugar and who wants to have tea or water instead, and that I have a knack for meeting these needs. "That gift makes people more comfortable," she said.

We local officers met weekly at our home so we could pray for the success of the monthly fellowship meetings and plan the meeting agendas. I loved those meetings, where I met the most wonderful women and continued to learn much from the leaders. Eventually, though, as the number of guests dwindled, we realized that the time for Aglow Fellowship meetings at Fremont was coming to an end.

Though we felt sad, the Lord soon had other assignments for us to complete. We realized that God had been training us to continue to minister in other areas, which required more faith and maturity. For instance, the Lord was training Jackie to be a pastor, and soon she began teaching Bible studies.

Mom's home going

On New Year's Eve 1981, my precious mother died of a massive heart attack at St. Joseph's Assisted Living Center at West Point. It was a shock, yet I had expected she wouldn't be with us very long. In the summer, when she was visiting, she couldn't remember details for more than two minutes, which really made me sad. I prayed then that she would be willing to go to assisted living because she really couldn't take care of herself any longer. Leo and Wilma kept telling me she would forget to eat the meals provided by Meals on Wheels or she'd forget to take her medication. About that time, she agreed to move to St. Joseph's. I remember telling God just before she decided to go, "Maybe it's time to take her home to be with You." He replied, "I'm not finished with her yet. She still has work to do for Me." I told Him, "When the time comes, make it quick so she doesn't have to suffer." I sensed that He would.

I knew she had problems with her heart fibrillating from time to time. The mortician said that her heart just exploded so she wouldn't have known what hit her. I was so relieved that the Lord had shown me that she definitely was born again. I knew she went to heaven immediately, which helped me to be stronger than I thought possible. I also knew that Jackie and other close friends were praying for me because I literally felt the Lord's strength and grace through the services. When Wilma and I went to St. Joseph's to choose a dress for Mom to wear in her casket, all the elderly people were crying, so we were able to comfort them instead of them comforting us.

When it came time to close Mom's casket, Wilma asked the funeral director to give me Mom's wedding band because Wilma had received Dad's wedding band. He said, "Oh, I don't think I can get it off."

I told him, "It will be alright to cut it off; I can have it fixed."

Through the years, Mom had gained weight so her fingers were larger. She could never get it off and it looked as though it had grown on her finger. A few minutes later, the mortician came up to me with Mom's ring, handing it to me with a big smile, saying, "It came right off her finger."

I knew immediately the Lord had done something special and told Him, "Lord, You did that for me, didn't You?"

He said, "I just wanted to bless you." Again I was amazed by His great love. Such a loving God we all have!

During the few short months Mom was at St. Joseph's Assisted Living, she had been going around to all the elderly people to cheer them up. She told me that several "old" ladies often grumbled at each other, so one day she patted them on their shoulders, saying, "Just forget about it. You both didn't mean it the way it sounded." I smiled because I knew they were younger than she was!

The nuns in charge of the home loved and enjoyed Mom because she was always so happy. She laughed and told them funny stories from her childhood. They didn't know that she was homesick and would cry in her room at night. Though she loved being with all the seniors during the day, most of them being good friends, she cried when she told me how she wished she could go to her home every night and sleep in her own bedroom.

After her funeral, I felt led to write a letter to all the seniors at St. Joe's, telling them why Mom was so happy and so kind to them, that it was Jesus within her that caused her to be so joyful. Then I added Scriptures with instructions of how they could have Jesus in their lives and how they could be certain of going to heaven when their time came. One of the nuns wrote me a thank you note, telling me the letter was beautiful and that they posted it on the bulletin board for all the residents to see. That's what God meant when He said He still had work for Mom to do. She was to be a witness about Jesus to all the residents.

God's healing power

Soon, we were hosting evening meetings in our home, this time playing videos of Charles and Frances Hunter's healing services. Their teaching drew quite a crowd. We often saw healings as we prayed for one another. Several neighbors received their salvation. We played those videos until the teaching series was complete and I learned even more from the Scriptures because of their teaching.

The Hunters taught us how to increase our faith. They said, "Faith comes by hearing, and hearing by the Word of Christ." (Romans 10:17 NASB). They added that we hear the Word by reading the Bible, which contains God's personal love letters to us. If we read it, seeking Him, and we believe and confess it, every promise in the Word is ours "because faith and promises work together," they said. I had seen many healings and miracles, all of which served to whet my appetite, and I continued to receive healing of various issues and challenges in my own body.

When we found out that Charles and Frances Hunter were going to be ministering at a meeting in Kansas City, we were so excited to attend. Karen, my niece, Lisa, and Karen's friend and I all drove the short trip to Kansas City.

We were blessed to be seated in the sixth row from the front for the first segment of their teaching. I had had neck pain for years, ever since I had foolishly jumped off the chicken barn roof when I was a child. Frances wanted someone who had neck pain to come up so she could show everyone how to pray for that condition. I ran up there, beating anyone else to the front. She called a friend to the stage who was a chiropractor to check my neck. He stated that I had two vertebrae out of place. Frances laid her hands on that area and commanded the vertebrae to move into place, in Jesus' Name. Then she exclaimed to the audience, "Would you believe that her vertebrae are moving under my finger?"

I was thrilled when the chiropractor checked me again and said, "They are in the right place now." What a thrill, having Jesus take care of me again.

The rest of the conference was filled with learning about different diseases and how the Lord uses us so He can heal others. The last night, they had us help pray by coming out of our seats and going to new people who had arrived for the last service. We were especially delighted that several people were healed when Lisa prayed for them. The few people I prayed for did not have serious conditions, but it was exciting observing and hearing of hundreds healed as all who attended the teaching for several days prayed.

Not long after that, during one of Karen's weekend visits home, the Holy Spirit taught us how to use the teaching we had received from the Hunters' healing seminar. After that, we felt more encouraged to pray for people, whenever we felt led by the Lord.

Eventually, the Lord showed Jackie that she was to be a pastor. Later ordained by Faith Christian Fellowship of Tulsa, she and her husband, Ken, started a nondenominational church of their own, Living Word. I became active in that congregation and Marv attended the Bible studies with me. With all the teaching we had received, as well as attending wonderful Bible studies at Living Word Church, the miracles in our lives were more frequent than ever.

"By His wounds you were healed."

1 Peter 2:24 NASB

I noticed one day that my throat felt as if something was lodged in it, like a huge pill. It began to hurt. I tried to dislodge it with water but nothing changed. I let it go for two weeks, being frightened all the while. I didn't see anything on the outside, so I assumed it was another cyst, as I had been told that the cysts sometimes come in twos or threes. I dreaded to go through surgery again. The last surgery back in 1973 had caused me the most pain I had had in my life, because a tracheotomy was needed. Recuperation with its complications had lasted for seven more months.

I knew I needed to have the surgery again or the cyst would just grow larger. I asked Kathy and Karen if they could take turns coming home to take care of Kevin and Kristy since Marv was still working at Hormel's. Karen was extremely busy with her job at Danielson's Floral; Kathy was also busy working at a summer camp.

After we set the date for surgery, I decided to read the Bible to encourage myself the night before my appointment. I asked the Lord for faith and courage but I also asked Him to take away the cyst. The next morning as I got up and dressed to see the doctor, it seemed to me that the lump was gone. When the surgeon examined my throat, he couldn't find anything. I was embarrassed and told him I was sorry that I had troubled him, but I had felt a lump in my throat for weeks. Obviously it wasn't there now.

He said, "It must have been a cyst and drained off in the middle of the night." I sure praised the Lord all the way home because I no longer needed that painful surgery. God had done it for me again.

Since then, I have had the cysts return in my throat three more times. All I do now is go to Marv. He lays his fingers on it, and as he prays in Jesus' Name, it always goes down within five minutes. Apparently, God has the fluid drain from the cysts. How wonderful to avoid surgery!

CHAPTER 33

GRADUATIONS, WEDDINGS, AND RETIREMENT

Ken received his associate degree in Agronomy in May 1982. After working for a lawn service company in Omaha, he had learned enough that he ventured out to start his own business in Fremont. He worked at Hormel packing plant as a gut-snatcher for ten hours a day, Monday through Friday, and then he worked on his lawn service business after work and on weekends. This pattern was learned from his own father who also worked at Hormel 50 hours a week, raised 1,500 head of hogs, and farmed 360 acres all at the same time.

Once when Ken was returning home from Lincoln late at night, he hit some black ice on the highway. He started to doze off behind the wheel and when his pickup started to slide, he hit the breaks in a sudden fright. This made the truck go into a high-speed spin, spinning in full 360-degree circles. The truck slid sideways down a deep embankment and ended up nose facing upward with the headlights shining into the snow-filled night sky. Ken had called out to the Lord to save him when the first spin occurred and he never hit any telephone poles or culvert at the bottom. He was able to put the vehicle in forward, drive through a farmer's bean field, and come out on a country road and back on the highway again. He thanked God for protecting him because he narrowly missed oncoming traffic and hit nothing when he went off the highway. Ken escaped a certain death without a scratch on his truck.

Wedding bells

On April 20, 1985, Karen married her sweetheart, Bob Birdwell. We couldn't have been happier. Bob was a stable, kind, hard-working, mature Christian man who fit right in with our family. We knew he could provide well for Karen with his work at the U. S. Postal Service.

I had been busy since December, sewing Karen's elaborate wedding dress and three of the four bridesmaids' dresses. Her bridal gown, with lots of lace ruffles, was not hard for me because I made a practice gown out of old sheets. I set up my sewing machine and gathered the 70 yards of fabric and all the equipment and supplies I would need to create all of the gowns in our basement recreation room.

The bridesmaids' dresses, with yards and yards of ruffles and lace were all a nightmare to sew because Karen didn't realize that the beautiful fabric, Georgette, would stretch like gauze. I had to shorten the ruffled skirts over and over because after they hung, the dresses stretched out longer and became uneven. Once again, God showed me what to do.

The Lord even saved Karen's wedding gown from disaster after it was completed. While working on a bridesmaid's dress, I had Karen's finished dress hanging on the basement stairs door. I decided to move it to get a better look at the hem of a bridesmaid's dress. As I inspected the bridesmaid's dress which was hanging where the wedding gown had been, I noticed the carpet was soaking wet. To my dismay, a water pipe had burst in the adjoining storage room, causing all the water to run under the stairs to the room where I was working. Had the wedding gown still been hanging there, the long train would have been totally ruined.

God answered my prayers each step of the way to get me through the difficult challenges I had with the fabric and getting those dresses to fit right.

When Kathy flew in the day before the wedding, she discovered the airlines lost the luggage that contained her shoes for the wedding so I had to guess at the length of her gown. The luggage was sent to our local bus station the following day. The wedding was at two in the afternoon, an hour away from our home. Ken's tux arrived four inches too short, which they discovered at the rehearsal the night before. We had a good laugh at Ken as he modeled his high-water pants, which came just halfway down his calf. The Lord took care of those crises in the nick of time as Ken's proper size arrived at noon. It is so neat to know that God cares about small things like wedding gowns, tuxes, and celebrations.

Right after Karen's wedding, I prepared for Kevin's graduation from high school. We had a lovely reception and open house for him. By this time, I felt like an old pro after all the experiences I'd had with receptions. All went well as Kevin and all of us enjoyed his relatives and friends who attended the celebration.

College for Kevin

Following his high school graduation in May 1985, Kevin kept thinking he wanted to attend Oral Roberts University. I was concerned about him because he said he really didn't know how to get there and what he was supposed to do about enrolling. When he left, my heart was so heavy because I worried about our young son embarking on this journey by himself. I would have given anything if Marv, Kristy, and I could have driven him to Tulsa, but Marv couldn't get a vacation then and Kevin needed to have his pickup down there to get around.

I held back my tears when he left because I didn't want to make it harder on him, but I cried after he was gone. I felt so sorry for him thinking how bewildered he would be, and hoping and praying he wouldn't get lost somewhere. I was so relieved when he called, telling us that the Lord guided him through all the unfamiliar steps he had to go through when he arrived. He adjusted well to college and really liked his new life at the university. There he completed his degree in Finance and Business Management, and graduated in 1990.

Following Kevin's graduating from ORU in 1990, he began his trek around the world on various missions and business trips that the Lord led him on. I remember so clearly how brave I felt he was to travel halfway around the world by himself and to trust the Lord to guide his every step. In 1992, after his worldwide adventures, Kevin felt led to open a store at Woodland Hills Mall in Tulsa. One of the many places he frequented was the former Soviet Union, which actually ceased to be the U.S.S.R. while he was there on his first trip. He had a deep fondness for this place and began bringing gifts and collectibles from Eastern Europe into the United States and sold them in his store, which he named Little Russia.

One day, a tall slender beauty named Zoryana came into Kevin's store to sample some of the delicious Russian chocolates. Kevin immediately noticed her, and that she deeply loved the Lord. To his great dismay and hers, he found he was out of chocolates. However, before she could get away, he quickly asked her to go out with him instead.

After many lovely times together, Kevin was officially smitten. Their romance blossomed into a beautiful Christian wedding on Nov. 9, 1996, in Tulsa. Zoryana ended up being the perfect wife for our son and a true gift from the Lord to our family.

Graduate school and marriage for Kathy

In 1984, Kathy moved to Laramie, Wyoming, to complete her master's degree in Education. It was a step of faith to resign her position, but God came through with a graduate assistantship weeks before she started school.

With her thesis complete and graduation done, she started work in Student Services working for a wonderful Christian supervisor who encouraged her faith and helped her grow professionally as well. In 1990, Kathy was offered a job in Billings, Montana, as the Director of the Upward Bound program. This is a federally funded program that helps low income youth get into college. She was blessed with some Christian coworkers as well as attending a wonderful church and Bible Study.

In May 1995, she met Cliff through some mutual friends at their church. There was a group that enjoyed hiking, camping, and spending time together. During this time, Cliff pulled a muscle in his back. God clearly told Kathy to lay hands on him and pray for him. Instantly, the pain was gone! Praise the

Lord! That summer, after many conversations and fasting and praying, they got engaged and were married March 1, 1996.

Ken and Helen meet and marry

Two years after Ken started his lawn service, the Lord told him to go to Missionary Training School at Tulsa and he decided to discontinue his business. In 1986, he received his B.A in Christian Ministry from Indiana Christian University under the late American apostle/evangelist Lester Sumrall in South Bend, Indiana. After completing Bible training, he embarked on mission work in the rural areas of the Philippines for 11 years. During that time, he made several trips to South Korea to minister to congregations in the Seoul area. During one tour, a church worker insisted that he must meet her sister, Helen Songsim, who was a pastor.

Ken met Helen when he was invited to minister in her fellowship, Agape International Fellowship. Both had been praying for a spouse. That day, they realized the Lord indeed brought them together. After the meeting, they talked for hours and hours at a local restaurant. They completely lost track of time and missed an appointment with a pastor friend that afternoon. In the taxi ride to the office, Ken proposed. They married in March 1997 at the U.S. Embassy in Seoul, Korea, and after marriage Helen came to the Philippines with Ken where she helped him in founding a Bible school.

Ken and Helen currently reside in Wonju City, South Korea, as international ministers, with the ministry 7K-Believers.

Kristy's graduation and marriage

In 1995, we traveled to Tulsa to attend the college graduation of our youngest, Kristy, who earned her bachelor's degree in Studio Arts and began working for CP Annie Productions in marketing and sales. In 1997, she received her pastoral degree from Rhema Bible College. Outside of work, Kristy kept busy ministering in Kids for Christ, an after-school Bible club, and in Jesus Revolution, a high school ministry.

In October of 2010, Kristy attended a conference at a Tulsa church. She went to gain additional knowledge and insight. However, noticing a handsome gentleman about five rows ahead of her, and how fervently he worshipped God, she became distracted. The next session, in order to pay closer attention to the speaker and to stay focused, she intentionally sat in the front row. As fate (or the Lord) would have it, this young man then noticed Kristy sitting in front of him. This time, he became distracted during the conference!

After a mutual friend introduced the two, Kristy and Casey began dating. Two years later, they married on May 12, 2012. Casey is everything Kristy had prayed for and more. He fit perfectly into our family, and we are thrilled to have him as a son-in-law. He is a testimony of God's goodness to send the absolute best if you trust Him and wait for His perfect timing.

The family business

After Ken left for school, Kevin decided to take over the lawncare business to pay his way through college, changing the name to "Lawngevity Lawn Care."

Once a month during spring and again in the autumn months, Kevin drove the eight hours home after classes on weekends, bringing a college friend along to help fertilize all of the lawns. Marv helped after he got off work at Hormel's. I was concerned because Kevin and his friend would drive back to Tulsa late at night, receiving very little sleep. I prayed Psalm 91 for their safety on those long journeys.

An unwilling secretary

Kevin asked me to take over the office work, including the accounting and phone calls, and told me to "act like I knew what I was doing." I was overwhelmed and fearful, having to learn about fertilizers, chemicals, and customer expectations, and I had to learn the routes to save time for the guys so they could be efficient. I worried we would lose all the customers with me at the helm. I learned a lot by frequently calling the university agronomists, who graciously taught me about weed sprays, grub chemicals, fertilizers, pre-emergents, even proper watering, seeding, and mowing. Plus, I had to cover sales, convincing new people we had a very good lawn service in the Fremont area.

Retirement from Hormel's

Upon graduation from ORU, Kevin wanted to pursue international business/missions. Marv had wanted to retire from Hormel's for years and farm fulltime but was concerned about making it on just one income. Kevin suggested he take over the lawn service to provide us a second income. So, in April of 1990, Marv retired from Hormel's, farmed full time, and took care of the lawn service on the side.

The work was hard because Marv would carry a 70-pound backpack weed sprayer, attacking the weeds individually as he walked all the lawns. Spreading the dry fertilizer looked easy, but to push a full spreader at a steady speed was tiring. A pedometer that Kevin and Marv each wore showed that they averaged walking 15 miles a day while carrying the backpack full of liquid herbicide or spreading all that fertilizer.

It got busy for me too because I had to do the bookkeeping and send out notices when we got home besides the usual household chores. At that time, each season, I was writing out over 2,000 invoices by hand with all of the customers' information and instructions. (Now it is all done by computer.) Marv needed me to ride with him all day in the van until dark to help him find the addresses as well as to blow fertilizer off the sidewalks to prevent staining when customers began watering their lawns. We had wondered why the customer base had gone down from other years but realized soon enough that the Lord was protecting us from having too much work.

After the first year, Marv realized that the busiest times for both farming and lawn care created a conflict; he turned the lawn care back over to Kevin in 1991.

I enjoyed selling our service, convincing prospects that we really were trustworthy and would do good work. I also enjoyed calling the people in the mornings, especially the widows who needed to know when the guys would arrive. They always were so sweet. Many of them were born-again Christians, but some were not yet. Always, they were lonely and responded favorably to my Christian witness, so I made many friendships. Kevin was happy that I would talk about the Lord whenever I felt prompted to do so.

Each day I prayed Isaiah 54:17 several times, adding the name of our company: "No weapon that is formed against you [Lawngevity Lawn Care] will prosper; and every tongue that accuses you in judgment, you will condemn." (NASB). I also prayed Proverbs 3:4. The King James Version reads: "So shalt thou find favour and understanding in the sight of God and man." I would pray: "Lawngevity Lawn Care has great favor, good understanding, and high esteem in the sight of (the customer's name) and the Lord."

Those Scriptures always encouraged me when I was stressed. The Lord turned many challenges around for us because of the promises in His Word. Eventually, in the 13 years, I learned so much about the business that I became quite good at it. The customer base grew large because Kevin and Marv provided such good work. Since Kevin took over the business, it has grown to 1,000 customers. He now has four arborists on staff, including himself. In addition to lawn care, the company now provides full tree care service.

Our last graduation

It was the day of Kristy's high school graduation, May 19, 1991, that Bob, Karen's husband, called to tell us they would not be coming to the ceremony because Karen was in labor with their first baby, Ryan Jonathan!

We were all so excited about our first grandchild, especially Kristy, who thought it a great honor to have him arrive on her special day. When Bob called with the wonderful news, we bragged to all of Kristy's guests that we were now grandparents. I almost had trouble focusing on serving the people, thinking about the new baby!

Proud grandparents

The very next day, laden with gifts for our new grandbaby, we hurried to the Lincoln Hospital to see Karen. As soon as she returned home, I drove to Lincoln to help her adjust to caring for her sweet little boy. It certainly was fun for me to help her in their lovely little home. Of course, I was privileged to manhandle that darling little dark-eyed boy until Karen was ready to take over her homemaking duties and care for her newborn. We couldn't seem to stay away that summer and went to see Karen's family often. They, in turn, came to Grandpa and Grandma's house frequently to show him off.

Off to college

It was a busy time as Kristy finished her final season with 4-H. Summer passed quickly as she prepared for college. She chose to major in Studio Art. The Lord showed her He wanted her to attend ORU, as Kevin had. Kevin advised her a great deal so it was not a hard adjustment for her, with the exception of moving so far from home.

The night before Kristy left for college, she wanted to say good-bye to a dear friend. The next morning, she told us an amazing story. She said that around midnight, she kept getting warnings in her spirit. "Be careful on your way home tonight. There is a drunk driver out there."

So she left and was driving carefully, when suddenly she saw a pickup swerve toward her. As the truck neared her car, she quickly steered her car as far to the shoulder of the road as possible. The truck was coming so close to her, she actually saw the form of the passenger and could see the driver in her headlights. She told us later that she was thinking, "How will my family bear it?" yet she felt peaceful. She said it felt like her car was floating through the air in slow motion as she braced for impact. In a fraction of a second, as quickly as she could blink her eyes, she saw the pickup behind her. It was about two blocks away, still driving on the wrong side of the highway. As she merged back onto the highway, she praised God all the way home for His protection and angels on assignment over her life.

When she told us her story, all Marv and I could figure was that angels must have picked up her car and then set it back. Then we thought of the wonderful promise in Psalm 91:11-12: "For He will give His angels charge concerning you, to guard you in all your ways. They will bear you up in their hands, that you do not strike your foot against a stone." We are still so grateful for that miracle.

Empty nesters

The day Kristy left for Tulsa, in August 1991, I began grieving because I knew motherhood would never be the same. Now it would only be by long distance. "Mothering is all I did for years," I remember thinking. "Now what will I do?" I cried for a long time after she drove off and then the Lord impressed upon me that I needed to go outdoors and help Marv, who was separating some sows to drive into the barn. The Lord continued, "Your answer is to keep busy."

I was amazed at how that little activity helped. God helped me adjust to my "empty nest," although there would be more work He would have to do on my emotions, which He took care of sometime later.

After all of our children were out of our nest, it once again fell to me to help Marv with more of the farm chores. Marv needed help in the barns with various jobs. We got hogs ready for market each Sunday afternoon for Monday morning delivery to Hormel's. I hated that job because it took me awhile to get myself smelling like a lady again after working in the stench. I had to man the gate, let the right hogs into the alley of our hog confinement building, and then help drive them into our pig mover (our pen on wheels) to transfer to our neighbor's trailer.

CHAPTER 34

MORE LESSONS FROM THE LORD

"Know then in your heart that as a man disciplines his son, so the Lord your God disciplines you."

Deuteronomy 8:5 NIV

One summer, the weather was quite dry. We needed rain so badly and of course I had been praying for rain; however, the Lord was about to teach me a valuable lesson. We didn't have center pivot irrigation on our west field, just a pivot pad (the slab of concrete to set the pivot on to hook up), so Marv thought it important to turn the wheels of the towers in order to tow them to the pivot pad on that field of soybeans. He said it was imperative to water those soybeans. I had prayed in faith for two inches of rain the night before, or so I thought.

The job we had to do was horrible. The heat was sweltering in the 7-foot-tall corn with no air getting to us in that hot sun. Marv had to jack up every tower in order to turn the wheels to a transport position and line up the power shaft with the U-joint. He had to pry the thick mud from the axles of each wheel with a crowbar after it had been circling around the irrigated corn field, and he needed my help to turn them. The mud was so thick, it was nearly impossible to get the muck out of the wheels. It took forever. Once there, he needed to change the wheels back to the original position in order to irrigate the soybean field. The longer it took, the more miserable I became in the 100-degree heat and I really complained.

Then I blew it! I whined to the Lord, "Lord, if You had just sent us the two inches of rain, we wouldn't have to go through all of this." Instantly, I heard a booming voice from somewhere outside of my head. "Yes, the Israelites complained and murmured too, and I killed them in the desert. I pour out My blessings upon you and still you're not satisfied."

Oh, was I scared! I knew He was right. I said, "Oh, God, You're so right. I am so sorry. Would You please forgive me for being so ungrateful? I do deserve to die. You are right." I really expected a lightning bolt to come down and take me out. I knew I was in deep trouble and in sin, and I felt much shame for being such a spoiled brat. Right after the Lord dealt with me, Marv decided to take a break.

We rode home on the tractor to have some lunch. What happened next really surprised me. Paul and Wilma came for a visit! They drove down to our farm to pick up some of our extra tomatoes and sweet corn we had offered them. After lunch, Paul went with Marv to help him in the field the rest of the afternoon while Wilma and I stayed in our nice, cool house to can some of the tomatoes. Guess what the Lord did! That night, we received a gentle two-inch rainfall. But only after He had taught me a lesson about murmuring and complaining against Him. And I am so glad He did. I certainly have never done anything like that again. Now I always remember to be grateful and tell Him so each time He does something for us or just for me, be it a small or large blessing. I never forget His love for me, His goodness, kindness, compassion, mercy, and forgiveness. I appreciate Him more than ever now and He is truly my wonderful Daddy.

The Lord also dealt with me about self-pity. I sure seemed to have problems with that. Always it was "Poor me, poor me" if things went wrong or I didn't get my way. Even though I was embarrassed by my attitude, I really couldn't seem to control those thoughts or words. The Bible calls it a stronghold from our enemy, the devil. About 10 years after my commitment to Him, the Lord was weary of my bad attitude. Every time I got into it, He would say firmly, "You are in self-pity again. I want you to repent of it and rebuke it." So each time I said, "I am so sorry. I ask You, Lord, to forgive me for my self-pity. In the name of Jesus, I rebuke the spirit of self-pity."

It took a while, but after about four months I finally recognized those thoughts before I would say them out loud. Now I have fewer problems with that bad habit. That was an ugly attitude, which must have been disgusting to those around me as well as to the Lord.

For most of my life, I have had trouble with worry about what I said wrong around people. I did not realize that it was a form of fear of man. I always hated to hurt their feelings but also, I was proud enough to want to be liked, and I wanted to look good to others. Each time I thought I had said something wrong to someone, those thoughts of worry and shame tormented me for days. It was so hard to forgive myself.

More infirmities

One day, I noticed a large lump on the base of my neck. This one felt rather hard, not squishy at all. I knew it was not another cyst, so I was concerned. I decided to pray for healing rather than go to the doctor. I showed it to my siblings at a family reunion and asked for prayer. Each day, every time I was in front of a mirror, I placed my finger on the lump and said, "In the name of Jesus, I command you to shrink and disappear. Thank you, Jesus, for taking it away." In two weeks and three days, it was gone. I was thrilled with His healing.

How grateful I am for proper teaching that we are to be careful to not speak out negative words or to look at the symptoms. Instead, we need to look at God's Word with His wonderful promises, knowing that Jesus already took heart disease when He was beaten and whipped. How grateful I am that I got to know our Lord's voice so I could trust Him.

I do believe we don't always have instant healings, even if we have faith in our hearts. There are times that it seems no matter how many times we confess and meditate on the corresponding Scriptures, our healings are delayed. There certainly have been times my healings came gradually. It may be that when we get into sin or have doubt and unbelief, we leave an open door to the devil who can put sickness on us.

If a problem comes back, I stand against it by standing on the Word of God. Mark 11:24 states, "Therefore I tell you, whatever you ask in prayer, believe that you have received it, and it will be yours." (ESV). The devil always returns to test our faith. Since he can't take our spirits if we belong to Jesus, he will try every trick to steal, kill, and destroy us while we are still on earth.

The only way to live is to have the Scriptures firmly planted in our spirits, particularly Scriptures that correspond with our needs, so that whenever problems come, we can be ready. Satan will see to it that we will have trouble. Romans 10:17 states, "Faith comes from what is heard, and what is heard comes through the preached word of Christ." (NET Bible). I found that hearing the Word of God is the key; we need to get enough Scriptures into our hearts so that they bring faith within us. Sometimes that takes time.

I have found that just saying the words over and over without meditating on them doesn't work; they are just empty words. But if we continue reading them out loud while meditating on them slowly so they sink in, even if it's just one Scripture verse, eventually the faith will be in our spirits rather than only in our minds. If belief is merely in our minds, it is just presumption. Unbelief is actually a sin and does not please God.

Chapter 35

On-going Learning and Training

"And I will give you [spiritual] shepherds after My own heart [in the final time], who will feed you with knowledge and understanding."

Jeremiah 3:15 ESV

Faithfully, we went to Bible study each week at our church, Living Word, where all of the people attending were committed to Jesus. The worship was glorious and the teaching was deep. We were learning so much, especially about God's will for healing and finances. At the same time, we were becoming rather dissatisfied with the short homilies at our local Catholic church. We were becoming increasingly hungry to learn more about the Bible, and that was not being taught at our parish.

Several years before, we had visited a large church in Omaha, Trinity Church Interdenominational. Marv felt comfortable there and I knew the Lord wanted me to attend where Marv wished to go because of Him wanting wives to be submissive to our husbands. We continued with the Bible study at Living Word with the Hartman's during the week and started attending Trinity on Sundays; Marv seemed to like large churches. We were spiritually fed and fulfilled and our faith in the Scriptures continued to grow.

Because of the teaching we received from Word of Faith, on divine healing and financial prosperity being God's will, and verified in His Scriptures, we were able to receive those wonderful promises. These led to the blessings and miracles He gave us. In our cases, we were even saved from early death as the Lord healed us both of heart disease. This was why we felt strongly to attend the non-denominational churches. Had we not known His will about healing, we would not have been able to receive our physical healings.

The Protestants or interdenominational people we met never taught against the Catholic Church. When a few people in Bible study groups we attended hinted at Catholics' wrong teaching, I was quick to defend those areas of the Catholic faith that helped me. I will always be grateful to the nuns, who tirelessly taught us many truths, and our priest, Father Virgil. We learned early on to discipline ourselves by the many rules and regulations. I believe that because of my early education, as the Lord showed me my bad attitudes and sinful ways, it was much easier to give up those habits.

However, I did notice some teaching that concerned me. I didn't quite understand why the Catholic clergy stated we would go to hell for not keeping the Holy Days of Obligation, which were Catholic (manmade) rules rather than God's rules. I am grateful to the Catholic Church for teaching us good morals, especially against sexual sin, and honesty and integrity with good values, using the Ten Commandments for our guide. I also learned to pray often and long because of all the times the nuns had us stop to pray at school. It is not a burden for me to pray long and often. Neither is it hard for me to repent and obey God when He convicts me of sin or a bad attitude, because I am used to the discipline of my Catholic days.

More tests

Soon the devil tested us again to see if we were really grounded and strong in believing God's promises in His Word. In the fall of 1998, the hog price fell far below what it cost us to feed them. We had a large farm operating loan from our bank and the only income we actually had was our Hormel pension check of $431.52. That was really scary, but we would encourage ourselves by remembering that we had been faithful to tithe where the Lord impressed us to give. In the meantime, we continued to go to our banker for more funds, and, of course, we prayed the Scripture promises.

The hog price fell lower than ever in the fall of 1999. We needed 34 cents a pound to break even, however we were receiving only 9 cents a pound for each critter. Because we were losing so much money, it didn't take Marv long to decide he had to quit raising hogs.

In the meantime, our friendly banker was happy to lend us money each month to pay for all of the feed until they were all ready for market. That really got us into a lot more debt with the bank. Soon we would see the wisdom in getting rid of those hogs and the work, besides avoiding more debt. So in 2000, our farm was free of animals except for our faithful Siberian Husky, Vanya, and eight cats.

CHAPTER 36

SUCCESSFUL HEART SURGERY

"Lord my God, I called to you for help, and you healed me."

Psalm 30:2 NIV

At the end of 2000, I saw that Marv was becoming more and more pale. I couldn't figure it out. He seemed to feel alright so I did not say anything. He had been walking three miles each day and was taking good nutritional supplements. The morning of February 23, 2001 was an unusual Friday morning.

Later, I found out from Kristy that she had noticed Marv's pale complexion as well when she was home for Christmas. The Lord told her to pray for her dad. "You need to pray for him. It's his heart and it is very serious and he is in unforgiveness."

She prayed for his safety and that he would forgive people easily from then on.

After Marv went outdoors to walk his one-and-a-half miles back and forth on our drive, he took a glass of milk when he came in and went to his office. Soon he came out to the kitchen where I was, sat down, held his chest, and told me, "I have terrible pain in my chest." I started praying, while laying my hand on his chest. "In the name of Jesus, I ask Your power to come."

I was greatly relieved that Kevin was right by the phone and lived only a mile away. He said he would be right over to take Marv to the hospital. Marv changed his clothes while I quickly packed a few things thinking that he would have to stay in the hospital. I kept repeating several Scriptures out loud and added Marv's name to them. "Our length of days is 70 years, but if by reason of strength 80 years" (Psalm 90:10), "Marv will not die but live and declare the works of the Lord" (Psalm 118:17), and "With long life, You will satisfy Marv and show him Your salvation." (Psalm 91:16). Those were the only ones I could think of at the time.

Kevin came within minutes, and as he drove 70 mph the seven miles to the Fremont Area Medical Center, I repeated those three Scriptures while sitting in the back seat. All the while I wondered how much time we still had and how much damage was happening to Marv's heart. We hit all the green lights, arriving at the emergency room faster than normal.

At first the nurses asked a few questions, and then looked at each other, "What do you think?" one said to another. They decided to give him nitroglycerin, which did not help at all. One asked, "From 1 to 10, how great is your pain level?" Marv hollered, "Fifteen!" When the doctor came in, she introduced herself as being in training in cardiology.

After she questioned the nurses, she stood there and said, "I don't know what to do." I was rather horrified while thinking, "OH, GREAT! We get one of those."

I said to her, "Doctor, I have prayed that God would show you what to do so whatever you decide to do will be the right thing." She thanked me while one of the nurses called our family doctor. All the while, I stood in front of Marv and kept repeating the three Scriptures to him quite loud. I didn't care what the nurses or the doctor thought. As I repeated to him, "God will satisfy you with long life," he said, "I'm not satisfied yet. I want to stay and take care of you."

When our family doctor came, he told me they needed to take an X-ray so I needed to leave. Kevin was waiting outside the door. We went to a tiny room nearby. He called our niece, Julie Todd, who alerted her parents, Betty and Richard, and Pastors Jackie and Ken Hartman. All of them arrived amazingly fast to be with us. By then many were praying for Marv. The doctor gave Marv a clot buster shot, which worked. It dissolved the clot and his pain eased. The doctor then came out to tell me that Marv had damage to his heart on one side and that area would "never come back again."

I remember thinking, "We'll see about that. God can bring it back." Marv was taken then to ICU for observation. After the nurses got him settled, they told me they would keep him at Fremont Hospital, and then an ambulance would take him to Immanuel Hospital at Omaha on Monday.

They said Marv was doing fine so I decided to leave the hospital to go home and change clothes and get some rest. I was shocked to discover a very bad ice storm came while we were inside.

It really hit us that God had delayed the ice until Marv was safely at the hospital. Marv most certainly would have died before we could get him there if we had to drive in that ice storm. How grateful I was for that blessing. I was able to get in to see him the next morning because the weather had cleared. His pain was gone and he was at peace. I stayed at a nearby motel so I could be near Marv.

On the following Monday, he was taken to Immanuel Medical Center in Omaha for his heart catheterization. I was shocked when the doctor told me he needed bypass surgery. I said, "Can't that be done with stints?"

He said, "Oh, no, he wouldn't live more than two months. Six of his arteries are 75 to 90 percent blocked."

How I dreaded hearing that news. I couldn't figure out why he was so bad off when we had been trying to eat healthy foods and take natural vitamins for almost 30 years. I realized, though, that he had endured terrible stress by working three jobs most years and that would have caused his problems more than anything. The doctors said his arteries would have been filling up for years.

Because of a low-grade temperature, Marv couldn't have his surgery done until Wednesday, February 28. Kevin and I talked to the surgeon the night before and told him we would be praying for him. He said, "Thank you! It is always 90 percent divine and 10 percent us," which comforted us. I was totally prepared emotionally. Marv and I had complete peace about it all and just knew everything would be alright. Kevin and Zoryana sat with me to wait.

During this time, the youth pastor from our church stopped by to pray with us. He was relieved, he said, that we were being so strong. He had expected we would be devastated with worry or grief. He read Psalm 91 and added a prayer. He was so encouraging. After he left, one of the nurses came to us and told us that Marv's surgery was delayed from 11 a. m. until 12:30 p. m. because of an emergency surgery for someone else. I told Kevin and Zoryana to leave since the surgery would take about five hours. The nurse promised to come out halfway through to tell us how things were going. I knew I would be alright waiting alone.

"O Lord, you have brought up my soul from Sheol; you restored me to life from among those who go down to the pit."

Psalm 30:3 ESV

Successful surgery

The surgeon came to tell us after five hours and twenty minutes that the surgery had gone well and explained that they were able to do two-in-one, so Marv actually had six arteries repaired with five sections of the vein taken from his left leg. I asked him about Marv's heart damage. He said, "Actually, that looked quite good. It may just come back again."

I thanked the Lord as soon as the doctor walked away. Before we left for the evening, we were allowed to go into ICU, one at a time, to see Marv. He looked so horrible that when Karen went in to see him, she ran out of the room crying. When Kevin saw how rough his dad looked after his heart surgery, he said, "I will never eat pie again." (He has since forgotten that vow.)

I went in last and was shocked because of all the tubes Marv had all over his body. It seemed I could only see the whites of his eyes, and his color was gray. I kept telling myself, "He'll look better tomorrow." And he did! The nurses had told me I didn't need to come until 10 a.m., when he should be feeling much better.

When I came back from the motel the next morning, they were already preparing to take him to a regular room. The nurses told me they were surprised he was doing so well. They had not expected him to be out of ICU until 2 that afternoon. All five days of his stay, they kept talking about how rapidly he was progressing.

Marv was dismissed the fifth day after surgery. I kept busy taking care of him at home, and a few weeks later, he was ready for physical therapy at our local hospital. We were both so grateful for the Lord healing him so well and so quickly. We were also glad we didn't have to worry about the hogs any more. Marv was instructed not to lift anything heavy for three months and that he would need physical therapy at the hospital for six weeks. Often Marv would say, "Had we still had those hogs, we would have had a terrible problem."

"The Lord will sustain him upon his sickbed; in his illness: You restore him to health."

Psalm 41:3 NASB

Here we go again

Three months later, the suture in Marv's left leg started bleeding on the inside, forming a clot, which traveled to his heart. He had the second heart attack the day after we had returned from his Uncle Charles' funeral in Minnesota. Again, Marv's pain was unbearable. And once again, Kevin took him to the hospital. I was at Kevin's home at the time, caring for our 1-year-old grandson. Zoryana had had an accident the day before, and had broken both wrists, so she couldn't care for little John. Since Kevin was close by, he jumped into my car and rushed away. I told the Lord, "I need to be with my beloved but I can't leave little John. Now Marv could die without me."

I heard the Lord say, "Call Sharon." In minutes, she and her husband, Gene, arrived. She watched John and helped Zoryana while Gene drove me home to get our pickup to drive to the Fremont hospital. This time neither Marv nor I were brave. Our doctor at Fremont gave Marv another clot buster and then he was placed in the ambulance once again for the emergency ride back to Immanuel at Omaha. As I watched the attendants close the ambulance doors, I saw Marv's bare feet on the stretcher. When the siren started, I sat in our car and cried. Then I drove home to gather some things for another stay near the hospital. I didn't have much faith this time; I was frightened and discouraged.

I said to the Lord, "I thought everything was already fixed, and now this. What can they do? I don't think he'll make it this time, Lord, unless You do a miracle."

The clot buster apparently worked and Marv did not need surgery when they arrived at the Omaha hospital. He noticed the pain stopped when the ambulance hit a bump on the highway. He was resting when I arrived. Four days later, an ultrasound was taken of his heart. When the surgeon and another doctor came in the next morning to see him, I heard the doctor tell Marv, "I wish everyone who comes in would be as easy as you. Your heart is working beautifully and you have absolutely no heart damage." Wow! Thank You, Lord! What wonderful news!

Before the doctors dismissed Marv, I mentioned that we had been driving a long way from Minnesota the day before. The surgeon stated, "You know, it seems that those who have been sitting for a long time while traveling seem to get more blood clots. When they travel by plane or bus, they need to get up every hour and walk around a bit to get their circulation going." I thought that was an interesting comment and have never forgotten it.

Chapter 37

Strange and Unusual Happenings

Over the years, we have witnessed so many miracles from our loving Father. If I wrote down every single one, this book would be more than twice as long! Following are some of the highlights.

When the painter from Omaha, Tom Ryan, told me about Jesus so many years ago, I enthusiastically asked the Lord to come into my heart and take over my life. Tom warned me then that I would have attacks from our spiritual enemy, the devil, and his demons. He told me about God's promises of protection contained in the Bible and that I needed to learn them as well as listen to the teachings of Christian teachers on the radio. He told me to join a Bible study group. I followed his advice, and soon began to realize what Tom was referring to when he spoke of our spiritual enemy.

"God is our refuge and strength, an ever-present help in trouble."

Psalm 46:1 NIV

Four months after committing my life to the Lord, we looked on helplessly as a hailstorm struck our crops. We were just sick as we saw the corn badly damaged. All that was left of the soybeans were 4- to 6inch stubble, the leaves totally stripped off by the hail. Marv knew it was impossible for them to grow back. The storm couldn't have come at a worse time. Besides the operating loan, we had just borrowed extra money from the bank to finish some work on the house. What would we do now?

Day after day, Marv arrived home from work, a depressed, angry, and discouraged man. I kept wondering why God would do this after I had committed my life to Him. As I prayed about it, I began to think about what Tom had told me. I remembered he said, "I need to warn you. We have an enemy out there called the devil. Now that you are 'born again,' the devil hates you. He will attack you and will probably try to kill you. Don't worry though, God is stronger than the devil and He is in control."

When Marv came home from work one day after the hailstorm, I told him, "I think the devil did this. There is really nothing we can do about the crops anyway. I think we need to just pray and trust God, and see what He can do for us." Day after day, I thanked God that He would help us pay our bills.

What a delightful surprise our Lord had for us! Soon we could see that the stems of the damaged soybean plants began sprouting again. At harvest time, those short, bare soybean stems were loaded with beans, so we harvested a normal crop, which at that time was 25 bushels per acre. We were thrilled because we had received our first miracle. We have had severe hail damage several times since, but the Lord always blessed us with fair crops in spite of the sick looking fields following the storms.

Another time, our neighbor Jack sold us some straw. After the guys loaded the bales into our hayloft, Jack gave Marv the bill and left. Marv came in and told me he wanted to pay Jack but didn't have the money in the bank. "I don't know what to do," he said. "I hate to borrow the $720 that I owe him." I said, "Well, let's just pray about it," and pray we did. We were pleasantly surprised when two days later we received a check from the Internal Revenue Service for $721 for overpaid back taxes (plus interest they owed us) from five years before. There it was! We were so excited the Lord came through for us again.

As we faithfully paid our tithes through the years, adding offerings beyond the ten percent, God graciously took care of our needs according to His promise in Malachi: "Bring the whole tithe into the storehouse, so that there may be food in My house, and test Me now in this," says the Lord of hosts, "if I will not open for you the windows of heaven and pour out for you a blessing until it overflows." (Malachi 3:10-11 NASB).

The Lord wants us to give to the poor. He states in Proverbs 21:13, "He who shuts his ear to the cry of the poor, will also cry out himself and not be answered" (NASB), and Proverbs 19:17, "Whoever is kind to the poor lends to the Lord, and he will reward them for what they have done." (NIV). In our case, most of those extra offerings went to the poor. God certainly provided and even multiplied as He gave back to us. He is such a good God and always keeps his promises.

"Among the gods there is none like you, Lord;
no deeds can compare with yours."

Psalm 86:8 NIV

The Lord did more mysterious but wonderful things for us throughout the years. One fall harvest we hired our friend John to haul our corn to market. We received a larger check from the grain company than Marv felt we were owed. Marv called them about the mistake, but the man said, "No, that was your corn. It's not anyone else's. I saw it all coming out of John's truck." Marv objected and said, "But that truck doesn't hold that much corn." The elevator manager still insisted that it was all our corn. Marv said, "Even our bin doesn't hold that much." The man said Marv needed to take the check because they really had received that much corn in Marv's name. So, we finally kept it, thinking that God just wanted to bless us. The only thing we could figure out is that God was pouring more corn into the truck as it was being unloaded. Praise His Holy Name!

"I will remember the deeds of the Lord;
yes, I will remember your miracles of long ago."

Psalm 77:11 NIV

Divine healing of pigs

While Marv continued to work in the shipping department at Hormel's, he was also extremely busy with our sows, baby pigs, and market hogs, which offered their own set of problems. It was quite common for babies to smother when a sow accidentally laid on them. It was also common for the smaller pigs to starve when they couldn't reach the mother's nipples when there were too many little pigs for her "faucets."

A few times, Marv decided to lay his hands on the babies and pray for them. You know what? They came back to life. One time, one of them did not "come back to life" so he threw the dead pig out of the pen as he went out to bring the mothers back in from feeding them. When he went to retrieve the dead piggy, he couldn't find it. Instead, he saw a little pig walking around the barn outside of the farrowing crates. He concluded that God had indeed brought back to life that baby pig, which he had prayed for about ten minutes earlier.

Most of the time, God honored Marv's prayers and the pigs were healed.

"The righteous cry out, and the Lord hears them;
he delivers them from all their troubles."

Psalm 34:17 NIV

Rescue from farm crisis

In 1985, the hog market dropped to its lowest in years. Interest rates went sky high. And Hormel's, the hog processing plant, lowered their salaries but increased the hours their employees had to work. Some weeks Marv worked 70 hours, yet got paid for only 36. We did a lot of praying that year, just for the Lord to meet our needs, which He did in the most wonderful and unusual ways.

That was the year when the bank needed to refinance our loan for the hog finishing barn we had built. Originally it cost $42,000. Besides that, we had to keep borrowing money just to pay the feed bills because the hog price we were paid was far below the breakeven price. This continued for months, from June on. Finally, in September, the prices started climbing up to the breakeven point. By October, we had racked up loans of $58,000.

It was a scary time and we knew we were in great danger of the bank foreclosing on our farm. Sadly, three of our neighbors lost theirs, even though they had inherited their farms. Meanwhile, I was terribly frightened but committed to pray fervently each day, trying to keep Marv encouraged. Many times he would come home with a negative report and I would feel nauseous from fear. Thankfully, I had learned by listening to Christian teaching that we should pray the Scriptures and the promises of God.

I didn't know many Scriptures at the time, so each morning I hurried to our bedroom and prayed His promises. I prayed, "Lord, You promised in Malachi 13:10 and 11 that if we bring our tithes to Your storehouse, You would open the windows of heaven and pour out a blessing so great we could hardly receive it, and You would also rebuke the devourer for us. We have been doing that, so now it's Your turn to do something about this situation."

Thankfully, we had good crops, so I paid the bank loan officer over $19,000 in October from the sale of the soy beans. A few weeks later, I wrote a check for $3,000 from the sale of the hogs when the price was somewhat higher. The banker handed me three of the bank notes, stamped "Paid." Marv did not sell the corn at the time, saving it to grind as hog feed. We continued to pray after that, knowing that we could still be in big trouble, especially if the bank did not refinance the hog building loan of $34,000.

On New Year's Eve Day, Marv looked at his records to see if he would have to pay any income tax for the year. Our income had been so much lower than what we needed to pay our bills. He called to me from his office, saying, "Elsie, come in here! Where did all these bank notes come from? There are 12 in here."

I said, "What? I don't know. I only brought home three in October, remember?"

He said, "Well, we'll have to go to the bank and show them these. They must have made a terrible mistake because these can't be our notes."

On January 2, Marv went to the banker who looked at all of our records. He said, "No, your records show that you are all paid up." We were astounded. Neither one of us had gone to the bank to pay more money on those loans, yet the banker told us we were all paid up. All we could figure is that angels must have gone in to pay off all those loans. We sure don't know, but our feed bills were all paid that year.

"And we know that God causes all things to work together for good to those who love God, to those who are called according to His purpose."

Romans 8:28 NASB

Part of farm life is weathering the storms that threaten our crops. One storm in particular reminds me how God provides. A tremendous storm came rushing through with warnings given on the news. I prayed against hail, wind, and rain damage, quoting Psalm 91 again, especially verse 10: "No plague or calamity will come against your dwelling" over our buildings and our land. I reminded the Lord that we had a covenant with Him, according to His covenant with Abraham. "Christ redeemed us from the curse of the Law, having become a curse for us – for it is written, 'Cursed is everyone who hangs on a tree' in order that in Christ Jesus the blessing of Abraham might come to the Gentiles, so that we would receive the promise of the Spirit through faith." (Galatians 3:13-14 NASB).

The wind was terrific. Many of our beloved Scotch Pine trees broke off, this time pulling down the power lines. Along our county road, for several miles, tall power poles snapped right off. The pea-sized hail, along with a few marble-sized mixed in, came down on our farm but stopped quickly. Kevin called from his cell phone on his way home from Fremont, asking how our crops were. I said, "Well, they're still standing and so are our irrigation towers." He shouted, "Mom, if they're still standing, then that's a miracle! Everything from Fremont south is totally bare from hail and wind. The fields are bare and every one of the center-pivot irrigation towers are turned over and totally ruined. Most of the power poles along the highway are all snapped off, and a large semi-truck is lying on its side. Everyone's crops are gone, Mom!"

When the storm passed, Marv turned off the power because of "hot" wires downed next to our outbuildings. Kevin came to man the chainsaw; his family helped me pick up the downed branches for Marv to haul away with the loader on our tractor.

After we finished clearing the downed trees, we drove around to look at our neighbors' losses. We were stunned how the larger hail had stopped at the county road right next to our field of corn, yet the neighbor's field across that road was all flattened. We felt so sad for them. Acreages next to us had a lot of damage. It seemed the storm skipped over us, then started again opposite our property, destroying most of the crops for miles. The weather report stated that "straight line" winds were 100 to 125 miles per hour and the storm caused serious damage for about 55 miles, 7 miles wide in some places. (One of our neighbors reported seeing a tornado bouncing up and down in the clouds.)

A day later, Marv checked another field we can't see from our farmstead. He found considerable wind damage with patches of corn totally broken off. Three of our towers on one center-pivot system were turned over. When the insurance adjuster came to assess the damage, he told Marv that the tips of the corn stalk tops were twisted too tight for the tassels to come out. With no tassels to pollinate the corn, there would be no corn at all in the field. Apparently, the winds were tornado-like rather than straight winds, or all of the corn would have blown flat and broken off.

We prayed the Lord would send His ministering angels to go to all the corn plants and untwist the tips so the tassels could pop out. In addition, Marv irrigated that field of corn. A few days later, he checked; all of the standing corn had tassels set on the tips. Though the other corn was still broken, what a beautiful sight to see the tassels coming out! We don't know if the tassels popped out from the irrigation water or if the angels did it, but it didn't matter.

Later, because half of the corn had broken off, the weeds grew and took over. When the time came to pick, there was absolutely none on that 60acre field. The rest of the corn crop and soy beans seemed to look quite good. However, when Marv harvested, he only received half of the normal crop. I had been asking the Lord about it. Then I believed I heard Him say, "I want to do a greater miracle."

Fortunately, Marv had purchased a good insurance policy. After the insurance check came, we realized that the Lord had blessed us again. The company paid us the current corn price when it was $4 a bushel instead of the lower price the corn would have sold for. We realized how much the Lord really blessed us and why He worked it out as He did. How grateful we were to the Lord even though we lost so many lovely trees from our windbreak.

"'For I know the plans that I have for you,' declares the Lord, 'plans for welfare and not for calamity to give you a future and a hope.'"

Jeremiah 29:11 NASB

Since that day back in 1964 when we first moved to the farm, we both had the dream of someday owning that farm. In the meantime, we bought several more parcels of land which were described as "inside 80's." These properties were not desirable by other farmers because they would have to cross our farmstead to be able to farm those fields. We always had peace about purchasing those fields. For years we tried to pay off the mortgage of the additional land we purchased. We prayed diligently that God would help us pay the mortgage, encouraging ourselves with the Scriptures we found in the Bible.

Each year it seemed one thing after another went wrong so that we could not make the payments. We always had to borrow more from the bank, listing it under "operating expense," thus going into further debt. We were simply spinning our wheels, which was disappointing and discouraging as we waited year after year.

For several years, the crop prices were low, as low as they had been in 1945, at $1.49 a bushel. The prices for operating were sky-high with the seed, fertilizer, chemical sprays, machinery repairs, crop insurance, and fuel, amounting to $100,000. This happened the same year as the latest storm. Marv had been as frugal as he could be and never bought new machinery, choosing to repair the old machinery instead.

That year, we were deeply disappointed when a local chemical fertilizer company, which we hired to spray our corn crop for weeds, overlapped the chemicals and burned our corn. Soon the field had large sections of yellow leaves that turned brown. Marv knew the crops would produce less than half of our normal yield due to the applicator's mistake; we were depressed. "Here we go again," we thought, knowing we may have to secure yet another large loan rather than make a payment on our farm mortgage.

The company made the same mistake the year before to our neighbor's corn and to another farmer we knew, but neither farmer was ever paid for their loss. Our neighbor warned us that we would not be paid for our damage either. However, I responded to Marv when he told me the news, "God showed me something. We have a covenant with God. He will pay us for our loss because He promised in His Word, Philippians 4:19: "But my God shall supply all your need according to his riches in glory in Christ Jesus." (ESV). We will get the money that company owes us. Let's just confess the Word (pray the Scripture promises) and not talk negatively at all. Then God can do it!"

The manager of the company stated that we would need proof before they would pay. In the ten previous years, Marv had sold his corn and soybeans to the same grain company in Fremont. They had all of our past records in their computer and were happy to find the information for Marv showing past crop yields. These records were proof that our corn averaged around 200 bushels per acre every year. In the current year, the corn yield average was only 65 bushels per acre. Not much was said when Marv showed his proof to the manager.

By Christmas, we still had heard nothing about the reimbursement check. I thought of the story in the Bible of the woman who bothered the king until he wearied of her request and granted what she wanted. So it is with prayer and determination to see it come to pass. We decided it was time to lean on the manager's supervisor, so every few days Marv called and stated that we still had not received our check.

Finally, on January 11, three months later, the check arrived in our mail. We hurried to our bank and paid off a large sum on our mortgage. What a joyful time that was! We now had hope again of realizing our dream owning this farm. The Lord had the insurance adjuster give us a fair assessment on the damaged crops the following year. We had enough money from the insurance check and the payment the year before from our chemically burned crops, so that we finally were able to pay off the mortgage. Praises to our faithful God! I cried with joy many times, as our Lord worked it all out and helped us realize our dream. God is so good!

"Praise our God, all peoples, let the sound of his praise be heard;
he has preserved our lives and kept our feet from slipping."

Psalm 66:8-9 NIV

Accidents will happen

God was trying to get my attention the Halloween Kristy and I had our car accident. When she was around 14 years old, I picked her up that Friday after school at her bus stop on the way into Fremont. Also on the way, I had planned to pick up something at a friend's home. One of her classmates had sprayed Kristy's hair bright orange and as we were talking about the party at school, we missed turning onto the side highway. As we passed the turnoff, she started getting fearful, almost wailing. "Mom, I don't want to go to Fremont. Mom, I don't want to go." I mistakenly thought she was embarrassed about her hair, so I replied, "It's okay, I am only going to the bank; then we will come right back."

Seconds later she screamed, "Mom, look!" I saw a car in the other lane, waiting for us to pass before trying to make a left turn, while another car was speeding too close behind. Just as we approached, a woman's car plowed into the young man's back bumper and pushed his car into our path. We were about 15 feet away. I braked as hard as I could, but we hit him broadside.

Just before the hit, I leaned over to try to hold Kristy back in some way.

The bench seat of our Chevy Impala was suddenly pushed back with a jerk, as if I had tried to adjust the position of the seat with the lever on the left side of the seat. Yet I had not touched the lever to adjust it. Someone or something pushed us back so that neither of us hit the windshield, and I totally missed slamming into the steering wheel with my face. Kristy's left leg flew up and hit the air conditioning vent, fracturing her leg. I must have opened my mouth in horror. As we crashed, I bit almost through my chin right below my mouth, which bled profusely, but that was all that happened to me.

I noticed that our car was badly damaged. I could walk so I managed to get to the lady to see what had gone wrong. She felt terrible but said she just didn't see the car in front of her. The young man's car was totaled as well, and he was not hurt. He was understandably upset because he had just made the last payment on his car.

Kristy and I were the only ones taken by ambulance to the emergency room, where the doctor put a temporary cast on her leg and sutured the inside of my mouth. As I thought about it, I realized that the Holy Spirit had been trying to warn us with a "check" in Kristy's spirit, but I had not understood why she was so uneasy. I also kept thinking about that entire seat suddenly pushing back on its own. Since we usually pray Scriptures of protection, I thought of angels pushing the seat back and remembered, "On their (the angels) hands they will bear you up, lest you strike your foot against a stone." (Psalm 91:12 ESV).

I was really concerned as to how Kristy would get up the steep stairs to her eighth-grade classroom with crutches. Kristy was still in too much pain to go to Mass with us on Sunday so she stayed home. She turned on TV to watch Richard Roberts. He announced, "There is someone out there who has been injured between her ankle and her knee. The Lord wants to heal you today. Just stand up and receive your healing." Kristy realized he was speaking to her so she jumped up. As she stood, she felt something like electricity go through her leg, and then the pain was gone. I took her back to the doctor the next day. He examined her leg again and decided that he could take the cast off already. She had no pain or weakness as she went back to class on Tuesday.

"Fear of man will prove to be a snare,
but whoever trusts in the Lord is kept safe."

Proverbs 29:25 NIV

Every day, whether I was doing household chores or sewing, I would listen to a portable cassette player. The Lord used it greatly as I listened to Bible teaching. Each day, I listened to worship music and a Psalm, which always calmed me down and encouraged me as I silently prayed.

One of the ministry women, Joyce Meyer, who has a gift of teaching, explained that those of us who have low self-esteem and have suffered rejection and abuse are constantly trying to please others. We can never say "no" to them because we are trying to buy their love and approval, wanting to please them so they won't reject us. I always worried about others getting upset with me. This teaching helped me tremendously because I could now see why I did what I did. God is not pleased when we try to impress others. He sees it as a form of control and idolatry. I was tired of being afraid of what people thought of me and what they might be saying against me. As I asked forgiveness, He used Joyce Meyer's teaching to give me hope that this bondage could be broken in me.

Final Words

The verse that the Lord gave to Marv and me is from the book of Micah:

"And what does the Lord require of you? To do justice, to love kindness, and to walk humbly with your God."

Micah 6:8 NIV

We have done our best to follow the Lord and share His Good News and all the wonderful miracles He has performed for us. The Lord has continued over the years to discipline me when He needs to teach me lessons or break strongholds of sin. Even when something has become an idol in my life, like having things or people become too important to me and mean more to me than Him, He makes me aware of it. I pray that my life story will be a testimony to the grace and goodness of my Lord and Savior, Jesus Christ.

Marvin's Obituary

My beloved husband, Marvin, went home peacefully to his Lord and Savior Jesus Christ, on Thursday, October 24, 2013. These are the words from his obituary:

Marvin was born on June 7, 1934 to John and Julia (Neels) Popken of rural Hooper, Nebraska. He received his education in Hooper. Following school, he farmed with his father. He married Elsie C. Luebbert May 16, 1956 at St. Anthony's Catholic Church in West Point, Nebraska. He was drafted into the U.S. Army on September 15, 1956, and was stationed in Augsburg, Germany.

After his discharge, Marvin worked in the Shipping Department at George A. Hormel Company in Fremont, retiring after 30 years of service. He and Elsie purchased a farm south of Fremont in 1963, which he farmed until his retirement in 2011.

Marvin's love of his life, Elsie, his family and grandchildren will miss him deeply. He was a devoted husband and father who was committed to a life of hard work and perseverance in order to give the best he could to his family. He succeeded in that and fulfilled his dream of leaving behind a Godly heritage to his children. His simple faith and life exalted the Lord through his lifestyle of integrity and honor as he put God first in all. His passions in life were first and foremost his wife and family but especially his grandchildren. He was excellent at making them feel like they were the most important people in the world, and to Grandpa they were.

Marvin's hobbies were very simple. He loved to farm, spend time with his grandkids, have his country fried steak at Farmer Brown's Restaurant and to give to numerous mission trips and Christian organizations. Through his generosity, these organizations have reached an untold amount of people with the gospel and love of Jesus Christ. He leaves behind a legacy of love for all who were touched by his life.

Marvin is survived by his wife Elsie of 57 years; five children, Kathleen and husband Cliff Grant of Stanwood, Washington; Karen and husband Bob Birdwell of Lincoln, Nebraska; Kenneth and wife Helen Popken of Seoul, South Korea; Kevin and wife Zoryana Popken of Fremont; and Kristeen and husband Casey Mitchell of Fremont; sister Betty Glodowski of Hooper; and grandchildren, Jess, Wade and Luke Grant; Ryan, Taylor and Grant Birdwell; and John, Grace, Samuel, Caleb and Benjamin Popken. He was preceded in death by his parents.

The funeral service was 2 p.m. Monday, October 28, 2013 at Living Word Church, 1110 N. Lincoln, Fremont. Pastors Jackie and Kenneth Hartman and Rev. Elmer Murdock officiated.

Burial was at Pohocco Lutheran Cemetery. Military honors were conducted by the Fremont Honor Guard of V.F.W. Post #854 and American Legion Post #20.

Memorials were suggested to Step Up to Life and to the Living Word Church. Arrangements were made by Moser Memorial Chapel in Fremont.

ADDENDUM

Marvin Fred Popken (b. June 7, 1934) and Elsie Clara Luebbert (b. May 4, 1935) were married May 16, 1956. Their children, Kathleen, Karen, Kenneth, Kevin, and Kristeen were all born in Fremont, Nebraska.

Kathleen Elizabeth Popken was born May 1, 1959. She married Cliff J. Grant, Jr. on March 1, 1996, in Billings, Montana. Their children are: Jess (b. April 27, 1997), Wade (b. November 27, 1998), and Luke (b. June 27, 2000).

Karen Anne Popken was born October 6, 1960. She married Robert Birdwell on April 20, 1985, in Lincoln, Nebraska. Their children are: Ryan (b. May 19, 1991), Taylor (b. July 31, 1994), and Grant (b. May 14, 2004).

Kenneth Gerard Popken was born May 12, 1962. He married Helen Songsim in March 1997, at the US Embassy, Seoul, Korea.

Kevin John Popken was born January 2, 1967. He married Zoryana Vysotsky on November 9, 1996, in Tulsa, Oklahoma. Their children are: John (b. March 7, 2000), Grace (b. September 14, 2002), Samuel (b. October 29, 2005), Caleb (b. November 17, 2009), and Benjamin (b. September 10, 2011).

Kristeen Lynne Popken was born July 15, 1972. She married Casey Mitchell on May, 12, 2012, in Fremont, Nebraska.

Elsie's family:

John Herman Luebbert (b. January 3, 1895) and Elizabeth Hagedorn (b. January 5, 1898) were married May 25, 1921 at St. Boniface Catholic Church, near West Point, Nebraska. They had seven children: Casper (July 22, 1922 – February 17, 1975), Leo (May 27, 1924 – January 7, 2002), Irene (May 28, 1926 – April 29, 1933), Fred (May 6, 1928 – June 1, 2005), Bernard (May 20, 1930 – March 12, 2011), Wilma (March 27, 1932 – September 27, 2015), and Elsie (May 4, 1935). As farmers, they resided in Monterey Township until John and Elizabeth retired to West Point in 1961. John passed away December 6, 1971 and Elizabeth passed away ten years later, on December 31, 1981.

Marvin's family:

John Peter Popken (b. September 14, 1898) and Julia Neels (b. May 30, 1911) were married June 6, 1932. John served in the United State Marine Corps. Upon returning home, he attended Midland Lutheran College in Fremont, Nebraska. The couple farmed in Dodge County, Nebraska and later retired to Hooper, Nebraska. They had two children: Elizabeth (February 14, 1933 – July 31, 2015) and Marvin (June 7, 1934 – Oct. 24, 2013). John passed away June 15, 1972 and Julia passed away two years later, on July 3, 1974.

About the Author

Elsie Popken grew up near the farming community of West Point, Nebraska. She and her husband, Marvin, farmed near Fremont until his death in 2013. Elsie was an active volunteer in her church, and other ministries, such as Aglow Women's Fellowship. Her heart for Jesus and her passionate desire that others know Him motivate her daily. Elsie resides in Fremont, Nebraska.

Made in the USA
Las Vegas, NV
23 October 2021

32941448R00122